The 33rd

DREXEL UNIVERSITY
College of
Arts and Sciences

Editor-In-Chief	Scott Stein
Senior Editor	Kathleen Volk Miller
Layout Editor	William Rees
Graphic Design	Courtney Sabo
Editorial Co-ops	Hannah Mindl Gittler Amanda Ryan
Digital Design Co-op	Brittany MacLean
Student Interns	Marquerita Algorri Kaitlyn Benesch Taylor Bush Maggie Heath-Bourne Jessica Laird Dana McCloskey Nicole McCourt Melody Nielsen Helen Nowotnik Scott Olsen Blake Pendergrass Elizabeth Pollack Glenn Reyes Michael Rodino Frankie Santoni Brooke Segarra Vidhi Vakharia

Sponsors

Drexel University
The College of Arts and Sciences at Drexel University
The Department of English and Philosophy at Drexel University

Dr. Donna M. Murasko, Dean, College of Arts and Sciences,
Drexel University
Dr. Abioseh Michael Porter, Department Head, English and Philosophy,
Drexel University

The 33rd Volume 6
Drexel University
Department of English and Philosophy
3141 Chestnut Street
Philadelphia, PA 19104
www.drexelpublishing.org

Cover photo by Courtney Sabo

Copies of this volume are available for $10 by writing to the above address.

ISBN 978-0-9820717-5-5

Thank you, thank you, thank you, and thank you to: Dr. Donna M. Murasko; Dr. Abioseh Michael Porter; all the judges from the Drexel Publishing Group Essay Contest, the Week of Writing Contest, and the First-Year Writing Contest (Jan Armon, Genevieve Betts, Ken Bingham, Ron Bishop, Valerie Booth, Roman Colombo, Ingrid Daemmrich, Dan Driscoll, Anne Erickson, Bob Finegan, Leonard Finegold, Marilyn Piety, Alexander Friedlander, Robert Gilmore, Despina Guthrie, Patricia Henry, Casey Hirsch, Monica Ilies, Rebecca Ingalls, Henry Israeli, Karen Kabnick, Marlin Killen, Michael Leone, Kristina Lewis, Deirdre McMahon, Christopher Nielson, Anne-Marie Obajtek-Kirkwood, Emilie Passow, Don Riggs, Donna Rondolone, Gail Rosen, Sheila Sandapen, Eric Schmutz, Dora Schnur, Jonathan Seitz, Fred Siegel, Errol Sull, Monica Togna, Brigita Urbanc, Marshall Warfield, Scott Warnock, Robert Watts); Department of English and Philosophy, especially Mary Beth Beyer, Eileen Brennen, and Nicole Kline; contest participants; Drexel Publishing Group staff.

Distributed by the Drexel Publishing Group
The fonts used within this publication are Archer and Avenir

Credits:

Cohen, Paula Marantz. "'For Truth, Justice, and the American Way': A Close Reading of an American Sonnet" is forthcoming in *The Southwest Review*.

Finegold, Leonard. Originally published (with more photographs) in *The Survivor* (Journal of Desert Survivors) Spring 2013 Volume 32.1. Photographs taken by Nicholas Blake.

Fox, Valerie. "Memo Regarding your Future" was originally published in *Apiary* (2012). "One Constant, in the Background (Shostakovich #5)" was originally published in *Ping Pong* (2013).

Hnaraki, Maria, Papoutsaki, Evangelia. "Dakos: An Island Bread" Anna & Godfrey Baldacchino (eds.) (2012). *A Taste of Islands: A Global Island Cookbook*. Charlottetown, Canada: Island Studies Press.

Ingalls, Rebecca. "The Student as Witness: Cultivating Creativity in the Yogic Body of Research" originally published in *Writing & Pedagogy* 4.2 (Fall 2012): 169-90. Photographs taken by Scot Crichton. "Pincha Mayurasana" (2012) "Kapotasana" (2013).

Israeli, Henry. "Swing" will appear in the Fall 2013 edition of *Harvard Review*.

Kane, Dawn. (2012) "A Sister School Journey in Africa." Retrieved from http://projectkenyasisterschools.com/2012/12/21/a-sister-school-journey-in-africa/

Levin, Lynn. "The Ask Sandwich" was first published in *Cleaver Magazine*, Issue .5, 2013 and was reprinted in *Schuylkill Valley Journal*, Spring 2013.

Millan, Harriet Levin. "Hang Up" originally appeared in *The Iowa Review*, Volume 42, 2012. "Urban Myth" originally appeared in *Great River Review*, Issue 57, Fall/Winter 2012

Obajtek-Kirkwood, Anne-Marie, "*Pat, Dave* and the others...by Helena Villovitch" is the English translation of a paper given in French: "Pat, Dave et les autres… selon Hélèna Villovitch" April 2013 at NYU in the realm of the SPFFA (Société des professeurs français the francophones d'Amérique du Nord) Conference.

Riggs, Don. "Serial Poet" originally appeared in *Press 1*, Volume 4 Number 2. Sept-Dec. 2010.

Rosen, Gail D. "Tiny Furniture more than a Small Film" originally published in *When Falls the Coliseum*, 2011. <whenfallsthecoliseum.com>

Spiers, Mary, (2011) Neuroenhancement: Do "Smart Pills" Have Limits?"[Review of the Film *Limitless*, 2011] *PsycCRITIQUES*, 56(31). Doi:10.1037/a0024650.

Stein, Scott. "A Knife to Set Things Right" originally published in a slightly different form in *When Falls the Coliseum*, 2008. <whenfallsthecoliseum.com>

Volk Miller Kathleen. "You Might Not Have ADHD: You Might Just be Tired" and "Remember Your Kids are Your Free Labor" originally published in *Philadelphia Magazine's Philly Post*, 2013.

Warnock, Scott. "Writing for Dummies: Standardized Tests are Destroying Education, Part 3 (of a Plethora)" originally published in When Falls the Coliseum, 2013. <whenfallsthecoliseum.com>

Welcome

The 33rd anthology is a visible expression of the College of Arts and Sciences' commitment to interdisciplinary scholarship and writing excellence. Within its pages is an eclectic mix of short stories, essays, and scientific articles written by students and faculty from fields across the University, from engineering to biology to English. This volume demonstrates the incredible diversity of Drexel scholarship: we are one institution composed of diverse perspectives. These unique perspectives enhance our community and have the power to inspire others to achieve new insights and innovations, whether that's writing the next best-selling novel or discovering a new molecule. But powerful stories and miraculous discoveries are nothing without the skills of communication. These skills allow us to share our ideas, our research, our vision, with the world.

Whether you dream of being an author, an architect, or an environmental scientist, your training starts here, with the tools of communication.

Donna M. Murasko, Ph.D.
Dean
College of Arts and Sciences

Preface

As is often noted, the Department of English and Philosophy has established a well-deserved reputation not only as a place where instructors of all ranks are passionate about teaching and learning—derived from classroom and other such experiences—but also as the one locale at Drexel where excellent writing is seen as a daily, achievable goal. Because our ultimate objective is to make excellent writing a defining characteristic of a Drexel education, we will continue to help our students understand that a fine blend of traditional literary skills and modern thought and practice will help to make them excellent, even outstanding, writers. We, the faculty in our department, have therefore set as our primary goals the achievement of the highest academic standards, the creation of a congenial atmosphere for our students, and a dynamic teaching and scholarly environment.

It is thus with immense pleasure that we present the sixth volume of this yearly anthology. In *The 33rd* 2013, we aim to encourage our students to fuse insights derived from their varied experiences and knowledge to create a document that truly should impress readers because of the complex web of writing the authors present, even with an occasional undergraduate self-consciousness.

Using varying approaches that, even in these early stages, reveal the complexity, density of texture and meaning, and the richness of vision and artistry that often characterize good quality writing, the students—guided by their very able instructors—have carefully demonstrated in print some famous words of wisdom by Diane Stanley, author and illustrator: "Good writing is clear thinking." What I now hope the students, again with guidance from all of us, will continue to do from this point on is to apply the other half of Ms. Stanley's statement: "Reading is how you learn what good writing sounds like."

We are particularly heartened by the efforts reflected here because scarcely a false note is struck in this volume. The pieces in the anthology—though varied—continue to demonstrate the relevance and importance of high quality writing and good reading habits. Taken together, the contributions by both students and faculty reveal that literary and cultural exchanges between these two symbiotic groups continue to develop and improve. The pieces collectively address in a readable format and at the undergraduate level some of the aesthetics, concepts, theories, and debates that inform the various levels and perceptions of our contemporary culture (both highbrow and popular); they also attempt (successfully, I think) to analyze the role of writing in shaping culture, beliefs, identities, and social practices.

My personal congratulations—as well as those of the whole department—go to all who participated in this laudable and practically useful project. To those whose selections were published, I would like to conclude by offering some words by the writer Enrique Jardiel Poncela: "When something can be read without effort, great effort has gone into its writing." Bravo!

Abioseh Michael Porter, Ph.D.
Department Head
Department of English and Philosophy

Table of Contents

Fiction

Creative Non-Fiction

Faculty Writing
Introduction

Contributors

First-Year
Writing

Introduction

The thousands of compositions written by students enrolled in the First-Year Writing Program at Drexel represent their extraordinary experiences and perspectives. Composed over weeks of reading, research, contemplation, rhetorical analysis, discussion, and revision, these compositions are a reflection of how students are learning to use writing as a tool for creative, complex inquiry, and are making their writing matter beyond the boundaries of the classroom: in the development of the self, in the crafting of proposals for change, in the building of ideas that lead to innovation.

The First-Year Writing category in this collection offers a showcase of some of the most excellent student work from this year. After a competitive multi-stage process of evaluating and narrowing down the submissions, the winners and honorable mentions are announced, and the awards are given at the English Awards Ceremony in the spring. I can say with confidence that these students, who hail from all corners of this institution, have made us proud not just as instructors and as a program, but also as a university that aims to create a culture of writing across the disciplines. We hope that these texts will serve as evidence to our writers and readers that—no matter what field you have decided to pursue—writing will be a critical tool for your exploration and success.

I want to thank the generosity of First-Year Writing faculty member Ingrid Daemmrich, sponsor of the First-Year Writing Contest, and the hardworking Drexel Publishing Group for bringing this book into being. I also want to extend my deepest gratitude to Department Head Dr. Abioseh Porter, Dean Donna Murasko, and Provost Mark Greenberg for their enduring support of writing pedagogy, innovation, and assessment. Finally, I want to especially thank our many beloved, wise faculty who continue to devote tireless inspired hours to make this program stronger each year.

Rebecca Ingalls, Ph.D.
Director, First-Year Writing Program

Tristan Winick

Culture of Personality: An Investigation of Bias Against Introversion in Western Society

Take some time to imagine Western society from the perspective of an outsider, perhaps one of a culture vastly different from our own. If this traveler were to observe for some time the daily interactions of our modern society, he or she might note its various technological advances, its relative affluence in a worldwide context, or the freedoms provided by its unique structure of government. Our hypothetical person may likewise come to expect hospitality from the denizens of our nation. This person may also notice how "loud" we can be, not only in a literal context, but in the sense that our cultural identity drives us to reach out to others and exhibit ourselves plainly for the rest of the world to see. To a certain extent, this mindset has great merit; by turning to the outside world, we kindle those around us, sharing our flame and allowing us to reap the benefits of cooperation. However, with every choice comes a price, and the price that we pay is the loss of introspection.

The introverts of the Western world are met with frequent criticism; they are often seen as aloof, occasionally viewed as conceited due to their lack of desire to interact with others, and, at worst, they may be wrongly diagnosed as mentally ill. Parents, mentors, and peers make endless attempts to bring introverted children "out of their shells," and inadvertently dampen their individuality in the process of conforming to society's expectations. Susan Cain, author of *Quiet: The Power of Introverts*, addresses this issue in her February 2012 TED Talk (the video of which can be found at www.ted. com/talks/susan_cain_the_power_of_introverts.html). She describes the discouragement of introverted behavior in Western society not only as a loss for introverts, but also as "our colleagues' loss, our community's loss, and at the risk of sounding grandiose...the world's loss."

The proof of Cain's statement is evident in our history; if one takes time to investigate our society's most creative artists, musicians, and authors, as well as our most brilliant thinkers, one will note that many of them were not what we would typically refer to as "social." Cain gives the excellent example of the famed naturalist Charles Darwin, architect of the groundbreaking theory of evolution, who, in Cain's words, "took long walks in the woods alone and emphatically turned down dinner party invitations" in lieu of solitude. The physicist Albert Einstein, the poet Emily Dickinson, Rosa Parks, a prominent figure in the 1960s American civil rights movement, and even many U.S. presidents—George Washington, Abraham Lincoln, and Calvin Coolidge, among others—were introverts. What might have become of these brilliant minds and influential leaders were they not given any time to reflect on their thoughts and experiences? The ideas presented above also lead to another, more significant question: if so much of what defines our culture was built upon the contributions of introverts, then why, in general, does Western society so greatly prefer the extraverted attitude?

Cain herself presents some ideas on the question at hand. Her interpretation of the preference towards extraversion in Western society has its roots in what she refers to as "cultural inheritance." A dramatic shift during the early 20th century, in which "we evolved from an agricultural economy to a world of big business," shifted our priorities from those of a "culture of character," which emphasizes the "inner self and moral rectitude," to those of a "culture of personality," where "magnetism and charisma suddenly come to seem very important," she attests.

The merit of Cain's interpretation is in its symmetry with our understanding of how people adapt to changing circumstances. In essence, she describes how the social and economic climate of an earlier era has left its mark on us as a culture today, which is consistent with countless other events throughout history. As her statement about "the 'new groupthink'" and about how many believe that "all creativity and all productivity comes [sic] from a very oddly gregarious place" seems to indicate, social paradigms have not only followed the trend of the previous century, but are increasingly tending toward an even more extraverted society. If one extends Cain's ideas, one might conclude that our current age of information and long-distance communication may be to blame for this upward trend of extraversion favoritism. Cain's interpretation is not the only one available, however.

Marti Olsen Laney, Psy.D., shares a differing idea of the reasons for bias against introversion in her book *The Introvert Advantage: How to Thrive in an Extrovert World*. Rather than attributing the bias to cultural climate, as does Cain, she describes the unfavorable status of introverts as a direct result of how extraverts interpret introverted behaviors. "Extroverts are so used to speaking off the top of their heads that they may be distrustful of more reticent introverts," and "[w]hen introverts speak with hesitation, extroverts may feel impatient" (Laney 50). Laney notes that introverts tend to shy away from promoting themselves, whereas "[extraverts] are their own best press agents" (189). As such, extraverts receive more credit for their contributions, and introverts tend to seem uncooperative or downright lazy.

Laney's interpretation takes a psychological and behavioral stance on introversion bias rather than a historical and cultural approach. In many ways, the behavioral approach is more specific, as it analyzes the interactions between introverts and extraverts on an individual basis, thus allowing one to draw specific details from said relations. On the other hand, one cannot use Laney's interpretation to explain why bias against introversion has been gaining momentum in recent years; its scope is too fixed in time and not generalized enough to project future trends.

In contrast to the prior two analyses, Christopher Lane presents a rather disturbing take on the issue of criticism against the introverted personality in the peer-reviewed scholarly journal *Common Knowledge*. He shifts the blame for this attitude to the pharmaceutical industry, alleging that, in order to exploit the populace, it branded such behavior as an illness in the form of "social anxiety disorder." As part of his argument, he recounts this story:

> Before you sell a drug, you have to sell the disease, so the various components of social phobia—bashfulness, fear of one's hand shaking while writing, undue concern about the opinions of others, and so on—first had to be sold as an illness. It took little time to persuade the professionals. In 1999, just nine years after drug trials for Paxil proved so disappointing that SmithKline Beecham considered shelving the product, the pharmaceutical giant received the first FDA license to market Paxil as a treatment for "social anxiety disorder" (393).

As Lane continues his article, he describes the alteration of the *DSM* (*Diagnostic and Statistical Manual of Mental Disorders*) over time, and introduces the idea that, in spite of the bias that has seeped between its pages, it "is treated today as the bible of American psychiatry and, increasingly, of worldwide standards for mental health" (396).

Although Lane makes no explicit statements regarding the favoritism of extraversion in particular, one can easily draw those conclusions based on the information included in his article. Using said information as a basis, it may be inferred that the general public, for fear of being branded with the stigma associated with mental illness, conformed to what the *DSM* and other psychological compendiums described as "normal" behavior. Those who operated outside of conventional behavior, in other words, the introverts, became particularly vulnerable to being labeled with mental disorders. "Buoyed up by celebrities lamenting their social awkwardness...specialists felt confident in attributing the increase in social phobia not to having lowered the diagnostic thresholds, but to bringing to our attention a problem far greater than anyone, including the sufferers themselves, had imagined" (397). This, in turn, reinforced the stereotype of extraversion as the normal, driving psychologists to alter the diagnostic criteria for existing mental disorders and to create new disorders. As well supported as these ideas are by the article, however, some are rather difficult to swallow; without Lane's extensive substantiation and heavy implications, as well as his large pool of sources, they would, admittedly, border on conspiracy theory. He wields the knowledge that his claims are on the threshold of the unbelievable as an instrument of surprise, shocking and startling his readers into contemplating the issue at hand.

Even if one extends beyond Lane's own research, there are sources that lend validity to Lane's claims. For example, a late 1990s study conducted by Leslie J. Francis for *The Journal of Social Psychology*, a peer-reviewed source, details the administration of the Coopersmith Self-Esteem Inventory to 602 16-year-old students of roughly even gender split. She notes "a significant positive correlation between self-esteem and extraversion" (140), and then goes on to state that "[t]hese findings imply that the image of high self-esteem assumed by the five psychologists who helped to select the original items for the Coopersmith Self-Esteem Inventory was associated with social conformity, extraversion, and emotional stability." As a final caution, she warns that "[s]uch characterization of self-esteem may implicitly discriminate against introverts."

A final attempt at understanding this issue turned me toward personal research. In a survey of 10 of my peers who were asked to answer two questions, the first of which asked if they were aware of a bias towards the extraverted personality in lieu of introversion in Western society, and the second asking the origin of this bias if one responded "yes" to the previous question, nine of the people polled indicated that they did indeed perceive a bias. Their answers to the second question varied, but most indicated that extraverts held more influence in society due to either the frequent vocalization of their opinions or aspects of capitalism/business-oriented society. Some novel ideas were suggested, however; one of the respondents indicated American traditions and holidays, which often involve fellowship and sociability, as a reason for bias against introverts (Winick 1).

As we draw this exploration to a close, one may be left with the impression that we have gleaned nothing of value, but I would personally have to disagree. Here we have a number of viable explanations for the stigma that our society associates with the label of "introvert," and although we have no definitive answer to our original inquiry, we may at least come away with a better understanding of some of the contributing factors. Clearly, there never will be a simple answer, and, likely, the favoritism of extraversion (and resultant bias against introversion) in our society is a combination of all of the aforementioned reasons.

Works Cited

Cain, Susan. "The Power of Introverts." TED. Feb. 2012. Lecture.

Francis, Leslie J. "Coopersmith's Model of Self-Esteem: Bias Toward the Stable Extravert?" *The Journal of Social Psychology* 137.1 (1997): 139-42. Print.

Lane, Christopher. "How Shyness Became an Illness: A Brief History of Social Phobia." *Common Knowledge* 12.3 (2006): 388-409. Print.

Laney, Marti Olsen. *The Introvert Advantage: How to Thrive in an Extrovert World.* New York: Workman Pub., 2002. Print.

Winick, Tristan. "Does Western Society View Introversion as Unfavorable and Extraversion as Ideal?" Survey. 18 Nov. 2012.

Nathan Tessema

Writing Across Languages

We've all been taught to write formally. At some point over the course of our academic lives, we've all been given tools and guidelines that we needed to follow in order to write and that we've come to see as conventional wisdom. Yet, how widespread are these writing practices, really? Are they universal or are they actually specific to those who speak our language? This issue lies at the heart of a much greater question: At what point do literature and language diverge?

I believe my background has greatly helped me to tackle this question. As an international student who grew up in Ethiopia, went to a French high school, and pursued higher education in the United States, I've been confronted with writing assignments in English, French, and Amharic (Ethiopia's administrative language). For each kind of assignment, my mindset was different because I knew that my writing would tend to a particular audience with specific expectations. Accordingly, I employed different styles and techniques for writing assignments in different languages. To help shed light on the relation between language and literature, I will delve into my personal experiences writing in these three languages to expose the differences (in style and technique) between formal writing in English, French, and Amharic.

I began my research by rummaging through my senior year baccalaureate essays. Specifically, I compared the introductory paragraphs of my essays because the introduction was truly universal in the sense that it was present in all of my writings, in all three languages. I hoped that analyzing the formats of these preliminary clauses would lead me to discern some of the stylistic differences I was looking to find. While my comparisons of English and Amharic introductions weren't as fruitful as I'd wished, the dissimilarities between French and English introductions were blatantly evident. Where English introductions underlined my presence as an author and insisted on the credibility of my experiences on the given topic, French introductions sought to eclipse me, the writer, and focused solely on the topic at hand, occasionally referring to me with the impersonal *Nous* ('we'). Moreover, French introductions explicitly defined the essay plan, using terms like *Dans un premier temps* ('Firstly') and *Ensuite* ('Next'), whereas English introductions merely presented the topic, only hinting at a plan.

These initial observations held true not only for the introductions but also for the entire essays: French essays (dissertations, commentaries) are highly objective. The author's presence is barely discernible; no mentions are made of personal experiences relating to the subject at hand. And from a structural perspective, the French essays' skeletons are made clearly visible by a great diversity of logical connectors ensuring transitions between ideas, arguments, examples, and oppositions. Both of these features, distinguishing French formal writings from their English counterparts, stem from the importance accorded to logos or rational thinking in French writing. The most fundamental principle I was taught as a student in French class was that logic took precedence over any preconceptions the author might have about the topic. Consequently, since there's only one logic common and identical to all humans, any discourse that's reasoned is universal and nonspecific to the author. The author's presence in a logical discourse therefore only undermines the quality of the logos in the discourse, tarnishing it with partiality: this is why the author's presence is minimal in French writings. The emphasis placed on the organization and structural coherence in French writings is also an indicator of the importance of logos.

Studies, consistent with these observations, have shown the consequences of this perception of logos on the choice of essay structure in French writing. According to *Foreign Language Annals'* "Key Issues in Foreign Language Writing" (Vol. 45, No. 1, 29-30), the privileged essay structure in University-level French curricula is the dialectic format, which enables the author to engage in reasoned self-deliberation by discovering arguments in favor of a thesis (*thèse*) and countering them with arguments of the antithesis (*antithèse*) with the purpose of ultimately formulating a synthetic conclusion (*synthèse*).

It's important to underline the fact that these observations are in essence comparisons. And as such, they are to be considered relatively, not in absolutes: while greater emphasis on logos is indeed placed in French writing, English writing is considerably invested in logos as well.

But what of formal writing in Amharic? After fruitlessly comparing my Amharic essays to my English essays, I turned to my lesson notes, searching for tools and styles that were exclusive to my native language. I discovered that Amharic had its own set of stylistic devices widely used to support assertions in formal writing. The two most interesting and best known stylistic devices are known as 'Teretna Mesale,' which are short proverbial sayings proffered at opportune moments when giving advice on a matter or summarizing a past event, and 'Qene,' which are two-verse poems with an explicit meaning concealing a hidden meaning. Both of these tools, initially part of oral traditions transmitted from one generation to the next, were incorporated into formal writing where they serve alongside rhetorical skills to test a writer's literary aptitude. The widespread use of these tools is very indicative of the weight accorded to traditions, be they written or oral, in Ethiopian literature. In *Research in African Literatures*' "African-Language Writing," analysts Barber and Furniss also discuss the importance of tradition in African literature (Vol. 37, No. 3, 1). Another noteworthy trait inherited from the impact of oral tradition is the striking emphasis placed on the sonority of words when providing descriptions or when adding contextual connotations. This characteristic is seen in the way terms are coined in Amharic; words often mimic the sounds to which they refer.

There are therefore a number of stylistic differences between English, French, and Amharic formal writing, with origins ranging from traditional influences to conceptions linking veracity with logic. Yet I feel these differences don't extend to anything other than style and technique. After interviewing some of my former classmates who shared these writing experiences with me, I discovered that this impression was shared. Two of my classmates made pertinent remarks concerning the form and content of writing (*le fond et la forme*). They stated that while the form differed from language to language, the content was the same because, rhetorically, they followed the same mental steps when confronted with any topic (evaluating arguments, researching references/examples, considering the most effective tools for the specified audience).

Nevertheless, despite the unity rhetorical skills confer to all kinds of formal writing, the plurality of formats in academic writing has become an issue in a day and age when globalization has created a close-knit global society characterized by close interactions between different cultures. Conferences, such as the one set in 2013 by the European Association for the Teaching of Academic Writing, illustrate the need for harmonization of academic writing formats. And while English has undeniably become the universal language of academia, this is only a palliative remedy masking the issue because a language is but a receptacle reflecting its speaker's culture; the root of the observed stylistic differences is not the language per se, but rather the cultural influences the language has been subjected to. The use of English as a universal academic language has magnified the scope of our audience to the entire world, but it has not exempted us from the job of identifying our kairos by immersing ourselves in world culture.

Works Cited

Barber, Karin. "African-Language Writing." *Research in African Literatures* 37.3 (2006): 1. Print.

EATAW. "Conferences—European Association for the Teaching of Academic Writing." Web. <http://www.eataw.eu/conferences.html>.

Reichelt, M., et al. "Key Issues in Foreign Language Writing." *Foreign Language Annals* (2012): 29-30. Print.

David Georgeanni

The Function of Form: The Role of Art in Society

One warm Saturday in April, I was helping my father repair the door of our woodshed. My father, a carpenter and a retired high school woodshop teacher, certainly knew what he was doing, but our "repair" was a rather ugly conglomeration of duct tape and heavy-duty staples. When I noted to my father how bad it looked, he responded with a phrase I've heard him use many times: "Form follows function." This saying, one of my father's favorites, conveys the concept that the way something looks is secondary to the purpose it serves. With this saying ingrained in my subconscious, I have always wondered about art. Art seems to be entirely about how something looks, as I've never been able to define a practical purpose that art serves. However, by the logic that form follows function, art should not exist if it does not serve a purpose. Therefore, I could not help but wonder: what is the role of art in society? The answer I found was deeper and more complex than I had imagined.

I decided that the best place to start looking for an answer to this question was the nearby Philadelphia Museum of Art, one of the most prestigious collections of art in the nation. At the Museum of Art, I met with Roberta Dranoff, a museum guide who agreed to field my questions about art. Though she was initially caught off guard by the broadness of my main question, she soon began to give an extensive explanation for the role of art in society. Dranoff first made clear the importance of the intellectual aesthetic feeling that art inspires. "It gives us a higher reason to live. It sustains us above the mundane. How do you feel when you walk in [the Museum of Art]? Art inspires a wonderful intellectual feeling." Dranoff explained that the "positive energy" that art inspires in people makes them more productive, which is directly beneficial to society.

She then elaborated on another direct benefit of art in society: the impact of aesthetic appeal in business. "If you were renting an apartment, say, would you prefer an extensively decorated space, or just a little box that just achieves its goal of providing shelter? The things that look nicer always sell better. Sure, it's important that things do what they're meant to do—but something that feels and looks good has a significant advantage," she elucidated.

At this point, Dranoff had given me some good leads for further research, but I wanted a little bit more. I asked her for an example of when and how art has influenced society in the past, and she immediately mentioned the Renaissance. She told me that art was a quintessential part of the movement that brought Europe out of the Dark Ages. She explained that, here again, art was used as a means to an end: Church-commissioned Renaissance art promoted and taught religious principles to influence churchgoers. As if this example had summed up her entire explanation, Dranoff concluded that art has had such an influence on so many areas of society because it has a way of inspiring the human heart and mind like no other medium.

At this point, I had a tremendous springboard off of which to jump farther into my research. I decided to start with Dranoff's point about art in business. I searched for articles concerning art and business and happened upon a source that fit my question perfectly: an article in the *Journal of Business Ethics* entitled, "Aesthetics as a Foundation for Business Activity." Written by John Dobson, Professor of Finance at California Polytechnic State University, the article explains how the ultimate justification of a business activity is aesthetics, a term referring to artistic taste and appreciation of beauty. As Dobson states, "Aesthetics provides a unified view of the nature and purpose of business that overcomes the incoherencies and inconsistencies of the ethical and economic view of business. As such, aesthetics also provides a justificatory mechanism for decision-making in business." He explains that all of the conventional criteria of a sound business decision are deeply rooted in philosophies concerning the appreciation of beauty, such as the link between beauty and excellence as described by Platonic philosophy. Since business decisions are thus so deeply dependent on the appreciation of beauty, Dobson concludes that while "the key words of the modernist business universe of the past 150 years may have been those of logic... the key words of the aesthetic business era will be such things as ... *compassion, community, beauty,* and *art*" (41-46).

At first, this viewpoint confused me. How can a business decision be "beautiful"? However, as Dobson made his case, I found that the term "beauty" extends beyond the physical. A business decision can be "beautiful" in terms of its morality and achievement. For instance, the decision of a business to contribute funds to the development of the surrounding neighborhood could be considered beautiful because it is an ethical approach that can help increase profits by attracting more customers to a newly more appealing area. This article helped me see that art and the appreciation of art have a bigger impact on business than just making products more marketable; art helps us appreciate beauty, and appreciating beauty can help improve our lives. The specificity of Dobson's article pleased me; to see such a concrete application of art and its appreciation to an aspect of society helped give me a glimpse of the answer to my question. However, the depth to which art and beauty influence business brought more questions to my mind. If aesthetics, the appreciation of art and beauty, is so fundamentally important in the basic philosophies of society, where else might it apply?

I decided to look into my original question in hopes of finding a broader, more general answer. I searched for articles concerning art and society, and I found an article that matched my search exactly: "Art and Society," an interview in the journal *Art Review* with Boris Groys, Professor of Russian and Slavic Studies at New York University and a senior research fellow at Karlsruhe University of Arts and Design. The question asked in the interview was quite similar to my main question: "Does contemporary art have a role to play in shaping social and economic development?" Groys explains that art does have a role to play in shaping social and economic development, as well as in political development, and that this role comes from the prominence of visual language in the contemporary world. As Groys explains, "By analyzing and interpreting this visual language, art is able to deeply influence our social and political behavior—and, thus, to influence the world development in general" (167).

This viewpoint was the sort of answer I expected to find. In this article, Groys focuses less on how art can help us appreciate beauty (as Dobson explained) and more on how art as a visual medium can have a significant impact on society in and of itself. Things like political posters and business advertisements use this universal appeal of art to foster social, political, and economic development. Groys's view brought back to mind the point that Dranoff had made about art's ability to inspire the heart and mind. At this stage, the factual information provided by the articles I found had brought me to as much of an understanding as reading could provide, but I wanted to see for myself. I returned to the Philadelphia Museum of Art and sought out Roberta Dranoff. I asked her where I might find works of art that would illustrate for me the inspirational power of art. She suggested I look in the Renaissance and post-Renaissance era galleries of European art. According to Dranoff, this was a time when the Catholic Church commissioned paintings to promote Christianity, and that such paintings should show me the effect they had on their audience.

Indeed, I did find such a work of art there. I found it in the European gallery, but a Spanish colonist in Mexico painted it; entitled "Saint Francis Defeating the Antichrist," it was painted by Cristóbal de Villalpando as a commission for a Franciscan convent in Guatemala. This work of art helped to drive the whole point home. It conveys a sense of true emotion—one of victory shared with Saint Francis; one of the overwhelming power of God; one of the benevolence of God, whose agent dispatched the greatest of enemies with a single clean blow. The colors are vibrant, and the imagery is moving: Elijah rushes in with a flaming sword as Saint Francis drives a saber through the heart of the Antichrist. I found myself inspired by this painting in a way that words could not achieve. Perhaps it helped that I am already a devout Catholic, but I could see on a personal level the same sort of inspirational power that art and its appreciation could evoke, as explained by all the sources I had found.

However, in all of my exploration, another question had emerged: what about ugly art? In my thought process, I had only really considered works of art that conveyed positive emotions, such as "Saint Francis Defeats the Antichrist." However, there certainly is an abundance of art in the world that conveys negative emotion through ugliness. In an art history database, I simply searched "ugliness," and I came upon an article entitled, "Disgust and Ugliness: A Kantian Perspective." Written by a Hungarian art historian named Mojca Kuplen, it was an extensive article exploring examples of ugliness in art. In the article, Kuplen differentiates between two concepts: disgust and ugliness. He explains that the "aesthetic purpose" (9), the intention of conveying beauty through art, is defeated by disgust but not by ugliness. As Kuplen explains, works that are disgusting repel viewers and by definition fail to be aesthetically pleasing, while works that are ugly can still be aesthetically pleasing but simply convey negative emotion by that means rather than positive emotion. He exemplifies graphic and violent sex scenes in artistic filmography as disgusting; they compel the viewer to turn away and even physically distance the viewer from the work. In explaining ugliness, though, Kuplen exemplifies works of visual art such as Francisco Goya's "The Disaster of War," which shows mutilated corpses as a means of conveying negative emotion about war while remaining aesthetically appealing enough to attract the viewer instead of repel the viewer (9). As Kuplen concludes, "While ugliness as a negative aesthetic partner of beauty is its proper opponent, disgust, on the other hand, is much more resistant to beauty than ugliness is... Disgust is the most hostile opposition to beauty, not because disgust would be the most extreme form of ugliness, but precisely because of its different nature. Disgust is a sign of an immediate failure. In contrast to ugliness, disgust fails without aesthetic examination" (9). This viewpoint certainly clarified the issue for me. Ugly art, just like "pretty" art, serves a purpose. As Kuplen explained, ugly art is still aesthetically pleasing—it still attracts the viewer. However, unlike "pretty" art, it conveys negative emotion instead of positive emotion. This all ties back into the ability of art to inspire the heart in a way that other means of communication cannot.

In all of my searching, I did indeed find an answer, if even a vague one. I have found that art's role in society consists of its ability to inspire and sustain the human heart and mind. This inspirational power fills people with positive energy, making them more productive. It calls us to search for beauty in everything, from an apartment rental to a business decision. It can influence the hearts and minds of many to think one thing or another politically, socially, or otherwise. Form does follow function, but now I understand art's function. Art's role in society, to inspire and sustain the heart and mind, is of a much higher purpose than I had imagined, and in understanding it, I can now seek to find a higher beauty in the world.

Works Cited

"Art And Society." Art Review 63 (2012): 167. Art Full Text (H.W. Wilson). Web. 9 Nov. 2012. de Villalpando, Cristóbal. *Saint Francis Defeating the Antichrist.* 1691. Philadelphia Museum of Art, Philadelphia, Pennsylvania. Web. 14 Nov 2012.

Dobson, John. "Aesthetics as a Foundation for Business Activity." *Journal of Business Ethics.* 72.1 (2007): Print.

Dranoff, Roberta. Personal Interview. 13 Nov. 2012

Kuplen, Mojca, "Disgust And Ugliness: A Kantian Perspective." *Contemporary Aesthetics* 9. (2011): 9. Art Full Text (H.W. Wilson). Web. 23 Nov. 2012.

Sam Cassel

Making a Miracle Ordinary

In the United States, 18 patients on the organ transplant list die every day, often after years of waiting ("Statistics"). This statistic shows no signs of slowing. The number of patients on the wait lists far surpasses the number of available donated organs, and this gap widens each year. In 2011, 28,535 transplants were performed in the U.S., yet there were 114,000 patients still waiting ("Statistics"). These patients' lives are controlled by their deteriorating health, yet the debate regarding how to increase donation remains at a frustrating stalemate. Many Americans find ethical dilemmas within current proposed solutions, other potential donors fear the power of the medical system and the government, and most commonly, grieving families struggle to agree to donate their loved ones' organs. These obstacles lead to the following question: through what means can the number of organ donors be increased without testing society's ethical boundaries or jeopardizing the population's trust in the healthcare system?

One of the most often proposed revamping of the organ donation system is called opt-out donation. Marni Soupcoff, a writer for Canada's *National Post*, explains that in such a system, all individuals within the country are assumed to be organ donors, unless one specifically fills out a form stating otherwise. To me, this proposal seems foolproof. It would incorporate into the system people who aren't particularly against organ donation, but just never bothered to fill out the paperwork. Currently, the only way one becomes an organ donor is to formally register, either along with one's driver's license or by visiting a donation registration website. Those who do not take the initiative to do so may have no particular reason against donation, and this system will include them. But by providing an opt-out option, the government is not forcing anyone to donate.

However, this proposal has faced powerful resistance. First, many Americans feel that this legislation is another government attempt to regulate the lives of its constituents. Others' opposition is fueled by their fear of an untrustworthy medical system. Before researching this topic myself, I found that many of my friends had declined registering because they feared that they would not receive all possible treatment to save them if a tragedy happened. So I wasn't surprised when Ms. Soupcoff highlighted that same fear. She explains that "it's the sort of gut feeling that would be engendered by a move to turn the tables on who gets the default say on the fate of a person's anatomy."

With that in mind, the potential fear generated from the opt-out proposal could cause this system to backfire. Thomas Murray, the director of the Center of Biomedical Ethics at Case Western Reserve University, argues that, should this legislation go through without proper education of the public, the panic raised could potentially worsen our current donor situation, with many frightened donors pulling out of the system (Nelson and Murray). Considering the steep shortage of viable organs the country is currently experiencing, this outcome is the last thing we want to risk. However, if we educate the public about why its objections are irrelevant, people might be more open to the opt-out option.

The fears concerning premature diagnosis of death are irrelevant due to legislation informally referred to as the "dead donor rule": the rule that defines death preceding donation. Carlos Gil-Diaz, a journalist of *Diario Medico* (Medical Daily), explains that in the United States and most European countries, there are two definitions of such death. The first is "traditional" cardio-pulmonary death, and the other is irreversible brain trauma, more commonly known as being brain dead (257). Here, the key word is "irreversible," and doctors are required by law to follow these guidelines. To disobey would not only lead to their dismissal, it would break the most substantial principle doctors live by: the "do no harm" ethic.

While we've determined doctors will not sacrifice a patient for their organs, many still find the opt-out system to be an invasive government decree. It may at first appear to be controlling, however, the government would actually be serving its number one role: to protect the people. Through the opt-out proposal, the government considers the needs of the dying patients on the waiting lists. However, the donors are not forgotten. The key point of this plan, the one highlighted in the title, is its opt-out option. One's wishes will still be respected, should religious or moral conflict prevent consent to organ donation, as long as one fills out the form.

Another solution, although more controversial, has been gaining ground in approval ratings as shortages grow larger: compensated donation. Within this solution, there are proposals to increase the number of live donors, and others to increase post-mortem donation, and both categories have their strong points and shortcomings. As a whole, compensation sparks emotions because it challenges the ethics of putting a set value on a human being. Many claim that putting a monetary value on an organ will indirectly put a value on the whole, and that putting a finite price on a human being erases one's dignity and worth (de Castro 143). There is value in this moral viewpoint. If we, as a society, were to put a price tag on a kidney, where is the line drawn? Can a value be assigned to all the other organs? Or maybe the whole body? Or even a life? This kind of definition is a fragile one to juggle. It contains not only the dignity and worth of a human being, but could potentially establish a starting point for a downward moral spiral leading to possibly a defined monetary value of life itself.

However, Dr. de Castro, a Philosophy professor at the University of the Philippines, views it a bit differently. He suggests that monetary compensation is comparable to the compensation of a neighborhood hero; that, after the deed was done, he was bestowed with a monetary reward for his good deed (de Castro 143). He also claims that commodification of organs is more ethically accepted by the public in certain scenarios than in others. He compares a man who agrees to donate his organs on the condition that his children will be entitled to private health insurance to a man who uses the organ donation money from his dead wife to build an expensive mausoleum for her. Most of us would agree that the former would be more highly accepted than the latter. The first expresses acceptable concern for his children's well being and the second expresses less accepted vanity. Overall, de Castro argues that ethics depends upon the taken approach, and "we have a responsibility to adopt a finely tuned rhetoric" to adapt compensated organ donations to the needs of society (de Castro 144). This made sense to me. Dr. de Castro provides an alternative viewpoint on compensated donation by using moral boundaries currently in place. Despite my personal advocacy of organ donation, I was still hesitant to agree with de Castro because I believe that compensating living donors has its own set of specific ethical and legal issues.

Priya Shetty, a writer for *The Lancet* medical journal, explains that the most opposed to this are doctors. They argue that it is in direct violation of the "do no harm" principle, describing it as the equivalent of paying people to maim themselves (1315). Doctors are also concerned that offering cash compensation would encourage people to donate hastily and for the wrong reasons.

Compensating living donors could trigger an exploitation of the poor. The least well off would provide more donated organs due to their lower economic standing. Simply put, they need the money more than the rich do, so they would donate a larger portion of the available organs. A legal organ market such as this exists in Pakistan, and in 2007, 70% of 2500 kidney transplants were supplied by the extremely poor (Shetty 1316). Instead of using compensation as an incentive to encourage altruism, it becomes a supplementary paycheck to the least well off, therefore confirming many doctors' fears that this system would be paying people to maim themselves.

This scenario introduces another prohibitive aspect of this argument: where would the money come from? If the compensation comes from the pockets of the recipient, the poor would be exploited further. The rich are better able to afford the life-saving organs they require, whereas the poor would struggle to pay the fees necessary to receive the transplant. If we add yet another cost to the recipient, it would make the operation only affordable to the wealthier. Ultimately, the rich would receive more and better care.

If the compensation doesn't come from the patient's pocket, it could be provided by either the hospital or the government. If the hospitals are required to provide the compensation fees, it would only be logical to assume the price for their care during transplantation procedures would increase. Wouldn't this exploit the poor as well? With the assumption that the lower socioeconomic class has less health insurance coverage and higher deductibles, this would cause the recipient to pay more out-of-pocket fees for their surgery, still undermining the less well off. That leaves the government as our other option. Surely, this would solve the problem of burdening the lower class with the additional cost of compensation. However, it would assume that the government has money to put towards an incentive-based donation system.

Arguably the biggest concern Americans have with compensated donation is the possibility of a legal organ market; they fear it would indirectly put a monetary value on a life. Currently, the US National Organ Transplant Act bans the sale of organs (Shetty 1315). Implementing a compensation system does not necessarily mean the U.S. would allow organ trade. However, Francis Delmonico, a professor of surgery at Harvard Medical School, explains that, "you won't be able to fix a price and ensure that price is the only game in town" (qtd. in Shetty 1316). It is easy to overlook the small distinction between giving a monetary reward to a live donor for their altruism and selling an organ. A fixed monetary incentive can easily develop into a competitive business market.

Despite some ethical concerns, allowing a legal market could positively impact the U.S. organ shortage. Advocates for a legal market point out that due to current shortages, many patients are turning to a fast-growing black market. An estimated 14,000 kidney transplants each year are provided by organ trafficking. Creating a legal market, if tightly regulated, would increase the number of available organs and decrease or even eliminate illegal sales (Shetty 1316). Dr. de Castro also argues in favor, explaining that an underground market doesn't ensure the safety of the recipient; there is no guarantee of proper pre- and post-transplant care (145). The black market is a terrifying aspect of the organ shortage; it is devastating that people turn to such dangerous alternatives. However, many Americans are not comfortable putting a negotiable value on human flesh. There must be substitutes for this drastic proposal.

In response to the shortcomings associated with live donor compensation, health policy experts have suggested focusing on the post-mortem donor, and more importantly, the donor's family. By law, a physician has no duty requiring him to discuss the patient's donor status with the family. However, in practice, the family always has the final say (Nelson and Murray). Due to the emotions surrounding the loss of a loved one, it is common for families to say no to donation, even if the deceased was a registered organ donor. To encourage consent, we could propose an incentive to the family such as a fixed monetary contribution to the cost of the donating individual's funeral (Soupcoff). A modest offer such as this would not mistreat any social class, would not risk the development of a market, and just might be enough of an encouragement to the family to reconsider its decision.

Spain has succeeded in attaining the highest organ donation rate in the world through similar means. This country has decided to promote the family decision for organ donation, and they do this through something called the "Family Interview." This interview is based on communication and compassion. Instead of trying to persuade a family to make the decision to donate organs, they focus on morals and values associated with the deceased as well as those associated with donation. This interview is also educational, allowing the doctor to properly inform the family of the legal definition of brain death, and what it means in relation to their loved one (Gil-Diaz 259). This knowledge and analysis of morals allows the family to make a more thoughtful decision, rather than act on raw emotion. However, this interview is founded on the idea that the family should never be pressured into agreeing to donation.

Since this system was implemented, Spain has experienced the highest donation rate in the world. Their deceased donor rate in 2010 was 32 per million population (pmp), as compared to the United States, trailing at 25.6 pmp (Gomez 1593). Obviously, this system works. Due to the compassion and patience provided to families, the medical system in Spain appears transparent and ready to serve the grieving. Never is it misconstrued that a conniving doctor wants the patient dead for his organs. This open communication gives the family comfort in their decision to donate, and has decreased Spain's donation refusal rates from 40-70% throughout the 1990s to just 15.6% in 2006—now the lowest in the world (Gil-Diaz 259).

Let's follow Spain's example, or better yet, become the example. On the course we're headed, the United States will have many more than 114,000 patients waiting for life-saving organs in the coming years. The organ donor shortage will not be fixed overnight, nor will it be fixed with one rule change, but it is obvious that altruism is no longer enough. It never was. The United States needs to educate its people, disprove the myths that evoke trepidation, and spread the truth about the importance of registering as an organ donor. If we can educate the population, the U.S. can implement an opt-out system without outraging the public or scaring donors away. We must take notice of the importance of the donor's family, and develop a program similar to Spain's "Family Interview." If we evaluate our morals, we will realize that it is hypocritical not to donate. We all strive to help others in our day-to-day lives; why not give the greatest help of all, and save someone's life? These patients can't wait much longer. Dedicate five minutes to registering, and America will be on its way to ending the wait.

Works Cited

De Castro, L. D. "Commodification and Exploitation: Arguments in Favor of Compensated Organ Donation." *J Med Ethics* 29 (2003): 142-46. NCBI. Web.

Gil-Diaz, Carlos. "Spain's Record Organ Donations: Mining Moral Conviction: CQ." *Cambridge Quarterly of Healthcare Ethics* 18.3 (2009): 256-61. Web.

Gomez, M. P., G. Paez, and M. Manyalich. "International Registry in Organ Donation and Transplantation 2010." *Transplantation Proceedings* 44.6 (2012): 1592-597. ScienceDirect. Elsevier V.B., 25 July 2012. Web.

Nelson, James Lindeman, and Thomas Murray. "Should Organ Donation Be Automatic Unless A Person Has Expressly Forbidden It?" *Health* (Time Inc. Health) 7.6 (1993): 30. Web.

Shetty, Priya. "Tax Cuts for Organs?" *The Lancet* 374.9698 (2009): 1315-316. Web. 17 Nov. 2012.

Soupcoff, Marni. "The Case Against 'Opt-Out' Organ Donation." *National Post [Canada]* 27 Sept. 2012, Issues & Ideas sec.: A17. LexisNexis Academic. Web.

"Statistics." *Donate Life America*. N.p., n.d. Web. 20 Nov. 2012. <http://donatelife.net/understanding-donation/statistics/>.

Danielle Kot Beng Hooi

My England is Very Powderful

Recently I met an international student from China, Yitong Wang, during an interview where he asked me about my life. Though he prepared for the interview, he had a hard time translating my words onto paper. I remember thinking, while I was sitting next to him, how hard he must be struggling with his assignments in class. At first I felt bad for him and so I asked if he would have preferred if the interview were conducted in his native language instead. He immediately shot me down and said, "No, I prefer to continue in English." At that moment I immediately had newfound respect for him. I relate this encounter with you because I want my readers to understand how easily some people take their language for granted and how hard others struggle to improve on a language that had very little meaning to us back in our home countries.

Coincidentally, I share a similar burden with Yitong. We probably shared the same fears the moment we decided to study in the United States. Personally, I used to spend sleepless nights worrying about my use of English before coming to the United States. Though I knew I could speak, read, and write in English, I constantly wondered if my level of English would meet the expectations required at Drexel. After studying here for a month, I realize that I had good cause to worry. Immediately after arriving, I was bombarded with writing assignments, which I was confident to take on at first. However, after receiving my grades for each and every one of them, I now know that I need to change the way I write in order to do better in class. Before I can improve on my writing, however, I must first understand how and why it developed the way it did. This brought me to my research question: "How does growing up in a country that uses English as a second language affect my writing?"

I decided to start my research by interviewing a friend of mine, Phuong Ha. I chose to interview her because of her unique educational background. Phuong is a Vietnamese who spent nine years of her life in Vietnam before moving to Malaysia. Both Vietnam and Malaysia teach English as a second language. However, when she moved to Malaysia, she studied in a British international school, rather than a Malaysian government school.

I conducted a video-call interview with her through Skype. I chose to have a face-to-face conversation with her rather than e-mailing her a bunch of questions because I wanted to be able to steer the direction of the interview when necessary. I explained that I wanted her to discuss the differences in the way she learned English in both countries. She replied, "I always felt that English was very watered down in Vietnam. We were taught very elementary English [...] how to construct sentences, simple grammar, and basic vocabulary. We only ever used English during our English class. Other than that, Vietnamese was used for every other subject. When I moved to a British school I was caught off guard when I was introduced to poems and novels." We spent the rest of the conversation discussing her views on her own writing. She explained that in Vietnam she never had to write long essays, so the idea of reflective writing or creative writing was foreign to her.

During the interview I felt like I could relate very much to her views on English writing. It occurred to me that I lacked writing practice as she did when she studied in Vietnam. "Practice is the key to success," as some would say. Sadly, writing was never given much emphasis in my school and so the only essays I was ever asked to write were for my exams. Even then, those writing assignments were rigid and had to follow a certain structure. So other than writing in my diary, the idea of creative writing for schoolwork was foreign to me. Beyond that, I could only use English during English class while I was forced to think and write in my national language during science classes, math, history, and so forth. After the interview, I wanted to compare my situation with other ESL (English as a Second Language) countries.

I went to Drexel's library's website which led me to ProQuest Research Library. From there I searched for scholarly journals that related to Writing for Second Language Learners. This eventually led me to "Opinion of Second Language Learners about Writing Difficulties in English Language." In this article, the authors Muhammad Shahid Farooq, Muhammad Uzair-Ul Hassan and S. Wahid researched the writing difficulties in the English language faced by second language learners. It was specifically about difficulties in writing the English language related to grammar, punctuation, vocabulary, and spelling for students with English as a second language. The study was conducted in Pakistan, where the primary language was Urdu. The results of the study showed that "...the most occurring difficulty in writing English language was that of rhetoric and grammar [...]. The most serious problems were that of vocabulary deficiency [...] and confusion in grammatical rules" (Farooq, Hassan & Wahid. 191).

Following the study in Pakistan, it occurred to me that just like my country, students lacked the proper foundation for the English language. The poor understanding of grammatical structure and the lack of vocabulary made it difficult for ESL (English as a Second Language) students to develop their writing skills. How are we to advance in more complex rhetorical writing capabilities when we do not know the basic elements of the English language? Personally, I admit I have always struggled with grammar, spelling, and punctuation difficulties. My schools focused more on how to communicate in English than understanding the key concepts of the language. So, if someone were to ask me to describe basic grammatical structure like present perfect tense, I would probably not know the answer. I started to wonder why ESL students had such poor levels of understanding English when it came to writing. The first thing that came to mind was the "technique of teaching." So the next question would be, "Which process of teaching would best mold a student's writing ability?"

I returned to searching through articles on the ProQuest Research Library and eventually came across "The Influence of Process Approach on English as Second Language Students' Performances in Essay Writing." The article, written by Timothy Kolade Akinwamide of Ekiti State University, explained that there are two different approaches to the teaching of writing. The first is the Product Oriented Approach: "This approach focuses on the product—the written text that serves as the model for the learner. It was believed that if a model text written by an accomplished and competent writer is given to students to read, the students imbibe all the good qualities of writing and thus become good writers" (Akinwamide 20). The second approach is the Process-Oriented Approach, which "focuses on the writer's potential for self-correction as a means of achieving success in writing. It involves several identifiable stages like, Prewriting, Writing and the Final draft" (Akinwamide 20).

According to the results of the research, students usually performed better under the Process Approach. Teachers need to move away from being a marker to a reader, responding to the content of student writing more than the form. After reading this article, I completely agreed with Akinwamide that the teachers shouldn't rely on the traditional approach while teaching a language. Personally, I was never introduced to the Process Approach while studying in Malaysia. I was usually just given an assignment, may it be an essay or a summary about a novel, and my teacher would mark whatever I wrote. In fact, I was usually encouraged to cram summaries and answers to specific questions to pass examinations. It was only after arriving at Drexel and attending English 101 that writing became more of an interactive process. Though I admit I am still struggling to accept this new concept of writing, it has helped me understand my own process of writing.

So, if the Process Approach has been proven to be more effective, why don't more teachers use this approach? There are a number of reasons why but I chose to look at it from the teachers' perspective. "Second language teachers of English language have their own limitations" (Akinwamide 21). It occurred to me that most English teachers in my country were once ESL students as well and had a similar English education as I did. So, it is possible that they too struggle with the language. Therefore it's possible that some teachers may either gloss over or ignore certain basic skills they find problematic themselves in the teaching processes. In fact, I was considered lucky because I went to a school in the city. Some teachers in the rural schools can't even speak English properly.

Beside the differences in the way writing is taught, I wanted to evaluate if there were any other factors that contributed to the differences in my writing from a student who uses English as a first language. Scrolling through articles again, one study stood out: "Cultural Factors in EAP Teaching—Influences of Thought Pattern on English Academic Writing." The author, Xiuyan Xu of China University of Geosciences, examined the influences of Chinese and Western thought patterns on English Academic Writing. Xu believed that due to the differences in historical background and educational policies, Chinese thought pattern differs from western thought pattern in many ways. This directly affects one's writing because of the relationship between language and thought. In one section of the paper, Xu wrote, "Chinese students rely heavily on memorization, which is a result of application of the same methodology when they were learning their first, native language. In order for one to learn Chinese, an individual must use memorization skills, which are the learning skills that they draw on in their later learning. This culturally constructed way of learning significantly affects Chinese students' learning English [...] this methodology of learning is generally incompatible when used in learning English." Xu goes on to explains that culture plays a huge role in the way we write and therefore in order for ESL students to improve on writing, we must first understand the cultural background they came from as well as understanding their use of their first language.

I agree with Xu's article in the sense that we cannot remove our mother language when learning to write in English. The difficulty most ESL students face is that they first think in their mother language and then translate it to English when writing. This becomes a problem because each language has its own set of rules, so a direct translation might distort the written message. Personally, English has always been my predominant language. So, thinking in English comes naturally to me. However, this concept applied to me when I was learning Malaysia's native language, Bahasa Malaysia (BM). Up till now, every time I needed to use BM, I would always translate the words directly from English. By doing so, I screwed up the grammatical structure of the sentence in BM. Like every other language, BM has its own set of rules, so a direct translation will lead to errors if you don't know how to apply those rules. For example, a direct translation of "school bus" would be "sekolah bas." However, in BM, the correct structure would be "bas sekolah."

So, does this mean that people who use English as a second language are forever influenced by cultural differences and therefore cannot improve on the way we write? With all this research on the problems faced by ESL students, I was positive that solutions were not far away. After scrolling through the World Wide Web with the keywords "English Second Language Today," I came across a documentary by CNN-IBN, titled "Why learning English has become a fad in China." This video showed that China was rapidly progressing and because of that, the use of the English language was given more emphasis. The Chinese government understands that in order to be relevant in the future, their people must master the English language. Today, the English-learning industry in China is worth nearly 2 billion pounds and there are more than 50,000 English-training organizations in the country (Chakrabarti).

After watching the video, it became clear to me that it is possible to improve English in countries that use English as a second language. As seen in China, children are being sent to English learning centers as young as two years old. Funding for the improvement of the English language has increased because the government sees English as beneficial for its country. With increased funding, better English language teachers are brought in from other countries; teachers are being trained to identify ESL issues and how to tackle them; more and more English learning centers are being built for those students who need extra attention outside of school. If more and more countries try to establish a better English education system, maybe the gap between ESL writers and native English language writers wouldn't be so vast.

From my research, I realize that there are many levels as to why my English writing is shaped the way is it. Education plays an important role. Without a proper foundation in English, one's writing is bound to suffer. Secondly, our first language is a major barrier to our development of our second language. In order to improve on my English writing, I need to either find a way to separate my thought process when I use the different languages or find a way to incorporate both the languages. The answer to that is still unknown to me but perhaps with more research I might come across a solution that would help me. It has also come to my attention that my country doesn't face this problem alone. However, as we have seen in China, actions are being taken to overcome the barrier to the English language. In fact, a few years back, my country passed a law to change all math and science subjects into English because it understood the importance of English on a global scene. So perhaps those students who benefit from this change will have a different outlook on this research question than I did.

Works Cited

Akinwamide, Timothy Kolade. "The Influence of Process Approach on English as Second Language Students' Performances in Essay Writing." *English Language Teaching* 16-29. Web. March 2012. <http://search.proquest.com/pqrl/docview/10091 62073/13A6872513894B5D6F4/3?accountid=10559#>

Chakrabarti, Sumon K, CNN-IBN. "Why learning English has become a fad in China." Video. 2 July 2011. <http://ibnlive.in.com/news/why-learning-english-has-become-a-fad-in-china/164029-2.html>

Farooq, Muhammad Shahid, Muhammad Uzair-Ul-Hassan, and S. Wahid. "Opinion of Second Language Learners about Writing Difficulties in English Language." *South Asian Studies* 27.1 (2012): 183-94.Web. 15 November 2012. <http://search.proquest.com/pqrl/docview/1023239824/13A6872513894B5D6F4/6?accountid=10559#>

Ha, Phuong, Personal Interview. 1 November 2012.

Xiuyan, Xu. "Cultural Factors in EAP Teaching - Influences of Thought Pattern on English Academic Writing." *Cross-Cultural Communication* 8.4 (2012): 53-57. Web. 4 November 2012. <http://search.proquest.com/pqrl/docview/1038461889/13A32DF6 A4394B5D6F4/3?accountid=10559#>

Zach Gregory and Paul Martorano

Lost In Transition

As 1976 came to a close, so too did the Cultural Revolution in China; however, the great nation did not walk away from this event unscathed. Despite its growth, the economy was inefficient, requiring increasing amounts of labor and money, and was on the verge of collapse (Field). If China's new leaders did not do something, this rising country would soon crumble to the ground. In 1978 a radical change was made to China's economy; China would adopt a new market economy that hybridized capitalism and socialism. Although the approach taken was "slow-but-sure," the results of the transition were dramatic. In rural areas of China, communes were disbanded and replaced by free markets, causing villages and towns to flourish (Suliman). By 2000, the average rural population's income had tripled from what it was in 1990 (the National Bureau of Statistics of China), causing the percentage of people in poverty to drop from 80% down to 13% (Ravallion and Chen). The agrarian areas of China were by no means the only places reaping the benefits of the economic change. The urban population's average income quadrupled (the National Bureau of Statistics of China), Gross Domestic Product (GDP) and exports increased, and inflation and unemployment stayed under 10% and 5% respectively (Suliman). The overall effect of the astonishing reform was an increased quality of living for many of China's nearly 1.3 billion citizens at the time (Klein and Özmucur). It was undoubtedly an exciting time to be a Chinese citizen, or so one would expect.

Despite the significant improvement to China's economy and overall living conditions across the board, the nation's average happiness actually declined significantly from 1990 to 2000. The amount of people who would describe themselves as very happy fell from 28% to 12%, and life satisfaction—the overall evaluation we make of our lives and an aspect of subjective well being (Feist and Rosenberg)—dropped from 7.3 to 6.5 (measured on a scale from 1-10). This trend of declining happiness held true for both the urban and rural population, as well as for all income groups (Brockmann, Delhey and Welzel). Happiness in transition countries, that is, countries with transition economies that are changing from a centrally planned system to a free market system (Feige), experience a decrease in average national happiness despite the improvement of living conditions.

China was not the only country facing this situation; in the early '90s the former countries of the Soviet Union began their own transitions. By doing away with government institutions and privatizing their economies, the countries were able to stimulate significant economic growth. By the late 1990s, the average GDP of eastern and central European countries had increased 40% since before the transition. The number of cars and phones doubled between 1990 to 2006 and 1990 to 2004 respectively, and the amount of people who owned computers rose by a factor of 30 during the same period (Guriev and Zhuravskaya). However, a series of surveys conducted by the World Value Survey from 1994-2003 found "self-reported life satisfaction ha[d] fallen during transition and [was] below the levels of life satisfaction in other countries with similar per capita income."

These findings went against decades of established ideas on happiness, including the Easterlin Paradox. The appropriately named paradox was spawned when Richard Easterlin posed the question, "Does Economic Growth Improve the Human Lot?", to which he received a surprising answer. Contrary to what the average person might believe, Easterlin found that happiness remains stagnant regardless of rapid economic growth. These results were revolutionary and heavily influenced economics (Angeles).

The paradox is explained by two ideas: "relative happiness" and "norm adjustment." Ruut Veenhoven, sociologist and accredited social psychologist (World Database of Happiness), summarizes these two ideas in his article "Is Happiness Relative?" He writes:

> Happiness results from comparison. The evaluation of life is a more or less conscious mental process and involves assessment of the degree to which perceptions of life-as-it-is meet the individual's standards of what-life-should-be. The better the fit, the happier the person...

> Standards of comparison adjust. Standards follow perception of reality. If living conditions are seen to improve, standards rise. If conditions are seen to get worse, standards are lowered. Adjustment follows with some delay.

Consequently, as one's standard of living improves, it should approach their expectations of what life should be like; however, that standard is constantly increasing. Hence an improving economy and better quality of life doesn't lead to a happier nation, according to Easterlin and his paradox. Still, though, China's and the former Soviet Union's citizens didn't exhibit static happiness through their economic transition; their happiness dropped significantly. So there must be more at play.

Hilke Brockmann, a professor of sociology at Jacobs University, and her team looked into three possible factors while they were investigating the mystery of China's disappearing happiness: anomie, political disaffection, and relative deprivation. Anomie—the state of society lacking social norms (Dictionary.com)—is common after massive reforms, especially one as large as the change China went through. Cities grew rapidly, people left the countryside for careers, and the Internet and cell phones became widespread. This can leave citizens feeling stressed and powerless, which ultimately leads to unhappiness (Durkheim). Political disaffection—unhappiness with the government—was another consideration, especially because people tend to be happier living in a democratic environment (Inglehart), so a lack of democracy may lead to people being sadder. Despite China's economical changes, politically China was more or less the same; political freedoms and civil liberties were still extremely limited, even in 2000 (Freedom House). One might wonder why the political institution would suddenly incite sadness when it had been around all along. Veenhoven explains that "political freedom is more important in wealthier nations than in poorer nations, whereas economic freedom has a stronger effect on well being in poor countries than in wealthy ones." The inverse of relative happiness, relative deprivation refers to people comparing their situations to others and seeing themselves as disadvantaged, resulting in lowered happiness (Brockmann, Delhey and Welzel). Although the change in economy helped China, it did not benefit all parts of China equally. In fact, one of the major problems with the transition was the inequality of the distribution of wealth (Field). *The World Bank Economic Review* reveals an important perspective of the transition:

> Despite the increases in the average output and income
> of Chinese citizens since the reforms, the gains have not
> been evenly distributed, and urban residents without
> rations and rural net consumers were hurt by the price
> changes. In addition, disparities in rural areas, which
> have always existed (Ahmad and Zou 1989), have been
> exacerbated as a result of the reform, with the irrigated
> coastal areas benefiting relatively more than others.

Consider the hypothetical situation of giving gifts to two children during the holidays. If one were to receive a better gift than the other, the child receiving the "worse" gift would feel disadvantaged and would be upset. In the end, one child experienced a decline in happiness though they both were better off than before.

Brockmann conducted a number of surveys on the rural and urban populations in China during the 1990-2000 decade. She measured subjective powerlessness, political distrust, and financial dissatisfaction to operationalize—to define a concept or variable so that it can be measured or expressed quantitatively—anomie, political disaffection, and relative deprivation respectively. Feelings of powerlessness did not increase by a significant amount in rural areas though they did in some urban populations, leading Brockmann to the conclusion that anomie did not cause the declining happiness in the rural population. However, anomie may have contributed to the unhappiness in urban populations. Political distrust had dramatically changed based on the population type. Distrust in the government increased significantly in the rural populations; however, it decreased significantly in the urban ones. Brockmann found, however, that the relationship between political distrust and life satisfaction that was apparent in 1990 had lost importance in 2000, leading to the conclusion that political distrust couldn't be responsible for the unhappiness.

Financial dissatisfaction showed the most promising results. Almost all of the rural population had become less satisfied with their financial situation and much of the urban population had as well. Additionally, financial dissatisfaction was the only one of the three variables to show significant increases in both populations and an increase in its negative effect on life satisfaction. Brockmann's data suggests that relative deprivation was the cause of China's unhappiness, as she explains in her report:

> To sum up, relative deprivation turns out to be the most
> promising explanation for two reasons: First, the climate
> of economic growth and top-driven income inequality
> seems to stimulate social comparisons, making many
> Chinese unhappy about their financial situation, even
> though they might be better off in absolute terms. Second,
> the income situation in 2000 played a more important role
> for overall life satisfaction than it did 10 years ago.

The same phenomenon occurred in the other transition countries; in nine focus-group interviews, conducted in nine Russian cities by the Institute for Comparative Social Research in Moscow (CESSI) and the European Bank for Reconstruction and Development (EBRD), one of the five factors found to contribute to unhappiness was increase of inequality and perceived unfairness of the new socioeconomic order (Guriev and Zhuravskaya). These cases of people whose income and quality of life are increasing yet their happiness declines are called frustrated achievers (Brockmann, Delhey and Welzel). Frustrated achievers aren't only influenced by those in their country; as these transitioning countries' economies increased so did their citizens' use of the

Internet and communication. One of the other five factors found to decrease happiness in transition countries during the focus-group interviews was "an increase in aspiration levels due to better information about the quality of life in high-income countries" (Guriev and Zhuravskaya). During one of the interviews a Russian citizen shared his perspective:

> I am sure that we will not live like normal people, our
> lifetime will not be enough to see the change for the
> better. Throughout my life I worked as an engineer, lived
> in a good one-bedroom apartment, and was satisfied with
> my life. But when my brother-in-law went to Israel and told
> us how he lived there, then we realized that life could be
> different. He has two cars and a house! In our country, only
> a director of a plant could live like that, certainly not an
> engineer. Only then I realized how badly we live.

Ultimately, it seems like the old cliché that money can't buy happiness really holds up, even when that money is billions of dollars in free-market-generated income. On the contrary, it actually brought sorrow. The unequal distribution of wealth in transition countries causes feelings of disadvantage, which depresses feelings of happiness. Furthermore, it creates these frustrated achievers whose unhappiness is only exacerbated by their increasing knowledge of other, wealthier countries. The famous 1990s rapper Biggie Smalls must have been referring to these countries as they were transitioning when he recorded "Mo Money Mo Problems." The sentiment is more elegantly put by English economist Arthur Pigou: "Men do not desire to be rich, but to be richer than other men."

Bibliography

Angeles, Luis. "A closer look at the Easterlin Paradox." *The Journal of Socio-Economics* (02/2011): 67-73. Web.

"anomie." Online Etymology Dictionary. Douglas Harper, Historian. 16 Nov. 2012. <Dictionary.com http://dictionary.reference.com/browse/anomie>.

Brockmann, Hilke, et al. "The China Puzzle: Falling Happiness in a Rising Economy." *Journal of Happiness Studies* (08/2009): 387-405. Web.

Durkheim as cited in Brockmann, Hilke, et al. "The China Puzzle: Falling Happiness in a Rising Economy." *Journal of Happiness Studies* (08/2009): 387-405. Web.

Feige, Edgar L. "The Transition to a Market Economy in Russia: Property Rights, Mass Privatization and Stabilization." *Skąpska, Grażyna* (12/2003): 57-78. Web.

Feist, Gregory J. and Erika L. Rosenberg. *Psychology: Making Connections.* McGraw Hill Companies, Inc., 01/2009. Web.

Field, Robert Michael. "China's Industrial Performance since 1978." *The China Quarterly* (09/1992): 577-607. Web.

Guriev, Sergei and Ekaterina Zhuravskaya. "(Un)happiness in Transition." *The Journal of Economic Prespectives* (2009): 143-168. Web.

Guriev and Zhuravskaya as cited in Brockmann, Hilke, et al. "The China Puzzle: Falling Happiness in a Rising Economy." *Journal of Happiness Studies* (08/2009): 387-405. Web.

Ingleshart as cited in Brockmann, Hilke, et al. "The China Puzzle: Falling Happiness in a Rising Economy." *Journal of Happiness Studies* (08/2009): 387-405. Web.

Klein and Özmucur as cited in Brockmann, Hilke, et al. "The China Puzzle: Falling Happiness in a Rising Economy." *Journal of Happiness Studies* (08/2009): 387-405. Web.

The National Bureau of Statistics of China as cited in Brockmann, Hilke, et al. "The China Puzzle: Falling Happiness in a Rising Economy." *Journal of Happiness Studies* (08/2009): 387-405. Web.

Ravallion and Chen as cited in Brockmann, Hilke, et al. "The China Puzzle: Falling Happiness in a Rising Economy." *Journal of Happiness Studies* (08/2009): 387-405. Web.

Suliman, Osman. *China's Transition to a Socialist Market Economy.* Westport, CT, USA: Greenwood Press, 09/1998. eBook.

Veenhoven, Ruut. "Is Happiness Relative?" *Social Indicators Research* (02/1991): 1-34. Web.

World Database of Happiness. *World Database of Happiness.* n.d. Web. 15 November 2012. <http://www1.eur.nl/fsw/happiness/>.

Daniel Schoepflin

NO-M-G: An Exploration of and Often Futile Resistance to Internet Jargon

As I sat in class, my attention quickly shifted from the droning lecture to my droning cell phone buzzing. I thought that perhaps would provide some interesting diversion, but was unprepared for the reaction my mind would have upon seeing the text I had received.

The letters in front of me appeared no different than a jumbled cacophony. "OMG! TTYL BFF!" What I was reading had to be some sort of frenetic code, right? It couldn't possibly have any meaning. It couldn't possibly be... *English*. And yet there they were—a series of largely incoherent letters that my friend had sent to me. Worse yet, I understood them perfectly. Worst of all, I was sending back nearly the same thing. I then started wondering, did these acronyms have any actual meaning? How did these words come into being on the Internet and how did they invade our face-to-face conversation?

The question of the morphing language of the Internet and the growing interdependence of face-to-face communication and cyberspace communication would help to define a generation. Generation Y and Generation Z grow up around the words and are characterized by this new growth and technology, and therefore the language that surrounds them. Furthermore, the development of the Internet language has accompanied a development of a new subculture of "memes" and media ("gifs," "movs," "jpegs," and the like). Finally, perhaps if I could discover the effect the Internet has had on our culture and language, then I could extrapolate and decide how one changes language and culture on a more global scale.

After settling down to establish the question more thoroughly and research the topic, I attempted to find a comprehensive look at the developing language of the Internet. Unfortunately, while I was researching, my phone vibrated time and time again with incessant text messages containing the above slang and jargon. Eventually, despite my distractions, I was able to find a paper written by a "cyber-linguist," Squires.

In her article featured in *Language in Society*, Squires sought to characterize the growing importance of Internet slang and jargon. In the article, Squires compares Internet "chatspeak" to "Pittsburghese," a dialect of

English in Western Pennsylvania (Squires). Both exist as a sort of subset of the English language, where common words are used in addition to those that would be considered totally foreign to an onlooker (or perhaps "onlistener"). While she acknowledges the similarities between the two, Squires indicates that the rapidly evolving nature of the communication on the blogosphere makes it much more difficult to analyze. She then seeks to categorize the "metadiscourse" (which she considers the development of communication as communicating is occurring) by analyzing the development of the words therein. As I read her article, I agreed with her sentiment that the use of acronyms on the Internet spurred the use of more acronyms and that the creation of unique phrases seem to have innumerable possible causes. She calls the youth of today "natively entrenched in digital technology" and explains that modern conversational language can be "weakened" by "chatspeak" as well (Squires). I agreed with her ideas about conversation, feeling that phrases such as "OMG" and "B/F" detracted from conversations and marginalized communication.

I wondered more and more about the conversation that had sparked my initial inquiry. Squires made me wonder about what had been said. Had anything of any importance actually been said? In the midst of all of the slang and jargon, was any meaning there? R. Goldsborough, an author for the journal *Teacher Librarian*, explains that there are "important" slang words and jargon phrases used on the Internet that have certain meaning (Goldsborough), at least in 2007. Unfortunately, Goldsborough's list was simultaneously outdated and incomprehensive. This illustrated Squires' idea that the lifespan of Internet words is short and they often change quickly.

Squires also raised a point that I found interesting. She brought to light the idea that the younger generation, which has grown up using "netspeak," is more likely to use the jargon prevalent on the Internet than the older generations. I then decided to do a little experiment. With the consent of those around me (a simple "ruok w this" or "Are you okay with this?"), I made a hidden recording of all of the instances of Internet slang and "memes" in a typical conversation. I found three cases of memes (e.g. "first-world problems" and "GO! BWAH!"), two cases of "OMG," five cases of "LOL," and four cases of the pesky "ZOMG" (a phrase which I apparently could not escape despite all of my efforts). All this took place within a relatively short time, indicating the prevalence of the words in our face-to-face conversation (Schoepflin).

After reworking the language of my searches in cyberspace to find information to strengthen my essay on the language of cyberspace, I found another appropriate article. Windham, a Ph.D. candidate at the George Washington University, successfully defended his dissertation in which he sought to illustrate the connection between use of social media, chat rooms, and instant messaging and adolescent psychosocial adjustment. He explained that many adolescents display dependence on electronic communication methods and that this largely affects their development (Windham). As I read the article, I took note of the profound effect that Internet jargon has on our lives, realizing that this may be the reason why it has entered our interpersonal daily conversation. His explanation that youths are more dependent on electronic communication and the deduction that I had made coincided with the idea of Squires that youths are more likely to use "chatspeak" in discourse. Ultimately, while the research of Windham differed from mine at first glance, I felt that they were inherently linked and knew that he could help me reach a conclusion.

I sat there, staring at my computer screen intently, and read through the articles I had gathered again. Something was missing from my quest. I seemed to try everything. The data I had found was leading me to a solution, but was not concrete enough for me to succinctly summarize it. Barring reading the papers backwards, it seemed that I had analyzed them as thoroughly as I was capable. ZOMG! Was I reaching an end to my search for knowledge? I was able to find a thorough characterization of the language as a whole, I was able to list the common phrases, I was able to show that the words developed, I was able to show that the use of Internet phrases and communications affected children, but I simply could not find the way that online jargon had permeated into our spoken word.

Far from ROFL-ing, I felt quite defeated. Ironically, while writing to a friend on Facebook, it seemed as though Mark Zuckerburg had given me the same insight he had had when creating his worldwide phenomenon. It was utterly electrifying. It was so simple that it was infuriating. The reason behind the adoption of the jargon of the Internet into our modern vernacular was intertwined with the Internet itself. The words developed as shorthand on the Internet and the popularity of the Internet and the words therein inspired their inclusion in our day-to-day speech.

Everything seemed remarkably clear, yet muddy. There should have been no impetus for the phrase "Obamacare" to catch on, but it did. A popular individual used it and his popularity coincided with its popularity. Similarly, there should have been no impetus for the phrase "ROFL" to catch on; however, as the Internet grew in popularity, "ROFL" did as well. The dependence on the Internet described by Windham spurred an increase in use of shorthand words on the Internet such as those described by Goldsborough, which, in turn, developed the ever-growing "metadiscourse" described by Squires.

The answer that I obtained was relieving, but unfulfilling. I felt as though I was missing out on some grander, deeper solution. However, I realized that while my research did not produce a satisfying result, it could continue developing alongside the Internet, the language on the Internet, and the English language as a whole. I was free to continue investigating, but could take solace in the fact that I had indeed discovered something about my BFF, the Internet.

As I sat behind another group of people having a conversation riddled with Internet jargon, I had to try to withhold my laughter again. "OMG!" someone yelled loudly. I could no longer contain myself. The corners of my lips turned upward, I took a deep breath, and I LOL'd.

Works Cited

Goldsborough, Reid. "Lingo for a techno age." *Teacher Librarian*, 34(5) (2007): 54,71. ProQuest Research Library.Web. 15 November 2012. <http://search.proquest.com/do cview/224877052?accountid=10559>

Schoepflin, Daniel R. Clandestine Recordings of Casual Conversation. 12 November 2012. Raw data.

SMS Services.N.d. Photograph. http://masterthenewnet.com/tag/text-messages/, n.p.

Squires, Lauren. "Enregistering Internet Language." *Language in Society* 39.04 (2010): 457-92. ProQuest Dissertations and Theses. Web. 15 November 2012. <http://search. proquest.com/docview/744520868/fulltextPDF?accountid=10559>.

Windham, R. C. "The Changing Landscape of Adolescent Internet Communication and Its Relationship to Psychosocial Adjustment and Academic Performance." (2007): n. pag. ProQuest Dissertations and Theses. Web. 15 November 2012. <http://search.proquest.com/docview/304871113?accountid=10559>.

Julia Turner

Another Fish, Please

Writing does not come easily to everyone. Many people struggle with writing throughout their academic and professional careers. There are a variety of reasons for the resulting carnage of the English language that occurs when some attempt to write. Common causes of inadequacy and resistance to writing include restriction by harsh guidelines, too much allowance provided by vague instructions, and distracted writing.

I am a prime example of a distracted writer. When I tried to begin this essay my brain shut down entirely. I tried a miscellany of techniques to focus my attention. I started by trying to write my ideas down on paper, where the Internet and "one quick game" of FreeCell could not distract me. I attempted to shut off the inner dialogue that focuses on everything except the task at hand. *I think Dasani is probably my favorite kind of bottled water...*

After about two or three hours, I had a good chunk of my composition completed, created a fine piece of artwork in the margin of my paper, and composed a list of possible things I could text to a boy.

Obviously, I was not getting anywhere, so I cleared my desk of distractions—and by distractions I mean everything except my desk lamp. I gave my cellphone to my roommate and finally opened a Word document. Despite all of my efforts, I still could not write. I could not form a proper sentence to save my life. The only reason I am making any progress right now is because my roommate is sitting beside me allotting me one Goldfish per complete sentence. Unfortunately, not every struggling writer feels the same way about Goldfish as I do, so I cannot imagine what persuades them to write. Going to the root of the problem, what is it that causes this resistance to and trouble with writing?

I should just text him. I think I'll go with #4 ("Whaddup, C-Money?"). It's cool. It's casual. He has to respond to a question...

Poor student writers, myself very much included in this group, habitually employ the use of one of the most exhausted, but seemingly successful, writing techniques: Give the grader what he or she wants. After the first few writing assignments, we have usually figured out what kind of writing the grader wants to see: "...students learn how to play the game of school..." (Carroll 7). For particularly stubborn students, the necessary flexibility of this technique becomes a problem. Students, along with submission to each grader's certain criteria for good writing, must be able to tailor their writing to the demands of each individual subject: "...various disciplines teach ways of writing that are not only different but, often, contradictory" (Carroll 7). The rules associated with the construction of a history paper will, undoubtedly, differ from those guiding the composition of a biology paper. For students, this means that their methods of writing are never fully appropriate or correct because they are constantly changing them to suit a new set of preferences. It seems that colleges and universities have taken steps to remedy the issue of subject-specific writing. An increasing number of college classes look into how a student can combine the techniques of every type of writing he or she has encountered. However, high schools and middle schools rarely take the time to explain to students how their writing methods can be applicable in every writing situation they face. The frustration that is associated with the constant adaptation of one's writing can certainly lead to a resistance towards writing.

Do we have any straws? That is the only thing that would make this bottled water better...

Just like writing itself, learning to write is a process. From grade school on up, we build upon the techniques and rules we learn each year. Most students' first introduction to formal essay writing happens in middle school; it is the first time students explore some of the most important writing techniques associated with the composition of lengthy papers and complex idea development. However, it is also the time when teachers are apt to "baby" students and let them get away with taking advantage of the term "artistic license." At Knickerbacker Middle School in Eastern Upstate New York, students were performing poorly on state-mandated English Language Arts tests, so a group of teachers took the initiative to revamp the English Department. They enhanced the use of peer review, self-assessment, and writing rubrics and even set up a competition between classes. As previously mentioned, middle school is a time for exceptions. While almost all of the students were expected to receive a score of three or higher on the rubric, a single student was given a different offer: "I made a deal with him and told him it could be our little secret. Since this student struggled academically and had had difficulties with writing in the past, I thought it would be fair that, if he received a two for every criterion, the whole class could still receive the reward" (Andrade et al. 11). The idea that students can be held to individual standards throughout their academic career is a nice thought, but it is simply unrealistic. Giving students exceptions in middle school does not prepare them for higher level learning where individual struggles have a much smaller, almost nonexistent role in evaluation. This allowance in the beginning does not encourage students to improve their writing or work harder to achieve work comparable to that of their peers.

It is not surprising that when these students reach a point in time when their individual writing dilemmas do not matter, some of them stop trying to create works with any literary value. Coming from a small school, academic flexibility is not a foreign concept to me. It was a known and accepted idea among my teachers that I was a big fan of math and that writing was not my strongest point. Before they actually had me in class, every English teacher knew that if I was given the slightest bit of "wiggle room" in an assignment, I would turn in a set of haikus about a character in the required reading. When Advanced Placement Literature was forced upon me by a merciless guidance counselor, I had an incredibly hard time. It was a distance-learning class, so the teacher did not know me and I was being graded in comparison to every other student in the country. After months of turning in subpar work and receiving appropriately subpar grades, I changed my techniques and forgot all about the fill-in-the-blank essay style I previously relied on. I have to wonder that if my writing reputation did not follow me through middle and high school, would I be a better writer today?

He hasn't responded yet. I've been ignored like a sad little impossible-to-open pistachio...

Writing can draw influence from an infinite number of sources. These influences can guide writing in unintended directions, restrict the freedom of idea development, and facilitate writing that brims with bias: "... variations—sometimes extreme—from [the] norm in terms of class, race, family background, religion, and family income [may] sometimes affect the students' writing, their understanding of writing, and their 'success' as they make their way from the first to the final year of college" (Bernard-Donals 337). As colleges are known to be relatively diverse, there are a tremendous number of different beliefs and ideals shaping the writing of the student body. These factors may dictate how or why the writing of a student veers from the path set by an instructor. In many cases, students are unwilling to bend their set of beliefs in order to conform to what the grader wants. It is not important that their writing is correct as compared to other works, but that it reflects the beliefs and standards with which they conduct themselves.

Dear Lord. He was probably bullied in middle school by some kid who called himself "C-Money." I've reopened a deep, deep wound...

For some students, words simply do not make sense. They do not fit together like how two numbers add up to a sum. Others cannot compose when restricted by guidelines while some cannot produce work without following exact directions. For many there are too many distractions or the motivation to write is simply not present. Every student is different. For some, a journey that is supposed to develop better writing turns into one that is a quest for the thing(s) that motivate(s) and facilitate their ability to write.

And after all of those Goldfish, he still hasn't responded...

Works Cited

Andrade, Heidi, et al. "Assessment-Driven Improvements in Middle School Students' Writing." *Middle School Journal* 40.4 (2009): 4-12. *ProQuest Research Library*. Web. 29 Nov. 2012.

Bernard-Donals, Michael. "REVIEW: Truth and Method: What Goes on in Writing Classes, and how do we Know?" *College English* 66.3 (2004): 335-343. *ProQuest Research Library*. Web. 2 Nov. 2012.

Carroll, Lee Ann. *Rehearsing New Roles: How College Students Develop As Writers.* Carbondale: Southern Illinois UP, 2002. Print.

Josh Weiss

Academically Creative

The topic of my second composition is written with the aim of figuring out the reason why I prefer creative writing to academic writing. While coming up with a way to construct such an essay, it occurred to me that I could utilize the very genre of creative writing in order to explore the matter. As a result, a play seemed like the most creative and enjoyable way to get my point across, not just for the writer, but for the reader as well. For the sake of this assignment, both academic and creative writing have been classified as fiction and nonfiction. This play consists of six different writers who represent either fiction or nonfiction. The conversation that ensues will hopefully solve the topic question:

Scene: *A room with four sides, but no door. Computer screens and flashing lights of all colors and sizes cover every available inch of wall. They are all making beeping noises at different pitches. Although five chairs sit in the middle of this cell-like room, six individuals are present. The types of chairs are a small black stool, a wooden rocking chair, a recliner, a desk chair, and a folding chair. Ray Bradbury is standing, scribbling furiously on his notepad with a No. 2 pencil, only taking time to look up and marvel at his surroundings. He also takes breaks to retrieve a handkerchief from his trouser pocket and dab at his sweaty forehead. Anne Frank, a young girl, is seated on the black stool, wearing a plain white dress with nice black dress shoes, cradling a small book in her arms. She is extremely pale and stares blankly at a flashing blue light. Malcolm Gladwell, sitting on the folding chair, is punching numbers into an adding machine that is perched on his lap. It continues to crank out rolls of paper with complex calculations on them. Harriet Beecher Stowe, an old woman, is sitting motionless in the rocking chair, eyes closed, breathing slowly. There is a blanket on her lap. The fifth individual is a petite woman wearing a red dress, clogs, and glasses. Her hair is black. She sits at the desk, grading a stack of papers with a red pen. Every so often, she snorts in amusement at the writing of one of her students. H.P. Lovecraft stands in the corner, wearing a pinstriped suit. He is wide-eyed and believes that no one else can see him. Somewhere outside the room, the song "Sympathy For The Devil" by the Rolling Stones begins to play. Lovecraft begins to snap his fingers to the beat and mumble the lyrics beneath his breath. Every so often, there is a clack! clack! clack! sound that is coming from nowhere in particular. Nobody pays it any heed.*

Bradbury: [*like a giddy schoolchild*] Incredible! Just incredible! I mean, just look at all this stuff! [*he dabs at his head with his handkerchief while breathing deeply*]

Stowe: [*being the wise old crone that she is, Stowe speaks softly without opening her eyes*] Ray, if you keep it up, you're going to give yourself a heart attack.

Bradbury: [*sarcastically*] Thanks, mom. But come on. This stuff is straight out of, well, science fiction. Just think of all the stories I could write based on this room alone.

Gladwell: Speaking of this room, where are we? [*he stops punching numbers on his machine long enough to take a look over both shoulders. Lovecraft still believes that no one can see him and continues to sing along with the Stones*]

Lovecraft: [*under his breath*] I rode a tank, held a general's rank when the blitzkrieg raged and the bodies stank... [*at this lyric, Anne Frank shudders, but does not look away from the blue light*]

Bradbury: [*for the first time, his excitement is replaced with confusion*] You know what? I have no clue. I distinctly remember that I was standing in a cornfield investigating crop circles. I was thinking of how it would make a great short story, but then there was this bright light. I must have blacked out because the next thing I remember was waking up in this room with you people. It was as if... [*he trails off into deep thought*] Guys? [*his initial excitement begins to return*] Do you think it's possible that we were... abducted by aliens?

Gladwell: Don't be preposterous! There's no need for that fictional nonsense. There must be a perfect explanation for where we are and why we're here. For the last hour, I've been trying to calculate different possibilities and extraterrestrials rank pretty low on the list. Also, you should know never to venture into a cornfield alone. [*he returns to punching numbers into his machine*]

Lovecraft: Pleased to meet you. Hope you guess my name... [*his fingers start to move in the fashion of playing a piano*]

Bradbury: Wait a second, pal. [*he points his finger at Gladwell*] Are you trying to discredit science fiction as a credible form of writing?

Gladwell: Of course! While you spend your days messing around with robots, time travel, and *aliens*, I'm actually making a difference in the world by helping people understand it. You should read one of my books sometime. May I recommend *Blink*, *The Tipping Point*, or *Outliers*?

Bradbury: [*turns to the others*] This guy is unbelievable! Telling me what to read! [*turns back to Gladwell*] All right, Mr. Smarty Pants, where do you think we are?

Gladwell: Well, according to my calculations the most likely explanation is... [*he pauses. The only sounds are the Stones and various beeps of the computers and lights around them. After a few seconds, Gladwell speaks*] Death.

Bradbury: Do you mean to tell us that we're actually d— [*He doesn't get to finish his sentence because at this moment the clack! clack! clacking becomes more prominent. Then, one of the computer screens turns on and its beeping becomes increasingly louder. Underneath the screen is a small slot. Out of this slot, a piece of paper prints out. Bradbury momentarily forgets his anger at Gladwell, and walks over to the flashing computer screen. He rips the piece of paper out of the slot and glances at it*]

Stowe: [*although her eyes are closed, she somehow knows of the paper's appearance in the room*] Well, Ray? What does it say?

Bradbury: [*puzzled*] It says, "URGENT: What is fiction? What is nonfiction? You have five minutes." It's signed with the letters J.W. Is that it, then? [*he turns the slip of paper over to see if there is anything written on the back*]

[Despite the time constraint, the time within the room does not follow the conventional rules of time and space. No one except the audience will be aware of this fact]

Lovecraft: [*his singing persists*] Just as every cop is a criminal and all the sinners saints...

Gladwell: J.W.? What's that? A person? An entity?

Bradbury: Perhaps it's a giant octopus-like creature with the wings of a dragon [*after hearing this, Lovecraft's singing comes to an abrupt halt and his eyes widen in fear. He begins to mumble some ancient chant while holding his hands on his head. The only recognizable word uttered is Cthulhu. The music outside the room continues anyway*]

Gladwell: What gibberish are you speaking now, Bradbury?

Bradbury: I saw a creature like that in a dream once. It was awful. Haven't gotten any sleep since, but more importantly, what are we supposed to do with this? [*he holds up the slip of paper*] It says we have five minutes to answer the questions, "What is fiction? What is nonfiction?"

Gladwell: And if we fail to comply? [*the clack! clack! clack! returns and a second piece of paper exits the slot. Bradbury walks over, retrieves the slip, and reads it*]

Bradbury: [*he swallows hard and speaks in a serious tone*] "Swift and prompt termination. Four minutes remaining. Sincerely J.W." [*he slowly walks to the recliner and plops down in it. He quickly glances at Lovecraft who is still muttering his ancient chant. Now all the computer screens are showing a countdown of four minutes*] We better do what it says, Malcolm.

Gladwell: [*he nods*] All right. If this J.W. can hear everything that we say, then I assume that we can answer the question verbally. Does anyone disagree to a scholarly conversation on the subject? [*silence. The woman grading papers merely snorts*]. Good. I'd like to get the ball rolling by answering the nonfictional part of the question [*he clears his throat and prepares to speak. Bradbury pipes in*].

Bradbury: Now wait just a second there, Buster Brown. Why do you get to go first? I was the first to read those pieces of paper and all you did was sit there with that oversized calculator on your lap! Now I suggest... [*he is cut off by Stowe*]

Stowe: [*in a harsh tone*] Ray!

Bradbury: [*defeated*] Yes, ma'am.

Stowe: Malcolm, you were saying?

Gladwell: Thank you Ms. Stowe. As I was saying, nonfiction is [*he uses air quotes*] "literature based on fact." Just look at some of my books....

Bradbury: [*in an exasperated tone*] We get it, you sold some books. Can we get past this already?

[*A robotic feminine voice speaks from the computer screens as the lights flash from blue to yellow to red*]

Computer: Three minutes remaining

[*This shuts Bradbury up, who looks down at his lap, embarrassed. He then pulls the lever on the side of the recliner, allowing the chair to bend backwards. He lets out a breath of air and speaks*]

Bradbury: Proceed...

Gladwell: As I was saying, just look at some of my books. *Outliers* is about how certain smaller factors can lead to larger success. I explore subjects such as: what made Bill Gates so wealthy or why The Beatles were such a successful musical act. [*Lovecraft stops chanting and finally speaks to everyone else in the tone of a small child*]

Lovecraft: No Beatles! Stones! [*"Sympathy For The Devil" is still playing somewhere outside the room. After this outburst, he looks down at his polished shoes, embarrassed*]

Stowe: [*her eyes are still closed, but she addresses Lovecraft*] You know we can see you, Sweetie? [*Lovecraft, still looking at his shoes, nods slowly, disappointed that he wasn't invisible after all*]

Gladwell: My books are based on fact, logic, math, science. They interpret what we see and do every day. They, they...

[*The clack! clack! clack! is heard again and the beeping gets louder again. All the lights begin to flash between red and blue. The beeping subsides and is replaced by the voice of a little girl; this is the voice of Anne Frank. Still sitting on the black stool, she squirms at the sound of her own voice. She drops the book from her arms and it falls to the floor with a small thud. On its cover reads the single word DIARY*]

Voice of Frank: I've reached the point where I hardly care whether I live or die. The world will keep on turning without me, and I can't do anything to change events anyway. I'll just let matters take their course and concentrate on studying and hope that everything will be all right in the end... [*there is silence in the room as the voice of Frank is replaced by the clack! clack! clack! and then feminine computer voice*]

Computer: Two minutes remaining. [*the timer returns to the screens and the lights flash all different colors now. Frank, still pale as ever, finally speaks. She does not look away from a flashing blue light. Her English is flawless with a hint of German. She speaks with the eloquence of a grown woman*]

Frank: It—It was horrible. We were up there for two years. I heard the stories of what they would do to my people, but I didn't want to believe it. How could a people—my country!—do such inhumane things to other living beings? It was something out of, well, fiction. Horror stories. Something you know too well, Mr. Bradbury. [*she looks at Bradbury with tears streaming from her eyes. Bradbury looks at her, in shock*] I wrote anything and everything I could in that diary. It helped fight the boredom, but more importantly, it... [*Stowe speaks now. Her eyes are open and she is sitting up straight in her rocking chair. She* *is staring at the computer screens. There is pain in her eyes. Her voice is clear and crisp]*

Stowe: ...It helped make sense of a complex world. [*she turns to Frank*] Writing down what you saw, Dearie. You weren't trying to escape. You were trying to make sense of it all by immersing yourself in it. Maybe then, life wouldn't be so scary. [*tears well up in her eyes as she produces something from under her blanket. It is a book, a copy of Uncle Tom's Cabin*] Men, women, children. All in chains. Sold into bondage. Born into bondage. When you live in a world as confusing as ours, you need to go out and learn something. Journalism, my friends. [*Frank runs to Stowe who accepts her with open arms as the little girl begins to openly weep. The old woman consoles her*] Shhh. It's going to be all right, Dearie. [*Soon, Frank quiets down and sits in Stowe's lap. Stowe gently caresses her hair like a loving grandmother would. Then, Lovecraft leaves his spot in the corner and walks over to the dropped diary. He picks it up, stares at the cover for a moment, winces in pain, and then hugs it to his chest. Next, he returns to his corner without a word. The computer voice speaks again*]

Computer: One minute remaining. Your turn, Mr. Bradbury. [*Bradbury stares at the computer screen countdown for a moment before speaking*] Sure. Fiction isn't based on fact. It's definitely not based on reality. Then why do I prefer it? [*he takes a deep breath and turns to face the others. They all look at him except the woman grading papers and Anne Frank, whose head is nestled in Stowe's shoulder*] Imagine exploring the greatest mysteries of the universe. Where do we come from? Who made us? What's our purpose in life? Fiction is the vehicle through which we can answer these existential questions. Furthermore [*he points his forefinger in the air*] we can achieve great things that could never be achieved in reality. [*the woman grading papers snorts*] That's where science fiction comes in. [*he looks at Gladwell, who is twiddling his thumbs*] We can meet robots, and live on Mars, and meet aliens. Fiction is not a waste of time. It is like architecture, constructing alternate realities that fulfill our greatest dreams and live out our worst nightmares. When reading fiction, the world of the author becomes the world of the reader. It can also serve as a façade for important messages that the public is not ready to hear. It is pure entertainment, short and sweet.

[*The computer speaks*]

Computer: Time has ended. Conversation status: satisfactory... [*the computer screens shut off and the woman who has been grading papers begins to laugh hysterically. The other characters look at her*]

Bradbury: What's so funny? Wait. Who are you? Have we met? [*the woman is still laughing*]

Gladwell: Ma'am! Compose yourself!

[*The woman composes herself, but giggles here and there. She puts down her red pen, takes off her glasses, and begins to clean them on her red dress*]

Woman: The name's Eileen. I'm an English teacher, mostly high school kids. [*she pauses for a moment to catch her breath*] You know I once had this girl in my class. I believe her name was Jeannie. Now, my class is based on reading novels and then analyzing them for things like imagery, symbolism, and analogies. I required this analysis in the form of a paper. You know what I'm talking about, the real procedural and academic writing that's all the craze these days. This was to prepare my students so they would be more proficient in their college essays. Whenever this girl would hand in her papers, she would include her own personal insights on the subject. At first, I thought I had no need for these opinions. "Save that for your creative writing," I would say. But then something funny happened. I began to realize that both academic and creative writing were both creative in their own ways. They each differ from person to person, each of whom has his or her own unique writing style. [*she finishes cleaning her glasses and puts them back on*]

Gladwell: [*to the others*] You bring up a good point, but that doesn't explain what was so funny. [*Eileen looks at Gladwell for a moment*]

Eileen: Does anyone really know where we are or why we're here? Has anyone else, but me noticed that clacking noise that's been going on and off?

[*The others look at each other, puzzled. Even Lovecraft tries to figure out an answer to her question*]

Bradbury: What are you driving at, Eileen?

Eileen: Look at it this way. How did we come to be in this type of room when most of you lived in different time periods? Why were we prompted to discuss fiction and nonfiction when the conversation was leaning towards death? Who is J.W.? [*Stowe is truly wise and understands immediately. She smiles*] Ms. Stowe is now on the same page, gentleman. Do try to keep up.

[*Then the lightbulb goes off in Gladwell's head*]

Gladwell: [*in utter disbelief*] Dear God. You're not implying that we're actually in a...

Eileen: Play, yes, Mr. Gladwell. I've been an English teacher for the majority of my life. I think I know a play when I see one.

Bradbury: So that clacking noise, it's just...

Eileen: A typewriter. Or keyboard. I'm not really sure, but that, ladies and gentleman, is our gracious writer, J.W. [*"Sympathy For The Devil" ends and Lovecraft begins to whimper. He hugs Anne's diary closer to his chest. Upon seeing this, Anne gets off Stowe's lap and walks over to the whimpering man in the corner. She holds his hand*]

Frank: There, there. We wouldn't want to ruin that nice suit of yours with tears, now would we? [*Lovecraft's crying subsides and he hands Anne back her diary, who accepts it with a smile. Stowe beams as the two disappear. The black stool disappears as well*]

Bradbury: Holy smokes! They just vanished!

Eileen: Ah, yes. It seems that this little meeting of ours is coming to an end. The writer is ending the play.

Gladwell: [*yawns*] Anyone else tired? [*he closes his eyes and begins to snore. He, the adding machine, and the folding chair vanish*]

Bradbury: [*he is now sitting forward in his recliner, his head in his hands*] I guess I'm not long behind [*at this moment, one of the computer screens lights up and a piece of paper exits the slot. Bradbury gets up, retrieves it, and reads it. He smiles and disappears. The paper flutters to the ground. It reads, "To infinity and beyond." Stowe stares at the paper a moment then sits back in her rocking chair*]

Stowe: It'll be nice to rest these old bones [*she closes her eyes and disappears, leaving Eileen alone in the room*]

Eileen: [*takes a deep breath*] Finally. Some peace and quiet [*she picks up her red pen and continues to grade papers until she vanishes. All the flashing lights turn off and the clack! clack! clack! is heard once more*]

Publishing Group
Essays

Introduction

Researching, thinking, and writing are at the core of the College of Arts and Sciences. No matter what field they're in, students must be able to research, to find and evaluate the best evidence and information on a topic. They must be able to think, to formulate original ideas and to take a fresh approach to a problem or question. And, of course, they must be able to write—excellent research and thought must be communicated to others to have value. After all of their reading and thinking about the work of others, students must make their own contributions to the field by writing.

The constant exposure to accomplished works published in their field of study can intimidate students when they sit down to write. Or inspire them. It may do both as students struggle to bring their own vision to the subjects they study and find the right words. Fortunately, this struggle often yields remarkable writing. The following works, selected from student submissions to the sixth-annual Drexel Publishing Group writing contest, exemplify a firm grasp of subject matter and a facility with language.

The essays in this section of *The 33rd* cover a host of subjects from a range of disciplines in the arts and sciences. The topics are as diverse as the students who wrote about them, but the essays all demonstrate originality and boldness as well as great skill in researching, thinking, and writing.

Virginia Theerman

Feminism and Changing Womanhood in Edith Wharton's *The Age of Innocence*

In the present day, the civilized world considers sexual discrimination an archaic and demeaning practice. However, not so long ago in American history women struggled for equality. Back in the late 1800s, feminists such as Elizabeth Cady Stanton and Susan B. Anthony worked to build support for women's rights in the face of extreme prejudice and despite the prevalence of the 'cult of domesticity' that kept women in the home. Edith Wharton, an author of the early 20th century, would take inspiration from this time period and the figures in it, making revolutionary changes in her own life, and encouraging the independence of women. Using late 19th-century New York Society as a backdrop for her novel *The Age of Innocence*, Edith Wharton uses the expectations of Victorian society and the contrasting characters of Madame Ellen Olenska and May Welland, along with Newland Archer's blindness towards women, to illustrate the concepts of feminism, the changing ideas of womanhood, and the underestimation of women.

In the Victorian era, the upper echelon concerned itself with widening the distance between classes by establishing strict customs and manners, especially when it came to the conduct of women. From a very early age, parents indoctrinated their daughters with the proper behaviors, means of dressing, and expectations for the future. Wharton well documents the life of a young woman in the 1870s throughout her novel with descriptions of "the invitations, visits, dinners, opera going, dances, and weddings that kept it [New York society] all in place" (Knights 87). Through her narrator Newland Archer's perspective, Wharton gives her reader insight to the everyday condition of women. Newland's shock when faced with Ellen Olenska's behavior at a party, where she speaks to the guest of honor, a duke, openly, then crosses the room alone to join Archer, defines the mindset of a society well-bound by convention. For, "etiquette required that she [Olenska] should wait, as immovable as an idol, while the men who wished to converse with her succeeded each other at her side" (Wharton 56). This statement contains the popular opinion when it comes to women—they should remain remote, untouchable, and "unblemished" by experience (Wharton 42).

These expectations bound average upper class society young women as they spent most of their public life in pursuit of husbands. Upon obtaining a spouse, society expected a woman to retreat calmly into the confines of her home, venturing forth only to position her husband or children in the spotlight (Eby [Cott] 64). In this way, the cycle of dependent women perpetuated itself. Throughout her novel, Wharton emphasizes the idea of generations of women, all part of this evolutionary process to create the newest set of young women. Her narrator thinks to himself: "And he [Archer] felt himself oppressed by this creation of factitious purity, so cunningly manufactured by a conspiracy of mothers and aunts and grandmothers and long-dead ancestresses, because it was supposed to be what he wanted, what he had a right to..." (Wharton 41). In this, Wharton uses parallelism to emphasize the whirling circle, the catch-22, that kept women trapped in the cycle of innocence and meekly docile kowtowing. She also takes advantage of the current events in her setting's time period; using Darwin's recently published *Origin of Species*, she will define the idea of each successive generation taking traits and behaviors from the previous generation.

Within the confines of the novel, this cycle of traditional Victorian women rarely broke down. The New York society that Newland so feared simply would not permit a breach in the worship of the high god of 'Form'—what falls within propriety, and what does not. The minor character of Lawrence Lefferts embodies this hypocritical deity as he "covers up his many affairs by pontificating about the holiness of the marriage bond" (Wershoven 63). This sets up the double standard that creates the conflict within the novel: that sexual life before marriage counted as experience for a man but remained 'immoral' for a woman (Eby 63). However, at the time, this standard applied to virtually every aspect of life—not just sexuality. If a woman gained independence, asserted an opinion on anything besides trivial matters of dances and dresses, or if she attempted to step out of the domestic sphere and descend from her pedestal, the entire society would malign, criticize, and discredit both her and her ever-precious reputation.

In *The Age of Innocence*, Edith Wharton uses the character of Madame Ellen Olenska to challenge these expectations of traditional womanhood, as she chooses to separate from her abusive husband, return to her childhood home of New York alone, and stick to her own moral code when she falls in love with Newland Archer, a man already engaged to another woman. Madame Olenska's eccentric life story, although it begins in tragedy, allows her to break the typical mold of a society girl and become the strong and independent figure that foreshadows the women who will characterize the 20th century. An orphan, Olenska fell to the care of the somewhat ridiculous and certainly unconventional Medora Manson, a woman well known for inadvertently making every wrong move under 'Form.' Society pities the young Olenska, even as they describe her as a "fearless and familiar little thing, who asked disconcerting questions, made precocious comments, and possessed outlandish arts" (Wharton 53). Rushed into marriage in her teen years to the foreign Count Olenski, a rich but abusive and cruel husband, Madame Olenska will choose separation and a return to the United States, specifically New York.

However, her idea of a simple homecoming to the friends and relatives who love her becomes a complicated intrigue defined by the silent use of etiquette in an attempt to make her return to "peace and freedom" less scandalous (Wharton 146). Unfortunately, her manners, formed by years of society life in Europe, do not follow the typical format laid down for the women of New York, nor the United States in general. Literary critic Clare Virginia Eby notes that "Ellen's oblivion to her lawlessness [meant] that she must be cast out" (59). Madame Olenska's independence threatens the tribal elders—she may pass on her dangerous ideas to the other women in New York, although nice women would never take her up on the offer.

Wharton uses Olenska's lack of inhibitions to represent the coming generation, a far more open-minded and independent crowd. This new woman thinks for herself, makes her own decisions, and refuses to adhere to the group mentality, "stay[ing] receptive to values not her own while remaining strong against the absorbing pull of collective standards" (Fedorko 98). Her strong will and independent spirit especially show themselves when she and Archer have declared their love for one another, despite his engagement to May Welland. In this scene she firmly refuses to become his mistress, saying, "In reality it's too late to do anything but what we'd both decided on.... I can't love you unless I give you up" (Wharton 146-147). Madame Olenska will not play the game of life by New York's rules: She has too much self-respect and confidence to ever betray her inner values by sinking to the level of hypocrites like Lawrence Lefferts. This unheard-of attitude marks her as extremely advanced for her time period. By asserting her choices, individuality, and determination over Archer, the man who should have taken the lead, Madame Olenska breaks the cycle of subservient women and sets up her own standard for traditional, or rather, untraditional, womanhood. This outlook on life will define the role of women as feminists fight for equal rights in the late 1800s, and inspire the predominating role of women as they search for individuality and a life separate from men in the 1900s.

Contrastingly, Edith Wharton will use the character of May Welland to define and fulfill the traditions of Victorian life through her courtship and marriage to Newland Archer, and in the way she runs their household as she becomes the perfect society woman. Wharton will also use the ongoing metaphor of the merciless Greek goddess of the hunt, Diana, to give the reader additional insight to May—her innocence, her determination, and her cruelty in trapping Archer. From the beginning of the novel, the author portrays May as everything a conventional woman should be: demure, polite, and modest, of good standing, pure, innocent, and pretty. From the reader's first glimpse of her at the opera as she gazes on the lilies of the valley (representative of purity) that Newland Archer sent her, to her appearance at the Van der Luyden's party as Diana, to her perfect society wedding, and to her final proclamation to Newland that she bears his child, May's façade of the perfect traditional woman almost never slips. Even as she tries to sacrifice herself for Newland early on in the novel, when she references her fiancé's old love affair and tells him he should not marry her at the expense of another woman, she cannot help but murmur like the perfect debutante. She demurely whispers, "I've wanted to tell you that, when two people really love each other, I understand that there may be situations which make it right that they should—should go against public opinion" (Wharton 128). However, the minute that Newland assures her of his affection she drops back down into her proper role—that of a young girl who knows nothing of such distasteful and worldly matters.

Later in the novel, after their marriage, Newland asserts that even that small spark of life that ran in her veins that day has gone; instead, "the blood that ran so close to her fair skin might have been a preserving fluid rather than a ravaging element; yet her look of indestructible youthfulness made her seem neither hard nor dull, but only primitive and pure" (Wharton 161). The reader can see "Wharton's deep feelings for this girl as the 'terrifying product' of the social system, who is schooled to be in a state in which she 'knew nothing and expected everything'" (Holbrook 23). May has fallen exactly into the pattern of existence presented to her by her mother, her grandmother, and her mother before that. This cycle has an effect on Wharton's narrator, who often exclaims that he will slowly turn into a copy of his father-in-law, because May has no experience of married life other than her own parents to draw on and build from. Granted, Newland often underestimates the true passion his wife has for him and for their station in life, but understandably so, as May does an excellent job of hiding her coarser feelings.

True to a proper Victorian woman's form, May also excels in controlling and manipulating the situations that surround her life with Newland. Well-versed in ways to appear innocent herself, she has also perfected the means of making all of the people in her life appear flawless. She will only hint to her husband that she knows he has feelings for Madame Olenska, but in the end her scheming, combined with the help of the tribe of family, will bring Newland's fantasies of a life with Madame Olenska tumbling down. He receives a shock when her entire plot comes to light with her revelation of her pregnancy, and the consequences:

> He felt that his wife was watching him intently. 'Did you
> *mind* my telling her first, Newland?'

'Mind? Why should I?' He made a last effort to collect himself. 'But that was a fortnight ago, wasn't it? I thought you said you weren't sure till today.'

Her color burned deeper, but she held his gaze. 'No; I wasn't sure then—but I told her I was. And you see I was right!' she exclaimed, her blue eyes wet with victory. (Wharton 291)

By looking directly into Newland's eyes, May proclaims that does not regret what she has done—she feels almost no shame whatsoever. He in turn realizes how much effort May has gone to in order to thwart his intellectual affair with Madame Olenska. Not only did May throw a goodbye party as a final farewell for the lovers, she outright lied to her cousin in saying that she carried a child before she could fully ascertain her condition. May knew exactly what effect this news would have. By revealing her pregnancy to Ellen, May reminded her that she, May, Archer's lawful wife, had proof of their marital relationship. Of course, as a strong-willed woman of high standards, Ellen instantly recognizes May's right to Archer, and backs down from her choice to become Archer's lover, even as she understands that this fulfills the result May hoped for. Meanwhile, when Archer learns of the pregnancy after the ill-fated dinner that separates him from Madame Olenska, he deals with the unpleasant revelation of his wife as a wiser and more complicated woman than he had imagined, and realizes that she has well and truly trapped him.

Throughout *The Age of Innocence*, the perpetual generations of women and the contrasts shown between Madame Olenska and May Welland depend entirely on the perceptions, actions, and opinions expressed by Newland Archer, the narrator. In fact, the *im*perceptiveness of Newland Archer truly defines the novel. For his blindness towards women and their capabilities will create much of the novel's main conflict. To begin with, Archer takes a pessimistic outlook on the unconventional attitude of Madame Olenska. He feels that she plays with fire by remaining her true self, by not conforming to the rules of New York Society. He also assumes that she will easily consent to breaking his engagement with May so that they might stay together. On both accounts he judges in error. While Madame Olenska lacks awareness of some of the social *faux pas* that she makes, her lapse in judgment results from a desire to stay true to her own code of values and manners by ignoring New York's nitpicky standards. On the idea of Newland's break-up with May, Madame Olenska also remains firm—she will not undermine the trust and love she has built up with her cousin and society in order to satisfy her own happiness. Oddly enough, Archer does a better (although still very poor) job *understanding* the motivations of Ellen Olenska than the motivations of May Welland, even though May fulfills the original idea of his ideal woman in every way. Although she may possess limited interest in new ideas about art, science, or literature, she does possess a great deal of knowledge about the current ideas surrounding society and morality, and has her eyes wide open to his motivations and decisions. Professor and critic Margaret B. McDowell puts it best:

> If he initially misjudges Ellen... he also misjudges May
> by viewing her as more limited than she is. Before their
> marriage, he simply assumes that she will never be
> capable of surprising him with 'a new idea, a weakness,
> a cruelty, or an emotion.'...He does not recognize the
> stratagems to which May resorts in order to keep him
> from leaving with Ellen.... [he cannot see] May as a
> woman instead of a stereotype.... [he] underestimates her
> intelligence, the extent of her worldly knowledge, her
> strength, and her capacity to fight for her interests. (91)

Ultimately, Newland, as a representative male figure who claims he has revolutionary ideas about the education and the sexual experiences of women, cannot get past his stereotypical role as the protector to the innocent woman, who knows little of the world and needs guidance. His inability to recognize his own hypocrisy leads to an underestimation of the women around him, and, in the end, the destruction of his own happiness.

Edith Wharton's exploration of the late-19th-century woman makes an interesting background and provides plenty of character development for her novel, *The Age of Innocence*. The habits, moral qualms, and scandals of vibrant Victorian New York unfold from the male perspective of Newland Archer, who vacillates between the woman he loves, Ellen Olenska, and the woman he has given his bond to, May Welland. Both women bring interesting histories and motivations to the story, despite the narrator's blindness towards their abilities and desires. What May lacks in innovation, she will make up in marital ambition, and what Madame Olenska lacks in conventionality, she more than compensates for with her passion. These two very different women make up the evolving woman that Edith Wharton saw in the 1920s and the woman who still searches for her own identity and place within or without society today.

Works Cited

Eby, Clare Virginia. "Silencing Women in Edith Wharton's *The Age of Innocence*." *Bloom's Modern Critical Interpretations: Edith Wharton's* The Age of Innocence. Ed. Harold Bloom. Philadelphia: Chelsea House Publishers, 2005. 55-69. Print.

Fedorko, Kathy A. "Kathy A. Fedorko on Ellen's Individuality." *Bloom's Major Novelists: Edith Wharton.* Ed. Harold Bloom. Broomhall, Pennsylvania: Chelsea House Publishers, 2002. 97-99. Print.

Holbrook, David. "*The Age of Innocence*." B*loom's Modern Critical Interpretations: Edith Wharton's* The Age of Innocence. Ed. Harold Bloom. Philadelphia: Chelsea House Publishers, 2005. 13-32. Print.

Knights, Pamela. "Forms of Disembodiment: The Social Subject in *The Age of Innocence*." *Bloom's Modern Critical Interpretations: Edith Wharton's* The Age of Innocence. Ed. Harold Bloom. Philadelphia: Chelsea House Publishers, 2005. 83-108. Print.

McDowell Margaret B. "Margaret B. McDowell on Archer's Limited View: May vs. Ellen." *Bloom's Major Novelists: Edith Wharton.* Ed. Harold Bloom. Broomhall, Pennsylvania: Chelsea House Publishers, 2002. 90-91. Print.

Wershoven, Carol. "Carol Wershoven on the Low Nature of High Society in Wharton's New York." *Bloom's Notes: Edith Wharton's* The Age of Innocence. Ed. Harold Bloom. Broomhall, Pennsylvania: Chelsea House Publishers, 1991. 62.65. Print.

Wharton, Edith. *The Age of Innocence.* New York: Barnes and Noble Classics, 2004. Print.

Christiny Martin

Earthly Delights and Delightful Frights

Hieronymus Bosch's "The Garden of Earthly Delights" is an overwhelming piece to look at, as well as think about. This work is 7'3"x6'5" at the center, painted with oils on a folding wood panel. When unfolded, the panel would stretch out to approximately a 12'10" width. Though this work was created between 1505-1510, during the High Northern Renaissance, Bosch's work is a standout from that of his Northern peers. Artists like Dürer were concerned with perfecting realistic natural detail. Meanwhile, Bosch was ahead of his time in creating this piece, being the only artist of this era to delve into an early form of abstraction.

From the outside, "The Garden" is deceptively drab. The outer panels are painted with what looks like a creation scene. The Earth is depicted as a flat disc of terrain. It bisects a transparent sphere, containing the clouds and other traces of the atmosphere—all painted in grayscale. The wispy figure in the corner of the blackness of space is God. He is creating the universe, or at least the Earth. Inscribed above the scene is a short biblical quote in Latin: "*Ipse dixit, et facta sunt: ipse mandávit, et creáta sunt,*" meaning, "For he spake and it was done; he commanded, and it stood fast" (Dempsey).

The inside of the panel is in stark contrast with the gray-blue-black of the creation scene. The bright pinks and greens, as well as the dozens of strange little figures create a sensory overload. Strange, organic-looking structures impaled by glass tubes give "The Garden" an almost psychedelic feel. The structures resemble containers and apparatuses used in alchemy, which makes one wonder if Bosch might have been exposed to some chemical fumes while creating the piece. The painting is full of intricate little details that have to be scanned panel-by-panel, or else they might be missed completely.

In the very first panel, God introduces Eve to Adam. They are the only human or even humanoid figures in this panel. Though this section is serene compared to the other two panels, something about it is still off. Adam and Eve are well behaved and placid in the presence of God, and everything appears normal, like a standard Genesis scene (aside from the giant, pink, bong-like structure behind them), but if one looks closely, one will find that the animals are off-kilter.

There are the standard lynxes, otters, elephants—but peppered among them are creatures that don't exist in the natural world. These creatures include unicorns, three-headed lizards and storks, a platypus-hawk hybrid, and what appears to be a duck reading a book. These oddities, hidden among their more conventional counterparts, could be a subtle foreshadowing of the chaos that ensues further in the narrative—specifically, in the very next panel.

In the center panel, which is the attention-grabber of the piece, the garden is overrun with men and beasts alike. But, many of the creatures have ballooned to monstrous proportions. Unlike the first panel, where Adam and Eve seemingly ignore the wildlife around them, their descendants in the second panel are engaging the strange animals in a variety of questionable behaviors.

Many of the human figures are seen riding around on livestock—pigs, goats, horses, cows—and other, fictitious creatures such as horned cats. One human figure is fed berries from the beak of a large bird, while they lounge inside and on top of what looks like a hollowed-out berry, also of gigantic proportions. A man carries a massive fish with a slit cut into its belly out of an enclosed structure, which makes one wonder exactly what was going on in there.

It is almost as if the humans have become like the strange beasts, interacting with them in a variety of peculiar, inappropriate manners, as well as interacting with one another in such a way. The figures engage openly in sexual activity. The panel is so complex that sifting out the explicitly sexual activity from the merely sensual is difficult. It takes a keen eye to spot the hidden gems. Several couples kiss and caress (one couple in the foreground, a handsy couple floating inside of a glass sphere, and an interracial couple kissing atop a mallard). There are a few implicitly sexual situations, in which tangled limbs protrude from various enclosures like a clamshell or a strange little shelter. However, near the burnt-orange enclosure, by the man with the fish, one figure anally penetrates another figure with a variety of different flowers. A little further back, three figures are sheltered beneath a canopy that is held up by a curved rod lodged in a female figure's anus. In the lake in the center of the panel, inside of a blue globe, one female figure touches the genitals of another female figure.

However, this piece is not a glorification of pleasure, sensuality, and brazen sexuality. In the third pane lies the hell scene. The background of this section is painted mostly in the same blue-grey-black as the creation scene of the cover, with dots of red and orange symbolizing hellfire and brimstone. The foreground is painted with a similar elaborate brightness as the first two panels, except the green grass is now barren dirt.

The descendants of Adam and Eve are made to pay for their sins in a variety of gruesome yet befitting ways. For their indulgence in "sinful" music and merriment, several figures are tortured and racked upon various musical instruments. One hangs crucified on a harp. Another is made to bear the weight of a giant horn on his back while a demon sodomizes him with a flute.

The same animals that befriended the humans reappear in grotesque forms. A pig wearing a nun's wimple forcibly kisses a man. A toad-faced demon in a bridal veil tattoos music notation on the buttocks of a flailing man. A giant rabbit carries a human figure over his shoulder on a pole. But the real star of the show is the bird-faced demon sitting atop a toilet, eating the damned souls and defecating them into a pit. He wears a helmet formed from a metal pot, secured to his head with wire. This figure, being the most prominent, could very well represent Satan himself.

Bosch's overall message is that indulging in sensual pleasure leads to damnation, and that path has been set since God created the first humans. However, he spends more time going wild with the different types of fantastical pleasures than representing the gravity of their punishment. The level of detail and layering Bosch puts in the center panel implies that he has given a lot of thought to these sinful behaviors, and might have even had fun imagining them, not unlike anti-gay politicians who appear to have contemplated the nuances of gay sex more thoroughly than one would expect. This may be the very same reason Bosch paints himself as a demon with a hollow abdomen in the third panel, staring out at the observer with a knowing "they caught me" look on his face.

Even with a basic understanding of theology, average observers would be able to discern the message if they studied the details close enough. But it's difficult to keep in mind that the moral is that society should NOT engage in these behaviors—especially when the theological aspects of the piece are painted on the smaller panels, in less detail. That means that "Earthly Delights," in essence, is about guilty pleasure. Sin is wrong and there are consequences, but Bosch makes the sin look so fun and inviting. He represents sin as slightly silly, as well (with people wearing fruit as hats.) Yet, to the average viewer, *still tempting.*

"The Garden of Earthly Delights" is particularly easy to relate to compared to other pieces of its time. Even though it condemns sin, it does so in a whimsical way. Hell looks like the cover of a Grateful Dead album. Bosch's piece lies in stark contrast to a work like the Isenheim Altarpiece, which was meant to be inspiring but was really more depressing. Bosch's use of color and shape makes the entire piece sensual and inviting, despite the message. The moral of the story is delivered, but without frightening the viewer to death.

Of course, this is an interpretation written in the age of science fiction and slasher films. The hell scene could have been the most nightmarish imagery to ever enter 16th-century Flanders. Still, this piece raises the question of whether or not Bosch thought sin might actually be worth the consequences. This question might have been answered by a depiction of heaven in "Earthly Delights," and whether or not its imagery was as intriguing as Bosch's hell. Likely, it would pale.

Works Cited

Dempsey, Charles. "*Sicut in Utrem Aquas Maris*: Jerome Bosch's Prolegomenon to the 'Garden of Earthly Delights'" JSTOR. Jan. 2004. Web. 24 Mar. 2012. <http://www.jstor.org/stable/3251834>.

Mik Schulte

The Rape Crisis in the U.S.: How to Improve the Justice System's Response to Sex Crimes

There has been a lot of talk lately in political circles about a war on women. Regardless of which side of the political spectrum is correct, the real war on women is much more intricate and nuanced than the Washington D.C cliché, and the toll of victims in this war continues to rise with each passing day. Every two minutes, somebody in the United States is sexually assaulted. That means that annually there are about 207,754 rapes in the United States. Nine out of every 10 rape victims in the United States are female; one out of every six American women and one out of 33 men have experienced an attempted or completed rape in their lifetime. This amounts to a total of 17.7 million American women, and 2.78 million American men, who have been victims of sexual assault or rape.

Victims of rape or sexual assault are three times more likely to suffer from depression, six times more likely to suffer from post-traumatic stress disorder, 13 times more likely to abuse alcohol, 26 times more likely to abuse drugs, and four times more likely to contemplate suicide. The harsh reality for victims of sexual assault and rape has received more public attention over the past three decades, thanks in part to television shows like the *Law and Order* franchise, *Cold Case*, and *To Catch a Predator*. Marlee Matlin, Charlize Theron, and Halle Berry have each won the Academy Award for Best Actress for their portrayals of victims of sexual assault. However, these issues were largely ignored by the general public until the 1990s, with feminist advocates becoming welcomed into the mainstream and not treated as part of a political fringe.

Feminist activist Kristen Bumiller notes that high-profile trials between the late 1980s and mid 1990s "reinforced iconic representations of victims (as innocent, white, and/or angelic) or sacrificed the actual victims for their failure to live up to this idealization." Furthermore, these characterizations of both victim and perpetrator "contributed to the crime control mentality by adding force to the belief that the maintenance of social order depended on ruthlessly castigating violent perpetrators who preyed on innocent victims." This 'crime control' mentality did lead to sweeping reforms in the 1980s and 1990s, ultimately culminating in rape shield laws and the adoption of the Violence Against Women Act in 1994, considered to be the "most significant accomplishment of the anti-rape movement." The "crime control" mentality has also had unintended negative consequences, causing several problems with the justice system's interaction with victims and perpetrators.

The current "crime control" mentality has divided much research on these ethical issues into sides. The solutions of one side, the victims advocacy side, are tailored towards getting justice for the victims at all costs without any regard for the accused perpetrator. The solutions of the other side, the constitutional scholars and those who believe that those who are accused of being sex-crime perpetrators are unfairly persecuted, fail to acknowledge the rights of the victims. Consequently, the divisiveness of the academic community on this issue has made it difficult for practical solutions to be proposed.

There are many ethical issues to take into consideration when seeking to understand sex crimes and how the justice system should best address them. This research seeks to frame the problems differently, and is intended to offer an alternative model to the current "crime control" approach; it seeks to balance the recommendations of the "victims advocacy camp" and the "constitutional rights of perpetrators camp." How would a model justice system respond to sex crimes? How should the system interact with the victims, the perpetrators, and the public? Are there additional responsibilities for judges and attorneys when working with sex-crimes cases? Are perpetrators and those accused of committing a sex crime being unfairly persecuted? These are the questions that this research seeks to answer, by suggesting, with some qualifications, replacing the "crime control" model with a public health model.

In discussing her research about sex-offender recidivism rates, Kristen Zgoba notes two interesting findings. First, that when writing law about sex crimes, legislators often "have succumbed to constituencies influenced by assumptions and myths associated with sex offenders, high rates of sex offense recidivism and stranger-perpetrated incidents." Second, that sex offenders report negative consequences when they are subjects of broad community notification measures, including being harassed by neighbors and being threatened; some reports include sex offenders being assaulted or being robbed. Contrary to mass media portrayal, an overwhelming majority of rapes and sexual assaults are not committed by masked strangers hiding in the bushes. Approximately two-thirds of rapes were committed by someone known to the victim, 73% of sexual assaults were perpetrated by a non-stranger, and more than 50% of all rape and sexual assault incidents were reported by victims to have occurred at home or within one mile of their home. The misconceptions about perpetrators of sexual assault and rape have led to many local jurisdictions enacting very broad community notification laws. As Chrysanthi Leon notes, these laws operate under the assumption that many perpetrators will reoffend, and also that they are inherently dangers to the general public, when statistics and multiple studies (Zimring and Leon,

2008, Hanson and Bussiere, 1998, and Harris and Hanson 2004) all indicate that many sexual assault and rape cases were perpetrated by acquaintances. In fact, the sex-offense recidivism rate stands at 5.3%, and "sex offenders as a group present low risks of sexual re-offense." According to RAINN, a rapist is more likely to become a serial criminal rather than a serial rapist, with only 46% of rapists who were released from prison being re-arrested within 3 years of their release for another crime, and with only less than 20% of these re-arrests for a violent offense.

Taken as a whole, these findings demonstrate the many misconceptions that exist about sexual assault and rape. The current "crime control" model for the justice system is chained to these misconceptions. Researcher Emily Horowitz combined crime statistics and survey data from the Federal Bureau of Investigation, the Bureau of Justice Statistics, and the Crimes Against Children Research Center. She then compared them to the frequency of media headlines with the terms "sex offender" and "sex predator" and found that legislators are influenced by a constituency which is subject to these headlines that enflame their perspectives. Thus, "these same enflamed constituents reading the headlines on a daily basis become enflamed jury members sitting behind the bench deciding the fate of a defendant who is supposed to be seen as innocent until proven guilty."

The studies of Horowitz, Leon, and Zgoba all assert that jurors are extremely prejudiced towards a person accused of being a sex-crime perpetrator. Combine these assertions with the "crime control" model that comprises the justice system today, and the result would be a situation where accused perpetrators would be convicted *en masse* without question. However, official national crime statistics do not bear this scenario out, which is one of the biggest failings of even the more neutral academic literature. Rather than ground the research in statistics and quantitative studies, much of the literature pursues ideological theoretical arguments that disregard statistical fact. Out of every 100 rapes in the United States, only 46 are reported to police. Of those, only 12 lead to an arrest, nine are prosecuted, five are convicted, and only three will spend even a single day in prison. This means that out of the roughly 207,754 rapes which are committed each year in the United States, only approximately 6,233 victims will see their rapist serve any jail time.

A model justice system should give the accused a fair trial, respect all constitutional rights that being a United States citizen affords, and then carry out a sentence. Nationally, sex offenders are subject to a variety of federal databases after being convicted, databases which were created under the Adam Walsh Act of 2006 and also "Megan's Law." These laws, while well intended, have strengthened a "crime control" mentality, encouraging the false assumption that just because somebody is a sex offender, members of the public are automatically in mortal danger. The main problems with broad community notification laws are twofold. First, there does not exist a similar provision for other groups of offenders. Rather, a sex criminal is treated under a separate legal standard, and enjoys less rights than the man who shot his grandmother, the man who savagely beat his wife, the woman whose house is secretly a meth lab, or the woman who drowned her children. The second problem with community notification statutes is that they perpetuate fear and hysteria. As RAINN notes, the majority of sex offenders are known to the victim, and coupled with the low recidivism rate for sex offenders, the vast majority of sex offenders are first-time offenders, and therefore were not previously registered. Public notification measures do nothing to decrease the rape rate. In fact, the rape rate has held relatively steady since 1993, with no measurable difference between communities with "extremely stringent community notification laws" and those without. The legislation often creates additional problems, and as researchers Stephanie Buntin and Ron Langevin note, "falsely lure the public into a sense of security at the expense of the constitutional rights of the [sex offenders], because the woman jogging terrified of being raped by her next-door neighbor who is on the 'Registry' has a better chance of being raped by somebody who isn't on the 'Registry' yet." Therefore, the intended benefits of community notification laws do not outweigh the unintended risks, and actually place the public more in jeopardy as a result of the false sense of security.

The defining characteristic of a public health model is that it is universal in nature, targeting everyone in the population instead of separating different risk levels between victims and the perpetrators of these crimes. Some researchers, including Christine Gidyck, note that universal approaches are useful, but more selective prevention methods aimed at targeting high-risk individuals are more cost effective. However, a change from a "crime control'"model to a risk management model would not address the many ethical concerns as they relate to the perpetrator, as such a model would protect the public at the expense of the constitutional rights of the perpetrators. A second reason against a more selective approach is that there is limited data demonstrating causal factors to sexual aggression. Simply put, it is unknown why some individuals are more prone to sexual aggression than others, and basing a model on an unknown would not be feasible. More research is needed to ascertain whether or not such links exist, and if it is determined that they do exist, then programs can be later developed to target these causal factors.

Developing a public health model requires a foundation comprised of the development, evaluation, and dissemination of individual-level prevention and risk reduction programs, as well as the broadening of advocacy efforts and prevention efforts beyond the individual level to encourage societal change. Violence against women is a societal and community issue, and no amount of legislation can be effective without societal change. The ideal public health model requires that researchers and community members operate using a bottom-up approach towards developing innovative programs, and also when communicating existing ones. The different parties need to be open to more innovative solutions, and accept that imprisonment and community notification are ineffective. Public health approaches to prevention dictate that in addition to individual approaches to prevention, efforts towards broad community change are needed, which requires that social norms be transformed. The theory which should govern this model should be that of social diffusion, which suggests that social change occurs when socially influential individuals ally with a specific cause. This is the same macro-level theory that has governed society's changed attitudes towards substance abuse and HIV/AIDS, and is the reason a public health model would be the ideal model for society as a whole. The success of this model depends solely on the willingness of society to change its mind about sex crimes and sexual abuse. Multiple studies indicate the growing academic support for this theory within health prevention literature, and these same principles must be applied to the sex-crimes issue.

The danger of current micro-theory-based public health model programs is that they target correlative instead of causative factors of sexual violence, similar to how programs which were designed to mitigate antisocial behaviors, such as the DARE program and the It Gets Better Project, have largely failed. The failure of these smaller programs is demonstrative of the need for a larger macro-theory-based public health model. This model would be comprised of four main tenets. First, that the public continue to be educated about the reality of rape and sexual assault. Increasing education is the first step to creating a successful public health model, including educating the public about general awareness, not just becoming hyper-aware when you discover that a convicted sex offender is living next door. Education is also crucial for understanding victims' responses, an accurate understanding of perpetrator behavior, and also that such responses and behaviors vary widely, and unlike with homicide, do not follow as many traditional patterns. This increased education is the most effective measure that can be taken to strengthen the justice system pre-trial. Education for how to lower an individual's risk for rape is also important, particularly on college campuses and in urban areas.

Coupled with an increase in education, more options need to be available to the justice system at sentencing. The first step towards creating these options is to end the mentality that all sex offenders are the same. Instead, a new sentence structure based on frequency and level of offense should be created. The first group would include first-time non- "sexually violent predators." The determination of whether or not an offender is a "sexually violent predator" is made by state review boards comprised of psychologists and other medical professionals. The distinction determines whether or not the perpetrator is more inclined than the average sex offender to reoffend. The proposed model would include increasing non-prison options for first-time non- "sexually violent predators" and would require medical evaluation, psychological counseling, and monitored community service. Furthermore, first-time non "sexually violent predators" should not appear on any public registry, because the chances that they will re-offend are extremely low, and as such, they should not be subject to the undue negative effects of being on a public registry. This diversification of options provides a better environment for the general public, victims, and perpetrators. Many first-time "sexually violent predators" serve probation or are only in jail for short periods of time. Therefore, requiring psychological counseling, medical evaluations, and therapy options would enable these perpetrators to get help they arguably need. Such help would overall benefit the community because it would decrease the recidivism rate for these offenders even further. However, any treatment that a perpetrator would receive should be separate from the legal process, and anything said within the treatment proceedings should respect doctor-patient confidentiality.

The second tier of sentencing options should correspond with existing sentencing guidelines for individuals who are not "sexually-violent predators" but for whom it is not their first offense. Rather than be committed to prison with no other options, these offenders should also be provided access to treatments if they wish. They should also be given earlier access to parole if they participate faithfully and willingly in the treatment and rehabilitation process, with the understanding that they will serve a longer probation time post-prison as well as an increased standard for monitoring. Further options that could be explored include sex-offender-only rehabilitation centers; or sex-offender-only housing, which would operate similarly to residential drug-treatment programs.

The limitations of this proposed model are as follows: the model cannot succeed without an increase in funding, both from private and public sources, which allows for the increased education and increased treatment options; societal commitment is key for the success of the public health model, and as with the HIV/AIDS and substance abuse crises, legislators are going to be the last proponents of any viable solutions because of the political risk it would entail; lastly, the model would be at risk for misinterpretation and could develop a strong negative reaction from victims advocacy groups, who are focused on the health and well-being of the victims, with very little concern for the rights of the perpetrators.

This proposed public health model would revolutionize how the United States justice system addresses sex crimes. The current "crime control" model does not work, and instead encourages public confusion and hysteria, and does nothing to address the causes and true nature of sex crimes. Until a model is implemented that addresses both the causes and effects of sex crimes, the rape rate will not decrease, and citizens are more at risk for sexual assault and rape. While it may not be politically convenient, it certainly is relevant, and in fact needed. The nature of the current political atmosphere with the upcoming election implies that rape and sexual assault will remain on the backburner of the political agenda, which is why it is important for academia to educate the general public, who must be the driving force behind the new model. Academics can propose models, but only the people can commit to them and encourage politicians to make changes. A public health model is most effective because it serves to protect the public, as well as integrates the public into the justice system. A stronger system serves all, and that is why radical changes are needed to strengthen it.

Works Consulted

Bumiller, Kristin. *In an Abusive State: How Neoliberalism Appropriated the Feminist Movement against Sexual Violence.* Durham: Duke UP, 2008. Print.

Buntin, Stephanie. "High Price of Misguided Legislation: Nevada's Need for Practical Sex Offender Laws." *The Nevada Law Journal*, Vol. 11 (2010-2011): 770-792.

Bureau or Justice Statistics. "Recidivism of Prisoners Released in 1994" (2002).

Bureau of Justice Statistics. "Felony Defendants in Large Urban Counties, 2002" (2006).

Casey, E.A, & Lindhorst, P. "Toward a Multilevel, Ecological Approach to the Primary Prevention of Sexual Assault: Prevention in Peer and Community Contexts." *Trauma Violence, and Abuse*, Vol. 10 (2009): 91-114.

Centers for Disease Control and Prevention. *Sexual Violence Prevention: Beginning the Dialogue.* Atlanta, GA. (2004).

Farrington, David P.; Jolliffe, Darrick. "Cross-National Comparisons of Crime Rates in Four Countries, 1981-1999," *Crime and Justice: A Review of Research*, Vol. 33 (2005): 377-398.

Federal Bureau of Investigation. "Uniform Crime Reports" (2006-2010).

Gidycz, C., Orchowski L., & Edwards, K. "Primary Prevention of Sexual Violence". *Violence Against Women And Children: Navigating Solutions.* Ed. Koss, White,

Kazdin. American Psychological Association. (2011) Print.

Gladwell, Malcolm. *The Tipping Point: How Little Things Can Make a Big Difference.* Boston, MA: Little, Brown. (2002) Print.

Horowtiz, Emily. "Growing Media and Legal Attention to Sex Offenders: More Safety or More Injustice." *Journal of the Institute of Justice and International Studies*, Vol. 7, (2007): 143-158.

Knight, R. & Sims-Knight J. "Risk Factors For Sexual Violence." *Violence Against Women and Children: Mapping the Terrain.* Ed. White, Koss, &Kazdin. American Psychological Association. (2011) Print.

Langevin, Ron; Curnoe, Suzanne; Fedoroff, Paul; Bennett, Renee. "Lifetime Sex Offender Recidivism: A 25-year Follow-Up Study." *Canadian Journal of Criminology and Criminal Justice*, Vol. 46, Issue 5 (2004): 531-552.

Lave, Tamara Rice. "Only Yesterday: The Rise and Fall of Twentieth Century Sexual Psychopath Laws." *Louisiana Law Review*, Vol. 69, Issue 3 (2009): 549-592.

Leon, Chrysanthi. "Contexts and Politics of Evidence-Based Sex Offender Policy." *Criminology and Public Policy*, Vol. 10, Issue 2 (2011): 421-430.

National Center for Policy Analysis. "Crime and Punishment in America" (1999)

National Institute of Justice & Centers for Disease Control & Prevention. "Prevalence, Incidence and Consequences of Violence Against Women Survey" (1998).

RAINN | Rape, Abuse and Incest National Network | RAINN: The Nation's Largest Anti-sexual Assault Organization. Web. 14 June 2012.

Rickert, Julia T. "Denying Defendants the Benefit of a Reasonable Doubt: Federal Rule of Evidence 609 and Past Sex Crime Convictions." *Journal of Criminal Law & Criminology*, Vol. 100, Issue 1 (2010): 213-242.

U.S. Department of Justice. "2005 National Crime Victimization Study." (2005).

U.S. Department of Justice. "2010 National Crime Victimization Survey." (2010).

U.S. Department of Justice, Bureau of Statistics. "1997 Sex Offenses and Offenders Study." (1997).

Zgoba, Kristen; Veysey, Bonita M.; Dalessandro, Melissa. "Analysis of the Effectiveness of Community Notification and Registration: Do the Best Intentions Predict the Best Practices." *Justice Quarterly*, Vol. 27, Issue 5 (2010): 667-691

Helena Krobock

Revolution of the Mind: Sigmund Freud and Psychoanalytic Theory

From ancient Greek philosophy of the soul, to the modern, cutting-edge research that entwines it with a diverse array of other fields, psychology is defined by an extensive history that has taken place over the course of several thousand years and throughout the world. Nevertheless, one image prevails as a symbol of the subject as a whole: the therapist's couch. As the number of references to psychology in the media increases, so does the number of sightings of this curious piece of furniture. The frequent association of psychology with a sofa symbolizes the vast influence of the movement from which the cliché originated—in its earliest years, psychoanalysis and its defining theories revolutionized psychology as an academic discipline and an applied science.

Fifty years prior to the era of psychoanalysis, the study of psychology became widely known as a scientific field. During the late 19th century, its earliest research was primarily concerned with the human brain, as psychology relied heavily upon physical, biologically based science. Renowned physicians, including Wernicke and Broca, studied the structure of the brain and discovered areas responsible for sensory and verbal function.[1] On the subject of mental illness, the few scientific explanations that existed were largely overshadowed by the widespread belief that psychological abnormalities, known at the time as neuroses, resulted from moral or spiritual failure. The majority of psychology's first students migrated from related fields. One such individual, Sigmund Freud, began his career as a physician, eventually studying neurological disorders that included epilepsy and aphasia. Following a series of case studies published in 1895, Freud developed an interest in what are known today as defense mechanisms. He spent four years engaged in both case studies and self-analysis, from which he crafted *The Interpretation of Dreams*. Freud's work was a major breakthrough in several respects. It revived the interest of the scientific community in dreams, which were previously dismissed as meaningless and of no value in understanding the human mind.[2] *The Interpretation of Dreams* was also groundbreaking

---

1 Myers, David G. *Psychology*. 8th ed. New York: Worth, 2007. Print.

2 "A Dream Science- Prof. Freud's Ingeious System of "*Psychoanalysis*"" New York Times 1 June 1913. Print.

in its use of introspection, or observation of oneself and one's mind, as evidence of the author's theories, which later led to criticism of its methods as unscientific."[3] Ultimately, however, the most revolutionary aspect of Freud's work was its theory of the unconscious mind, which became the foundation of psychoanalysis itself.

Initially, *The Interpretation of Dreams* faced a cold reception in the psychological community of Europe. Only a few hundred copies were sold in the eight years following its publication in Germany. Furthermore, it was barely mentioned, much less reviewed, in any major scientific journals or periodicals. Despite the criticism it gained on the rare occasion that it was acknowledged, the book became known as one of Freud's most famous works, inspiring an entire movement in the psychological community. During this period, Freud and several colleagues formed the Vienna Psychoanalytical Society, a group dedicated to the discussion and dissection of his work.[4] It eventually resulted in the creation of the International Psychoanalytical Association (IPA) in 1910. The IPA played a crucial role in training psychoanalysts and disseminating Freud's writings among not only the professional psychological community, but also throughout mainstream society.[5] Freud's teachings reached even further following the translation of *The Interpretation of Dreams* into English by Dr. A.A. Brill in 1913. With increased availability to a diverse group of consumers, psychoanalysis became a phenomenon in the Western world.

The fundamental theory of psychoanalysis attributes human behavior to motives of which we are unaware. They are located in our unconscious, a Freudian concept that is believed to exist below the threshold of self-awareness, yet be responsible for the majority of our mental processes. These drives often conflict with our inhibitions, which prevent us from fulfilling desires that we perceive to be socially unacceptable. As these "wishes" go unfulfilled, they become evident to us during altered states of consciousness, including hypnosis and dreaming. If a drive will cause significant distress in our psyche, our mind alleviates the threat by disguising the offending motive before we become aware of it. To exemplify this premise, Freud theorized that dreams consist of two parts: manifest content, or the literal, symbolic interpretation we can recall; and the latent content that is the true "meaning" of the dream

---

3 Robinson, Paul A. *Freud and His Critics*. Berkeley: University of California, 1993. Print.
4 "The Psychological Wednesday Society." *Sigmund Freud - Life and Work*. The Romanian Association for Psychoanalysis Promotion, 2002. Web. 07 Feb. 2012. <http://www.freudfile.org/psychoanalysis/wednesday_society.html>.
5 "From the Individual to Society -- Sigmund Freud: Conflict & Culture (Library of Congress Exhibition)." *Library of Congress Home*. United States Library of Congress, 23 July 2010. Web. 24 Jan. 2012. <http://www.loc.gov/exhibits/freud/freud03a.html>.

and an unfulfilled wish. He also explained that forgetting dreams is a defense mechanism that protects us from particularly disturbing drives that are poorly concealed by manifest content.

With the new psychoanalytic perspective came a new view concerning the cause of mental illness and new methods of treating it. As opposed to the prevailing ideas that neuroses result from biological, moral, or spiritual factors, the theory of psychoanalysis proposed that unmet needs in the unconscious can lead to psychological disturbances. By psychoanalytic logic, if neuroses originate as unacceptable desires that cannot be readily completed, simply committing a person to an asylum cannot effectively treat their illness, regardless of how humane the environment; therefore, it also called for different methods of diagnosing and treating mental illness. By enabling patients to express thoughts openly and to replace repressive self-criticism with nonjudgmental self-observation, free association became a particularly popular technique among doctors to access unfulfilled wishes in the patient's unconscious. Freud believed that free association should allow the patient to share his or her natural, uninterrupted train of thought and preferred to have the patient lie on a sofa as he sat in a chair behind it; thus, the famous image of the "therapist's couch" was born. Psychoanalysts also utilized altered states of consciousness in delving beneath the surface of the patient's awareness. Hypnotism often took place during therapy because it could allegedly bring forth repressed thoughts or memories, while dream interpretation became a widespread practice in the medical community and beyond. After a neurosis was diagnosed and its cause pinpointed, treatment focused on resolving internal conflict by acknowledging and, if possible, fulfilling unconscious wishes.

The impact of applied psychoanalysis was evident during the height of its popularity at the turn of the century. An article from the *New York Times* likened its role in understanding mental illness to the significance of "the microscope to pathology."[6] The article also indicated that Freud's theories were already put into practical use in state asylums by 1913, its year of publication. Essentially, psychoanalysis led to the earliest form of psychotherapy, or treatment consisting of interaction between a client and therapist that focuses on resolving problems. As Freud departed from organic medicine, psychoanalytic therapy became one of the first methods of treatment concerning the mind as opposed to the prevailing techniques that involved the body, such as restraint, skull drilling, and herbal remedies.[7]

---

6 "Dreams of the Insane Help Greatly in Their Cure." *New York Times* 2 Mar. 1913. Print.

7 Foerschner, Allison M. "The History of Mental Illness: From "Skull Drills" to "Happy Pills"" *Student Pulse* 2.9 (2010). *Academic Articles. Online Academic Journal - Student Pulse.* Student Pulse, 2010. Web. 27 Jan. 2012. <http://www.studentpulse.com/a?id=283>.

Despite its resonance in the psychological community, psychoanalysis also encountered significant criticism. As previously mentioned, its foundation, *The Interpretation of Dreams*, did not follow an entirely scientific method of research. Instead, Freud selected certain cases and used personal examples to support himself. In fact, he was accused of ignoring evidence that contradicted his theories because these procedures enabled him to do so.[8] Many critics also disagreed with the extent to which Freud credited sex as the root of unconscious drives. The flaws in Freud's work led many of his students to branch from his teachings and to develop independent ideas that are rooted in the fundamental theories of psychoanalysis. Carl Jung established the concept of the collective unconscious, a part of the personal psyche that contains the experiences of the entire human species and thus explains why certain images and symbols are universal. Meanwhile, Alfred Adler theorized that, instead of sex, our most powerful drive is the motivation to overcome inferiority.[9]

Criticism of psychoanalysis also brought a new perspective to the forefront of psychology. Behaviorism, which emerged during the 1920s, sought to define psychology strictly as "the science of behavior."[10] Whereas psychoanalysis relied heavily upon introspection and the study of internal processes, behaviorism dismissed the value of each since neither can be observed and interpreted via objective, scientific methods. Almost fifty years later, humanistic psychology united each perspective by placing equal emphasis on the studies of internal processes and observable behavior.

Psychoanalysis faltered in popularity as interest in the biological and neurological perspectives was renewed by the development of shock therapy, the frontal lobotomy, and psychosurgery in the 1930s. In the following decades, developments in psychopharmacology marked a shift in the field from psychoanalysis to physical medicine once again. Though its time was over, psychoanalysis had made for itself the reputation of a perspective that led to an undeniable revolution of thought throughout the field of psychology.

In a later edition of *The Interpretation of Dreams*, Freud introduces the text by writing that, "insight such as this falls to one's lot but once in a

---

8 Robinson.

9 Boeree, George. "Freud and Psychoanalysis." *Shippensburg University*. Shippensburg University, 2000. Web. 22 Jan. 2012. <http://webspace.ship.edu/cgboer/psychoanalysis. html>.

10 "Humanistic Psychology Overview." *Association for Humanistic Psychology*. Association for Humanistic Psychology, 2001. Web. 01 Feb. 2012. <http://www.ahpweb. org/aboutahp/whatis.html>.

lifetime."11 Indeed, his theories of psychoanalysis were likely his most vital contribution to psychology. Freud's ideas led to the development of an entirely new perspective, the influence of which has endured throughout the history of psychology and has set the stage for further growth. The psychoanalytic movement also changed the application of psychology in diagnosing and treating mental illness by introducing new methods that targeted the mind rather than the body. Had Sigmund Freud not written his revolutionary theories of the mind, psychology would not exist as we know it today—less extensive, perhaps less advanced, and certainly without one of its most famous images.

References

"A Dream Science- Prof. Freud's Ingenious System of 'Psychoanalysis'" *New York Times* 1 June 1913. Print.

"A Science Odyssey: People and Discoveries: Freud's Book, *The Interpretation of Dreams*" Released." *PBS: Public Broadcasting Service*. Public Broadcasting Service, 1998. Web. 07 Feb. 2012. <http://www.pbs.org/wgbh/aso/databank/entries/dh00fr. html>.

Boeree, George. "Freud and Psychoanalysis." *Shippensburg University*. Shippensburg University, 2000. Web. 22 Jan. 2012. <http://webspace.ship.edu/cgboer/ psychoanalysis.html>.

"Dreams of the Insane Help Greatly in Their Cure." *New York Times* 2 Mar. 1913. Print.

Evans, Rand B., and William A. Koelsch. "Psychoanalysis Arrives in America: The 1909 Psychology Conference at Clark University." *American Psychologist* 40.8 (1985): 942-48. Print.

Foerschner, Allison M. "The History of Mental Illness: From 'Skull Drills' to 'Happy Pills'" *Student Pulse* 2.9 (2010). *Academic Articles. Online Academic Journal - Student Pulse*. Student Pulse, 2010. Web. 27 Jan. 2012. <http://www.studentpulse. com/a?id=283>.

Freud, Sigmund. *The Interpretation of Dreams*. 4th ed. New York: Modern Library. Print.

"From the Individual to Society—Sigmund Freud: Conflict & Culture (Library of Congress Exhibition)." *Library of Congress Home*. United States Library of

---

11 Freud, Sigmund. *The Interpretation of Dreams*. 4th ed. New York: Modern Library. Print.

Congress, 23 July 2010. Web. 24 Jan. 2012. <http://www.loc.gov/exhibits/freud/
freud03a.html>.

"Humanistic Psychology Overview." *Association for Humanistic Psychology.* Association
for Humanistic Psychology, 2001. Web. 01 Feb. 2012. <http://www.ahpweb.org/
aboutahp/whatis.html>.

Myers, David G. *Psychology.* 8th ed. New York: Worth, 2007. Print.

Robinson, Paul A. *Freud and His Critics.* Berkeley: University of California, 1993. Print.

Simon, Linda, and Saul Rosenzweig. "Freud, Jung, and Hall the King-Maker: The Historic
Expedition to America (1909)." *The American Historical Review* 99.2 (1994): 669.
Print.

"The Psychological Wednesday Society." *Sigmund Freud—Life and Work.* The Romanian
Association for Psychoanalysis Promotion, 2002. Web. 07 Feb. 2012. <http://www.
freudfile.org/psychoanalysis/wednesday_society.html>.

Zaretsky, Eli. *Secrets of the Soul: A Social and Cultural History of Psychoanalysis.* New
York: Alfred A. Knopf, 2004. Print.

Evan Higgins

Being Black

Introduction

"It is not who you are underneath, but what you do that defines you"
—Batman/Bruce Wayne in Batman Begins.

This quote is important to understand how my views and beliefs are shaped. According to Batman, he is a hero not because he a multibillionaire Bruce Wayne, but because he goes out at night to put the criminals of Gotham away, to stop them from causing harm to its citizens, while being the foremost champion of the law. Like Bruce Wayne, I cannot be defined by my appearance, the color of my skin, or the actions of others who other people use to represent me. You should define me by what I do when the time for action occurs. I say this because my color of skin has been a defining factor. It is important to understand and offer another side of the story within black America. This story is often ignored and/or not acknowledged by society as a whole. No one understands the plight of African-Americans. We are subject to the stereotypes that are portrayed by the media. There is something deeper that is taking place within America that I want you to see. I have changed the names of the characters within these pages to protect them from your judgment.

Generation after Generation

My mom came here when she was seven. My grandmother left her country of Trinidad and Tobago to give her daughter an opportunity to live a better life. My mother was not wealthy in Trinidad. My grandmother saved up her money to pay for a flight for her and her daughter to come to America. Even once they were here, money was still an issue. My mom told of times my grandmother went from job to job trying to find somewhere to work since she would have been considered an unskilled laborer. My mom had my two sisters and struggled to raise both of them since she was doing this alone.

My dad's story was completely different but had the same result. He came to America to be reunited with some of his family after leaving Guyana. He felt there was nothing there for him and that America would provide him with opportunities to become wealthy. My dad worked plenty of odd jobs while here including being a physician's assistant and the treasurer of his church. My parents met during a session of a New York City initiative to get people to attend college. They would push each other and both land jobs as accountants in the financial district. My mom worked for an insurance company while my dad went on to work for E.F. Hutton.

After all of their successes, the recession in the late '80s and early '90s hit them hard. My dad lost his job at E.F. Hutton through no fault of his own (they were forced under due to several scandals and later bought by Smith Barney). What made this worse was that they had just purchased a house with all of their savings and they had a child on the way (which turned out to be me). My mom found a job working the books for a wealthy watchmaker who sold watches to Robin Williams and other famous actors. My dad spent a year looking for a job until he landed with Morgan Stanley.

When telling my parents' story, I feel that what they have done is absolutely irrelevant to me. Not that I am not appreciative of the values they have instilled in me or even what they have sacrificed on behalf of me, because I am. However, when I enter a room, no one sees my parents. They see another black male, put together by the stereotypes of society. I have already been judged on my ability and skill level and these perceived notions have formed untrue opinions about me.

Perception vs. Reality

My first co-op was as a finance intern at a campaign office for a Congresswoman. It was a small home office where everyone keeps their stuff in the open I was at my co-op, sitting at my desk doing work. There was my boss who was the office manager, myself, and two other co-ops and the finance director. On this particular day, there was a commotion in the office.

"Hey, has anyone seen my wallet?" my boss asked the office. There was utter silence because we were trying to make calls to constituents asking them to donate money for attending a function held by the Congresswoman.

He asked us again, "Seriously guys, has anyone seen my wallet? I cannot find it." We all stopped and stared at each other because we hadn't moved from our workstations all morning. We looked at each other, then looked back at him and started laughing. It was funny to us because he wasn't the greatest of bosses. While we were doing all of the "busy work" around the office, he would be playing World of Warcraft, a PC game. We felt mistreated every time we caught him playing.

While we were laughing, he retorted "Hey Evan, empty out your pockets. Maybe you took it!" Do you know about that awkward silence that takes place when someone does something that isn't funny? It was all over the office. I immediately felt the gaze of the other co-op students fall on me. I felt I was doing a monologue on Broadway

One of the co-ops responded to my boss: "Did you ask him because he was black?"

His face immediately began to turn red with embarrassment. I had thought the exact same thing. Why was I singled out? I always dressed neatly when I went to the office even though jeans were okay; I wore khakis because to me this was still a job. I don't have tattoos that cover my body and I remember telling my boss that when President Obama won, I wanted to get involved more in politics. So then why did he single me out? What was his rationale? I never asked him and he just laughed it off. But we talked about this during our lunch break.

"Hey Evan, I wonder if Jeff knew what he said was offensive?"

"He did, but the question remains, why accuse me? I don't sit by his stuff," I replied.

"Maybe because you are from Brooklyn?"

"Why does that matter?"

"He could think you are a bad person because of where you grew up."

"If that's the case then why do people in the suburbs and woods own more guns than urban populations?"

"Good point, Evan."

We discussed it a little bit longer and decided to change the topic to something more fun. In case you were wondering if I had his wallet, the answer was no. It was in his bag.

This notion that blacks and whites are on an even playing field is a mockery to my intelligence and I ask the people reading this to realize the truth: as long as you remain oblivious that the light that is cast on African-Americans continues to be negative, I will be subject to such treatment. The question I ask myself every day: Do I deserve this?

Friend by Day, Thug by Night

On my last co-op I took the school shuttle to Center City. The company that I worked for had me at Comcast working on various projects. I rode the shuttle with six other people and we called ourselves the 8:15 crew. We laughed and joked about plenty of things and we became good friends during the six months that we rode the bus together. Whether it was work-related, friend-related or anything Philadelphia-sports-related, we had funny stories to share with each other.

It was the summertime, so I found myself at the gym staying in shape. When I usually left the gym, it was dark outside. On this day, I was in sweats and a T-shirt and I was walking home when I spotted Ashley from our 8:15 crew walking towards me. Anyone that knows me can tell you that I am in no way, shape, or form a "thug" or someone you should fear. But nonetheless this was how the conversation went:

I said, "Hi Ashley!" as I waved my hands to get her attention. We made eye contact, so I began to slow down to talk to her. However, she sped up her walking. I said it again a little louder, thinking she had headphones in. Same results happened. Now she was a couple of steps away from me. I was still waving at her and she walked right past me. I turned around and said to her:

"Oh, okay, walk right past me, Ashley...."

She responded with a look of bewilderment on her face.

"Evan... Oh my gosh!" You could tell that she genuinely did not see me.

"Oh so now you see me?"

"No, I didn't recognize you."

I paused for second. I am a very sarcastic person and I wanted to make sure she felt really bad for what just happened.

"So, because I don't have on a shirt and tie, you didn't recognize me?" I knew exactly where this was going to go—a comment about my skin.

"It was dark outside and I didn't really see you with the all-black on."

I shook my head in disbelief.

I replied, "Ashley, I have on all-gray right now." She looked me up and down and laughed. I continued: "Okay, then, see you tomorrow at 8:15." We went our separate ways. As I walked home I couldn't help but think that she didn't recognize me. You would have thought my face morphed into something inhumane the way she walked passed me. It was like the clothes I wore for work defined me and that anything else was deemed threatening. Nevertheless, I learned a valuable lesson—people are afraid of me.

Taxicab Confessions

Since I am 22, I am no longer limited to just going to house parties. I can explore the nightlife in Philadelphia. On this occasion, I was with T.O. and Premier and we went to Recess Lounge. If you do not know or have never heard about Recess lounge, it is a nightclub in Old City that is frequented by people with tastes in house/hip-hop/Top 40 and Electronic music. It is also frequented by many of the famous Philadelphia athletes. The best feature of Recess lounge is that while other places close at 2 a.m., Recess closes at 3:30 a.m. It was our last weekend of co-op before senior year and we agreed that Recess would be a great place to celebrate the beginning of senior year. We decided to wear shirts, ties, and slacks, signifying to ourselves that we were growing up. We were on our way home and were outside waiting for cab.

I started talking, "Guys let's get a cab and get out of here." It was pretty chilly outside and we didn't have on any jackets.

Premier said, "Imma get this cab here," referring to the cab that was approaching us. As he gestured for the cab to stop, it drove by him to pick up five white people who were exiting Recess. As they tried to all get in his cab, I walked over. The driver started to move up. Premier then tried to talk to the driver, who proceeded to roll up his window and drive off. We both turned to T.O., who was from Philadelphia, for an explanation.

"Don't worry, guys! It happens to me all the time."

For a moment Premier and I were in a state of bewilderment at what was just said to us. I felt that no one should be okay with this happening to them. What was essentially said to our faces was that this particular cab driver would rather go without a fare than pick us up, which insulted me.

"What you mean?" Premier yelled out of frustration. "This is some BULLSHIT!"

I chimed in, "Really! If I were back home (I am from New York) we would have gotten a cab to take us from Manhattan to my house in Brooklyn."

We debated with one another about what we had just experienced. All the while we were trying to flag down a taxi. Eventually we got one to stop. We were still arguing when we entered the cab.

Still stunned, I said, "I still cannot understand how you sacrifice a fare. I mean, don't you get paid based on the number of fares you have in order to make the cab drivers have a stake in the success of the business?" The two others nodded in agreement.

But T.O. countered with his argument. "I have been here all my life and this is very common to me. I agree that this is not cool in any way and the fact that I am used to this isn't good either, but..."

At this point, our cab driver decided he wanted to give us his "honest opinion." I guess he felt comfortable because of the topic of our conversation.

"Listen, can I be real with you guys for a moment? I honestly took a look at you guys and I was leery of picking you up. I didn't want you guys to get to your destination and ditch me."

For a moment there was silence in the cab. We couldn't believe the words we had just heard. I have never felt less than a person in my life. This cab driver was willing to "enlighten" us on his take of our situation. As he persisted on with his theory, my rage grew.

Premier replied to the driver, "I don't know how you could say that. We each pulled money out our pocket and had it in our hand to wave cabs down and we still couldn't get a cab."

I followed up, "It wasn't like we were coming out of some hole in the wall. Recess is a well-known establishment and the way we are dressed should more than indicate that we were willing to pay for our fare."

He replied, "It's happened before to me. People have just hopped out of my cab once they reach their destination. There was nothing I could have done. I understand how you guys feel, believe me, but I don't blame him. I just had someone jump out of my cab a few weeks ago and, like, I saw you guys and took a chance."

As we rode home, I began to wonder about the environment that I had been going to school in for the past five years. Wondering what other stereotypes people have placed on me based on their "experiences." I wondered if when people see red-headed males on their campuses, are they afraid that they will shoot them because the suspects in the Newton, MA shooting and the Aurora, CO shootings had red-hair? Or is it something deeper?

Conclusion

"I have a dream that my four little children will one day live in a nation where they will not be judged by the color of their skin, but by the content of their character." –Martin Luther King, Jr.

What can we do about these situations? How do we address this phenomenon that is taking place within our society and move forward? Dr. King said these words 50 years ago. While progress has come, it seems that his words have fallen by the wayside. In a country where the discrepancies between the quality of education available, extracurricular activities along with income disparity between minorities and whites have continued to increase, I wonder what place myself and other minorities have in a society that pits the odds against me to succeed so early. Better yet, how many people do not want such things to exist?

Grant Grothusen, Vaughn Shirey, Zachary Stockmal

Crying Over Spilled Milk: A Study into Maintenance Issues in Drexel Residence Halls

Humans are capable of distinguishing a multitude of smells, with roughly 5 million olfactory sensors in the typical human nose (Fox 1). This might be why Drexel University students living in Millennium Hall recently experienced something both unusual and unpleasant on their treks down the northwestern stairwell. An odor most foul permeated the air, striking and sickening any soul trapped in this new spiral of hell. Many questioned the source of the smell. Had someone gotten sick? Was there spoiled food hidden in one of the many alcoves? It was not until recently that the mystery of the smelly staircase was finally resolved, but the inconvenience in the lives of many students highlighted a pertinent issue at Drexel. The shoddy state of maintenance in Millennium Hall and other residence halls is linked to student disrespect and action needs to be taken towards its improvement.

As the story goes, a resident living on an upper-level floor was in possession of a forgotten carton of milk that had been left in a refrigerator over winter break. The student's roommate decided to make devious use of the milk's disgusting possibilities. The dare was laid out: drop the rancid milk carton down the middle of the northwestern stairwell to the ground floor far below. The deed was done. Immediate remorse brought those involved down to the ground floor to attempt a cleansing of the area and their consciences. The scope of the damage was too great for them. The rest is history.

This incident, which student residents of Millennium Hall were responsible for, affected everyone who attempted to use the stairwell. The awful smell of rotten milk permeated far above the area of impact. Since taking the stairs was no longer a good option, elevator traffic increased greatly over this time period. When the elevators did finally arrive, they were full to bursting with students. The southeastern staircase, unfortunately, did not offer a remedy to this problem either, as it does not lead into the lobby of Millennium Hall. The southeastern staircase ends at the second floor, and this caused abnormal and increased traffic and noise on a normal residential floor where students were trying to sleep. All this uproar came from the misguided actions of disrespectful students.

This specific incident is only one example of a much bigger problem in Millennium Residence Hall. The smell, after some time and plenty of suffering, eventually subsided. However, many student residents still have a general disrespect for the maintenance of their living spaces. Peer pressure is a fundamental root of this disrespect. Betsy O. Barefoot of the University of South Carolina's National Resource Center for the First-Year Experience and Students in Transition describes the student's peer group as being "the single most potent source of influence on growth and development during the undergraduate years" (Barefoot 15). Unfortunately, as in the case of the spilled milk, this fact can manifest itself in the form of students influencing one another negatively.

Ironically, it is precisely these negative influences on behavior that Drexel University is trying to combat through its living learning communities. A learning community is formed when two or more cross-curriculum academic courses are linked so that the same students enroll in each course (Barefoot 15). The hope is that "students participating in learning communities experience greater social connection" (15). In recent times, learning communities have expanded outside of the classroom. On residential campuses, some learning communities can be linked with residential life, so that students can deepen their connections with one another while also living together in a single hall or on a single floor of a hall (15).

Millennium Hall is home to the Honors Living Learning Community (LLC). Most residents of the hall are also members of the Pennoni Honors College at Drexel University. These students had to display outstanding academic achievement in order to be invited into this prestigious society. They are expected to be models for the character and habits of the ideal Drexel student. Yet, even in the Honors LLC in Millennium Hall, there is still a significant amount of deviant behavior, and bad habits are all too visible. A look inside of any floor's communal kitchen will quickly confirm the latter. Disgusting used dishes are left in the sink, mold growing on remnants of food long forgotten and left sitting untouched by any cleaning initiatives. Not only are the appearances of such atrocities utterly disgusting, but the possible health issues posed by them are real as well. For example, based on the results of meta-analyses conducted by Fisk, Lei-Gomez, and Mendell, "building dampness and mold are associated with approximately 30–50% increases in a variety of respiratory and asthma-related health outcomes" (Fisk, Lei-Gomez, and Mendell 284). In the floor lounges, trash is left scattered on the floor, waiting to be picked up during the professional maintenance crew's daily morning run-through.

These littered objects create obstacles that must be carefully navigated when traversing through. Chances of falling and causing serious injury are high, especially as late students rush through to get to class. The stairwells and elevators are scribbled with discomforting profanities. The typical roll of toilet paper tossed down from a high floor has the potential of sending a student unlucky enough to be in the wrong place at the wrong time tumbling down the cold, hard metal stairs. All of these issues in Millennium Hall act as impediments towards academic success, as well as serious health and safety hazards. Members of the Honors LLC in Millennium Hall are expected to display responsible, respectful, and intelligent character at all times, yet they often fall short on all three fronts. Even now as legal adults, many students still expect others to clean up after their messes, while their lives go on without even a passing concern towards general safety. It is apparent that more than simply academic achievement goes into the determination of a student's responsible (or irresponsible) habits regarding dormitory maintenance during his first year living away from home.

When students have issues or behave poorly at school, the most common reasoning heard is, "It is the parents' fault." While this statement is not entirely true, the fact cannot be avoided that parents do have an effect on the well being of their children. While few would actually admit it, many teenagers leaving home to live at college will inevitably miss their parents. This is the only way of life they have known. As of now, Drexel University and many other colleges do not make this issue a part of their focus when trying to help students ease into college life. Students are encouraged to study hard and get lots of sleep, but University 101 professors forget to mention that students used to work during the day, and then get tucked in at night.

In the *Journal of Adolescent Research*, two members of the York University psychology department, Maxine Gallander Wintre and Mordechai Yaffe, published an article entitled, "First-Year Students' Adjustment to University Life as a Function of Relationships with Parents." The article explains that students are affected psychologically by the type of parents they had, or more specifically the method of parenting their parents enforced. These psychological effects carry on, influencing the student's academic and social endeavors in college. According to the article, there are three types of parenting that students are familiar with:

> "Authoritative parents (who are both demanding and responsive to their children), authoritarian parents (who are demanding but unresponsive), and permissive or laissez-faire parents (who do not place high demands but are responsive)" (Wintre and Yaffe 4-5).

Authoritative parenting is recognized as the most beneficial form of parenting to a student. Psychologically speaking, "Authoritative parenting has a positive impact on psychosocial maturity" (7). Authoritative parenting produces the best students academically and socially. These students have a healthy respect for their living community and the members of it. These students (the three authors of this paper included) tend to prefer tidy areas and desire cleanliness in their daily lives. This is because through authoritative parenting these children have learned to demonstrate mutual reciprocity. According to Wintre and Yaffe,

> "Mutual reciprocity is used to describe relationships wherein individuals perceive each other as relative equals, respect each other's point of view, and are involved in ongoing and open communication" (5).

Mutual reciprocity can be defined by the student cleaning up as a way of giving back to Drexel and the maintenance staff that have respectfully provided a home for the student. The biggest perpetrator of disrespect among college students would come from youths who were raised by laissez-faire parents. This type of parenting produces a child who will not have respect for new people and environments because he was never taught to respect his parents or his home. Students who had laissez-faire parents are most likely to make messes of places and disrespect their living community. This is because these students have never been taught a different way, or have simply never developed a sense of respect in their household. These students need to be encouraged to respect their living area and the people around them, despite this being difficult for them to do because of their upbringing.

Another consideration is whether or not the issue occurred based on the student's living situation. Students who live in a double-room dorm or a six-person suite have a different lifestyle; it might have been possible that this difference of locale would influence a student's respect toward their living community. In an interview with a local student, Steve Licari, who lives suite-style in Van Rensselaer Hall, Mr. Licari had unfortunate information to share:

> **Interviewer:** *"Personally, I live in a double-room style dorm room. There are 17 floors in my building. This distance can maybe make people feel disconnected, and this is why they show a lack of respect towards the dorm. Does living in a suite-style influence your decisions about general cleanliness or respect towards your living community?"*
>
> **Mr. Licari:** *"No. My room is pretty messy. (Laughs.) There is just as much garbage on my floor as there is at any other dorm on campus, regardless of the living style. Sometimes you might find a certain floor to be cleaner, like the floor with very studious students, and you'll find a floor that's*

*trashed because it's the 'Party' floor. Regardless of where
you go it really ends up being the student's decision, not
the area in which they live."*

Many students at Drexel University share the opinion of Mr. Licari. From this evidence, it can be theorized that the living area does not affect how a student treats his living area. The issue of respect falls down upon the student in any situation of dorm maintenance. It is up to the students to make or not make messes, and if they do make a mess then to clean it up. The student may have difficulty getting used to mutual reciprocity if his parents never enforced it in the household. Further action needs to be taken to get these students to understand the importance of respect and to contribute to a cleaner and healthier living community.

It is clear that the problem of respect at Drexel University is not one that will resolve itself overnight. While many students would argue that a combination of initiatives from Drexel's administration would be needed in order to attempt to correct issues, ultimately the initiative should be taken by the students who call these residence halls home. As a student, one needs to be aware of his or her actions and what effect those actions might have on others that share a living space. Many students fail to realize that they are no longer responsible for only their well being. In fact, health and safety issues concern the entire building of residents. What is needed from the student body at Drexel is a greater sense of respect for each other, and for the school as a whole. Students can achieve this by reverting back to grade-school standards on respect. Stop and think, "Is what I am about to do right? Am I making life easier for others? Did I really think about this?" Only when students develop this type of consciousness can they evaluate themselves effectively in potential scenarios. This type of thinking encourages mutual reciprocity, which is something that needs to be cultivated in the habits of Drexel students. Programs put forth by Drexel in events such as Freshman Orientation or the UNIV-101 classes can aid this cultivation.

Drexel's issues are not only concerned with the disrespectful students. Currently, respectful students cannot find an effective way to report maintenance issues in the dorms. Drexel's online submission system for maintenance requests is unnecessarily complicated. It consists of two separate websites, one containing instructions for submitting a request, the other providing the actual form for submission. Users of Drexel's facilities must submit their name, e-mail, phone number, as well as a selection from a dropdown menu of various issues. The problem with this setup is that it frustrates students before they can manage to submit a maintenance request. To resolve this issue, Drexel should integrate the instructional site into the actual submission site. Providing access to a succinct, all-in-one website would reduce the amount of back-and-forth browsing that users would have to undergo in order to submit a request. This would allow the respectful students to act on a problem that arises in a Drexel Living Community, an opportunity that up until now has been burdened with difficulty.

The issue of maintenance at Drexel University is one that must be addressed immediately and effectively. No one should have to find themselves trapped in a smelly stairwell ever again. The residents of Millennium Hall have experienced firsthand the consequences of letting students act on their disrespect. This disrespect comes from a negative influence on the student's behavior, be it from questionable parenting or the work of their peers. As a leading university, Drexel owes it to the respectful students to initiate a program that will deter the disrespectful students from acting on their poor behavior. College is the time when children become adults, and the first year is the most difficult to handle, as well as the most influential on the students' behaviors for the rest of their lives. This plan has acknowledged the issue in full detail, and if enforced in the Drexel community will produce a better living environment for all residents.

Works Cited

Barefoot, Betsy O. "The first-year experience." *About Campus* 4.6 (2000): 12-18. Web. 11 Feb. 2013.

Drexel Business Services. "Maintenance and Vandalism Information." *Drexel University.* Drexel University, 1 Jan. 2013. Web. 10 Feb. 2013.

Drexel University. "DrexelOne." *Drexel One Student Tab.* Drexel University, 2013. Web. 10 Feb. 2013.

Fisk, William J., Quanhong Lei-Gomez, and Mark J. Mendell. "Meta-analyses of the associations of respiratory health effects with dampness and mold in homes." *Indoor Air* 17.4 (2007): 284-296.

Fox, Kate. "The Smell Report." *SIRC.* Social Issue Research Centre, 20 Nov. 2009. Web. 20 Feb. 2013.

Licari, Steve. "Do the Students' Living Styles Affect Their Respect for the Campus?" Personal interview. 13 Feb. 2013.

Yaffe, Mordechai, and Maxine G. Wintre. "First-Year Students' Adjustment to University Life as a Function of Relationships with Parents." *Journal of Adolescent Research* 15.1 (2000): 9-37. SAGE *Journals.* Drexel University, Jan. 2000. Web. 13 Feb. 2013.

Allison Tipton

Paying for Treatment Before it is too Late: The Case for EDNOS

Twenty-five million: the number of people estimated to have eating disorders, including anorexia nervosa (AN), bulimia nervosa (BN), and binge-eating disorder (BED), in the United States alone. However, there is also a silent epidemic of those who display many of the symptoms of a full-blown eating disorder but do not meet all the criteria to receive a diagnosis of anorexia or bulimia nervosa. Instead, these individuals are often diagnosed with EDNOS, or eating disorder not otherwise specified. Despite the fact that those with EDNOS may be just as sick psychologically as those with a full-threshold eating disorder, they are often denied what little treatment those with a diagnosis of AN, BN, or BED receive. Rather, they must wait until their weight is "low enough," or they have been sick for "long enough," before they can get the treatment they need, at which point they may be fully entrenched in the eating disorder. In order to prevent the development of full-blown symptoms, provide the best chance of recovery for those suffering, and ultimately save money, insurance companies should cover treatment for those presenting with EDNOS.

Anorexia nervosa (AN) is defined as a mental illness in which a person has an intense fear of gaining weight, refuses to maintain a weight of at least 85% of what is expected for their height, is obsessed with weight and shape, and, if a female, experiences a loss of her menstrual cycle ("Eating Disorder Diagnostic..."). If any of these criteria is not met—for example, if an individual has lost a lot of weight but still weighs more than 85% of her expected weight or if a woman displays all of the other symptoms of AN but still has her menstrual cycle—that person cannot be diagnosed with AN, but instead is usually labeled as having eating disorder not otherwise specified. Similarly, if someone displays the classic symptoms of BN, including episodes of uncontrolled eating to a point of discomfort and unhealthy compensatory methods such as self-induced vomiting, excessive exercise, or laxative use, but has not been bingeing and purging for at least three months or at least two times a week, that person is not considered to have BN, but rather eating disorder not otherwise specified.

Those diagnosed with EDNOS may not display the extremes present in AN or BN, however much research points to the fact that they are suffering just as much, especially individuals with subsyndromal AN (SAN). According to Grange and Loeb, "Research has found distress, impairment, and psychopathology in SAN to be equivalent to AN," suggesting that SAN is just as serious as AN and reflects the same disorder, just at perhaps an earlier stage (30). Those with SAN also have comparable levels of psychological comorbidity compared to those with AN, and often deal with the same medical complications (McIntosh et al. 57). Similarly, those characterized with subsyndromal bulimia nervosa (SBN) also suffer greatly, as "[o]ther than binge and purge frequency, few differences on eating and general psychopathology measures were noted between SBN and BN" (Le Grange and Loeb 30). With such similarities between SAN and SBN and their full-blown counterparts, it makes sense that insurance companies would pay for treatment for those with EDNOS, and yet they rarely do.

In fact, even a diagnosis of AN is not always enough for an individual to receive adequate treatment. Though the BMI cutoff for a diagnosis of Anorexia is 17.5, Magellan Behavioral Health, Inc. will not pay for inpatient treatment unless an individual has a BMI of less than 16. Anthem Blue Cross is even worse, only paying for inpatient hospitalization when a patient has a BMI of less than 15 ("Will Health Reform Provide...").

Considering the similarity of symptomatology and psychopathology between sub-threshold and full-blown eating disorders, it is not surprising that many of those initially diagnosed with EDNOS eventually go on to develop AN or BN. In fact, according to various longitudinal studies, anywhere from 8% to 50% of patients with "partial eating disorders" are eventually diagnosed with AN or BN, and many others remain at the sub-syndromal level (Le Grange and Loeb 32). While it is clear that not everyone who exhibits symptoms of EDNOS ends up developing a full-blown eating disorder, a substantial percentage do. Thus, it makes sense for insurance companies to pay for treatment early on when symptoms of an eating disorder first appear, even if a person is characterized as having EDNOS. This is especially relevant since past research has shown that the length of illness is an important predictor of outcome for those with eating disorders. According to a study by Ratnasuriya, Eisler, Szmukler and Russell, the length of time an individual is sick before receiving treatment for AN or BN is negatively correlated with the chances of a good outcome, or recovery (496). Similarly, Herzog and colleagues state that, "Among these predictors (of poor outcome in AN) are very low body weight and long duration of illness..." (846). In addition, recent empirical research has shown that the earlier on a person receives treatment in the course of his or her illness, the better the chances at recovery, especially for adolescents presenting with AN. Perhaps the best illustration of the importance of early intervention comes from studies of the Maudsley family-based treatment program for adolescents with AN. This approach to treating AN is one of the most successful to date, with 90% of patients showing good outcomes at a five-year follow-up date. However, this high rate of recovery only stood for young patients (adolescents) who had been sick for less than three years (Le Grange 142). Clearly, it is very important to provide treatment early on for those with eating disorders before the individual becomes entrenched in the eating disorder and chances of recovery plummet.

Although insurance companies may argue that paying for treatment for those with EDNOS will cost them a tremendous amount of money, intervening only when people become "sick enough" likely ends up costing them more. Although, as aforementioned, not everyone diagnosed with EDNOS goes on to display a full-blown eating disorder, a significant number do, and once someone progresses into AN or BN the prognosis becomes grimmer and the level of care needed is often much higher. Without early and intensive treatment, AN and BN often become lifelong disorders that require repeated mental and physical hospitalizations, largely as a result of medical complications of the disorders. For example, in more than one-third of those diagnosed with AN, the disorder ends up being chronic, and the individual recovers and relapses again and again (Le Grange and Loeb 142). For those with AN, medical complications of the illness include disrupted heart rhythms, fertility trouble, osteoporosis, damaged nerves, gastrointestinal issues, and in the worst cases, multi-organ failure which often results in death ("Anorexia Nervosa."). Sadly, AN has a high mortality rate, with nearly one in five sufferers eventually succumbing to the medical or psychological effects of the disease (Nielsen 206). Similarly, there are many physical health problems that can result from BN, such as tooth decay, erosion or rupturing of the esophagus, dehydration, and an imbalance in electrolyte levels which can lead to cardiac arrest. ("Anorexia Nervosa"). The medical complications of AN and BN often require costly hospitalizations, and in some cases long-term physical care for the patient. In fact, it is estimated that the yearly healthcare costs for AN and BN are $6,045 and $2,962, respectively. These numbers are likely a very low estimate since they only include hospitalizations in which the diagnoses of AN or BN were used to bill for services, missing many cases in which patients were hospitalized for things like dehydration (which was caused by the eating disorder) and charged under that diagnosis (Crow and Peterson 400). Obviously, the cost of dealing with the medical problems that AN and BN can lead to is significant and could possibly be avoided if insurance companies provided treatment for those in the throes of EDNOS. The sooner the disorder is treated, the shorter the period of time an individual will likely spend sick and the less cost overall for his or her medical treatment. In addition, if those with eating disorders are treated early on, it is possible that many of the medical complications of full-blown eating disorders, as well as the cost of care that comes with the medical complications, could be avoided altogether.

Although the cost of treating the medical problems caused by eating disorders is significant, it pales in comparison to the hefty cost of treatment for the psychological symptoms of the disorder, which for inpatient or residential treatment can range anywhere from $1,000 to $2,000 or more a day! The earlier on symptoms are caught and treated, the more likely a patient is to only require one inpatient hospitalization, or to be successfully treated as an outpatient. However, the longer a person has an eating disorder, the worse their chances at recovery become and many patients end up spending their lives going in and out of residential treatment centers and racking up between 10 and 20 stays at specialized eating disorder centers. Over time, the cost of psychological treatment for those with treatment-resistant eating disorders can reach hundreds of thousands of dollars, a cost that insurance companies could likely avoid in many cases by allowing for earlier intervention.

Ultimately, all sides would benefit if insurance companies covered adequate treatment for individuals diagnosed with EDNOS. Perhaps the most meaningful benefit would be for the patients and their families, who would no longer have to fight to get treatment, but could instead focus their energy on helping the sick individual recover. However, insurance companies would profit as well through money saved in not having to pay for repeat hospitalizations in chronic eating-disorder patients and avoiding many of the costs associated with medical complications of severe AN and BN. By insurance companies granting treatment to those with sub-threshold eating disorders, those individuals who are suffering will be given the best chance at getting better, the cost of long-term treatment will decrease, and lives will be saved.

Works Cited

"Anorexia Nervosa." www.health.nytimes.com. *The New York Times*. 2011. <http://health.nytimes.com/health/guides/disease/anorexia-nervosa/complications-of-anorexia.html>. Web. 30 March 2013.

Crow, Scott J. and Peterson, Carol B. *The Economic and Social Burden of Eating Disorders, in Eating Disorders*. 6th ed. Eds. Maj, Mario, Halmi, Katherine, Jose, Juan, Ibor, Lopez, Sartorius, Norman. Chichester: John Wiley & Sons. 2003. Print.

"Eating Disorder Diagnostic Criteria From DSM IV-TR." www.casat.unr.edu. University of Nevada at Reno. 2012. < http://casat.unr.edu/docs/eatingdisorders_criteria.pdf>. 10 March 2013.

Herzog, David B. MD, Nussbaum, Karin M. MD, Marmor, Andrea K. AB. "Comorbidity and Outcome in Eating Disorders." *Psychiatric Clinics of North America* 19.4 (1996): 843-859. Web. 27 March 2013.

Le Grange, Daniel, Loeb, Katherine L. "Early Identification and Treatment of Eating Disorders: Prodrome to Syndrome." *Early Intervention in Psychiatry* 1.4 (2007): 27-39. Web. 10 April 2013.

Le Grange, Daniel. "The Maudsley Family-based Treatment for Adolescent Anorexia Nervosa." *World Psychiatry* 4.3 (2005): 142-146. Web. 10 April 2013.

McIntosh, Virginia V. W., Jordan, Jennifer, Carter, Frances A., McKenzie, Janice M., Luty, Suzanne A., Bulik, Cynthia M., & Joyce, Peter R. "Strict Versus Lenient Weight Criterion in Anorexia Nervosa." *European Eating Disorders Review* 12 (2004): 51-60. Web. 22 March 2013.

Nielsen, Soren MD. "Epidemiology and Mortality of Eating Disorders." *Psychiatric Clinics of North America* 24.2 (2001): 201-214. Web. 28 March 2013.

Ratnasuriya, R. H., Eisler, I., Szmukler, G. I., and Russell, G. F. M. "Anorexia Nervosa: Outcome and Prognostic Factors After 20 Years." *The British Journal of Psychiatry* 158 (1991): 495-502. Web. 20 March 2013.

"Will Health Reform Provide Coverage for Eating Disorders?" www.thingprogress. org. Center for American Progress Action Fund. 2012. < http://thinkprogress.org/ health/2012/03/06/436763/will-health-reform-provide-coverage-for-eating-disorders/>. Web. 26 March 2013.

Amanda M. Busch

The Unholy Birth of Playing God

"The benefits of biomedical progress are obvious, clear, and powerful.
The hazards are much less appreciated."
—Leon Kass

Human nature is a very fickle concept. We can say it is human nature to cling to life, avoiding pain and death at all costs. We can say that it is in human nature to advance, given a few accidents of personality and time. We can even say that it is human nature to protect oneself from harm, even at the cost of many others. What then happens when an advanced society falls into the hands of a shameful opportunist, whose thirst for power overcomes logic and morality, in pursuit of the "ideal" human nature?

Germany's history has been marked by outstanding technological achievement and scientific reasoning, but marred by the atrocities committed during the Third Reich. It was during the rise of the National Socialist German Worker's Party that utilitarian thought consumed the medical and academic fields, powered by the military's influence and provision, leading to horrific human experimentation that has cast shadows on the early history of psychopharmacology and neuroengineering as a whole. This essay will discuss Germany's rise to technological power as a chemistry giant, its place at the international vanguard in the field of psychology, the abuse of psychotropic drugs and human experimentation during the Nazi Regime, and the subsequent technological and social impacts on Neuroengineering and the field of medical research.

Although the first industrial revolution brought mechanization to many industries, the period after 1870 was a revolution of "science-based technologies, [which] altered not merely how goods were produced and consumed but also how industrial society evolved" (Misa 128). The cotton mills, which eased the labor to produce cloth, were now honing their abilities to make finer, mass-produced textiles. With the increased product demand came an interest in different colors and hues to make for consumer quality and entrepreneurial gain. German chemist August von Hofmann saw the promise of surplus coal tar, and employed a laboratory at the Royal College to find a use. In 1865, student William Perkin, who was working to create quinine (used to combat malaria), accidentally found that his research byproducts, when combined with alcohol, could dye cotton cloth purple (Misa 129-130). From that moment, the German chemical industry focused all research and development on this lucrative possibility. By analyzing and manipulating the chemical structures of dyes, researchers were able to create hundreds of colors, leading Germany to supply 88% of the world market for synthetic dyes by 1913 (Misa 133). Out of this boom in synthetic chemicals came some of the most important German chemical companies: Bayer, Hoechst, and Badische Analin-& Soda-Fabrik, known as BASF (Misa 130). Such scientific and economic development, however, would come at an astronomical cost. According to Thomas Misa, "the synthetic chemical empire led to the German chemical industry's direct involvement with the First World War and its appalling entanglement in the Second" (134). In the tumultuous fallout of the chemists' war, the top eight German chemical companies joined to form the superconglomerate, I.G. Farben, which would later become one of the most heinous abusers of human rights in pharmaceutical experimentation during the Second World War.

German academic research reached the apex of its golden age in the 19th century. The birth of modern pharmacology occurred in 1860, when it was introduced as a school of medicine by Rudolf Buchheim (Lopez-Munoz 389). Buchheim's student, Oswald Schmiedeberg, is seen as one of the pioneers of psychopharmacological research, a precursor to Neuroengineering. Schmiedeberg introduced urethane as a hypnotic agent in 1885. Between 1921 and 1926, Otto Loewi (a doctoral student of Schmiedeberg's) discovered the properties of acetylcholine, the enzyme which elicits nerve response in most organisms, by stimulating the vagus nerve in a frog heart. This breakthrough led other researchers, such as Hermann Fuhner, to experiment, leading to the "development of neurotoxic agents as chemical weapons by the Nazi scientific apparatus" (Lopez-Munoz 389). One of the most abused chemicals during the regime was injectable sodium hexabarbital, commonly called Evipan, which became a widely used anesthetic (Lopez-Munoz 390) and was used by Dr. Josef Mengele in his experiments on twins at Auschwitz (398).

Though modern psychology students are well aware of the research of Sigmund Freud, his challenging concepts would have been impossible without the work of neurohistologists and neuropathologists in the later 19th century. The propagation of the anatomo-clinical school of thought led to the understanding that biological lesions on the brain caused mental defect and disorder. Carl Wernicke published the first accurate description of schizophrenia and the resulting psychosis in 1900 (Lopez-Munoz 391). Along with the rise in understanding of mental disorder came the advancement in care facilities for the mentally disabled, with 16 university psychiatric clinics, 187 public and 225 private asylums in 1911 (Lopez-Munoz 392). Coupled with the advancement of pharmaceutical research, a motivation was born to synthesize neurologically targeting drugs to combat various mental diseases. It was not lack of knowledge or ability to create said medicine, but one overwhelming issue: lack of human test subjects.

The Darwinist perspective of natural selection and survival of the fittest appealed to the well-educated scientific minds of early 20th century doctors and researchers (Annas 168). Darwin's work also played a huge role in the creation of the German national eugenics movement, powered by the Nazi party and its leader, Adolf Hitler. With social acceptance of these theories, Germany all but welcomed the founding of the German Society for Racial Hygiene in 1909. These theories continued to flourish, further popularized by Ernst Rudin's findings that mental diseases, such as schizophrenia, were hereditary, as well as incurable (Lopez-Munoz 393). "Academic science, military power, industry and clinical medicine, including psychiatry, were woven together so tightly" (Lopez-Munoz 389), it's no wonder that "by 1942, about half of all physicians in Germany were members of the Nazi Party" (Annas 168). If requested, researchers were required to perform any medical tests to any specification required and on any subjects (voluntary or not). Those in opposition to the party or its demands had to remain silent and comply, or face imprisonment, experimentation, and certain death. Ten psychiatrists were killed for these reasons, John Rittmeister being the most well known (Lopez-Munoz 394).

A vital founding father of biomedical engineering and current professor at the University of Pennsylvania, Herman Schwan, researched the dielectric potentials of biological materials, following his extensive work at Siemens in Berlin, Germany (Schwan 1). Though he was a firm, but silent, opponent of he Nazi regime, Schwan stayed in Germany for the duration of the war. Due to his involvement in various research circles, he was witness to colleagues being pressured into human experimentation at the camps. One such colleague, also an anti-Nazi sympathizer to whom Schwan was covertly giving information, was caught: "[He was] asked by the Nazis to try certain drugs on concentration camp inmates and participate in human experiments. He refused to do so, and for that they put him in the camp" (Schwan 1).

"Horrifically inhumane" does not begin to describe the human experimentation during the Third Reich. "Some such specialists [of the medical field], apart from other criminal acts, did not hesitate to make use of their psychotropic agents available at the time in their criminal activities and in their repeated violations of basic human science" (Lopez-Munoz 388). The most atrocious cases were those in which concentration camp prisoner "subjects" were induced into a diseased state, such as malaria, typhus, or schizophrenia, and then "treated" with pharmaceuticals created by sectors of I.G. Farben and other companies. In very few cases were there volunteers for these experiments; instead, prisoners were brought into the camp infirmary, injected with Evipan to subdue, and then operated on.

Despite Germany's standing as the world leader in psychiatry prior to 1933, the eugenics movement led many medical professionals to see the mentally disabled as a threat to the future of the country. Due to the hereditary nature of these disabilities, published by Rudin and other researchers, many doctors wished to end the "circular madness" of schizophrenia, epilepsy, manic-depressive psychosis, and congenital afflictions of blindness, deafness, and mental weakness (Lopez-Munoz 394). The conglomeration of the Sterilization Act (1933) and active euthanasia of affected parties to make room in hospitals across Germany with the inception of the war was termed Operation T4 (Lopez-Munoz 394). Few, if any, voluntary parties existed to investigate pharmaceutical solutions to mental disease. Prisoners at Dachau, under the infamous doctor Sigmund Rascher, were subjected to large doses of mescaline "to assess the hidden schizophrenic behavior of inmates or to actually induce it" (Lopez-Munoz 398). The result of psychopharmacueticals in the form of barbiturates was a temporary lapse to a "state of immobility... [which] allowed a therapist to access unconscious information in the patient" (398), leading to the birth of "narcoanalysis," or the use of pharmaceuticals to elicit and unveil unconscious thought.

Malaria and typhus were spreading with extreme speeds in German-occupied countries during World War II, prompting many pharmaceutical manufacturers to research new cures. The psychological effects of these afflictions were also points of interest. Dachau concentration camp was the location for the malarial experimentation on over 1,084 prisoners from February, 1942 to May, 1945. Each month, three to five prisoners were exposed to mosquitoes carrying malarial strains, and contracted the virus. Blood was then drawn from these patients and injected into other subjects to maintain a constant source of the virus (Spitz 103). One patient, Father Leo Miechalowski, testified against the doctors responsible on November 13, 1945, a mere seven days before the beginning of the Nuremberg Trials. In his statement, he detailed that it took two or three weeks before his first malaria attack, after which he was treated with neo-salvasan, quinine, atabrine, and Perifere during different attacks (Spitz 107). "All of a sudden my heart felt like it was going to be torn out. I became insane. I completely lost my language—my ability to speak" (Spitz 107). When he repeatedly refused to be injected any more, the attending physician Dr. Ploettner, under directive of Dr. Claus Schilling, said, "I am responsible for your life, not you" (Spitz 108). This situation exemplifies the disregard for human rights and life in the pursuit of pharmaceutical research at this time. Of the prisoner subjects, 30 died directly from malaria, and 300 to 400 deaths were caused by complications and side effects of the pharmaceuticals (Spitz 106).

The typhus experiments at Buchenwald were even worse, as detailed by Vivian Spitz. The existing Weigl vaccine was expensive and complicated to produce, so cheaper alternatives using chicken egg yolks were investigated (200). The investigating physician, the infamous Dr. Ding-Schuler, organized multi-scale experiments for about 40-60 patients each (200). Starting in January of 1942, subjects were cut and infected with contagious lice, carrying the typhus culture (201). In 1943, subjects were injected, intravenously or intramuscularly, with blood containing the virus (201). According to prosecution witness Dr. Eugen Kogon, the experiments were carried out in Block 46, a "dreadful place" where "an experimental person did not only have to expect death, and under certain circumstances a very long drawn out and frightful death, but also torture and the complete removal of the last remnants of personhood" (203). Through the reuse of infected blood cultures, the infection grew to its most extreme state, causing "cases of raving madness, delirium, people would refuse to eat," ultimately leading to an estimated 95% mortality rate (203).

Without a doubt, these experiments were the applied means of mass extermination, or thanatology (McNeill 22). Though they seemed scientifically based, most of the scientifically contributive findings were lost when tons of documents were destroyed after the Allied invasion of Germany. As a result, most of the positive lingering effects are found in the judicial and ethical systems, rather than medical advancement.

In the mid 20th century, "medical experimentation became just one more tool of political power" (Lopez-Munoz 396). The resulting Nuremberg Trials were but a small victory next to the astronomical loss of human life and abuse of ethics by doctors, researchers, and military personnel involved in the Nazi regime. The German doctors and scientists defended their work, arguing that "the sacrifice of a few lives was necessary to save the lives of many; that they had acted under superior order" (McNeill 23). All involved medical personnel violated the Hippocratic Oath, which holds the rights and life of the patient above all else in medical practice. In the flurry of trials, Dr. Schilling (Malaria experiments) was sentenced to death (Spitz 105), 24 managers and personnel served six months to eight years in prison for their involvement with experimental testing, despite 15 tons of documents being destroyed upon Allied victory in 1945. Some war criminals were never brought to justice; Dr. Ding-Schuler of the Typhus experiments committed suicide, and many other doctors either evaded capture or were acquitted due to destroyed documentation. As a result of these trials, the Nuremberg Code was written as a guideline for future research practices, seen as the "Ten Commandments" of ethical human research (Annas 167).

To this day, the fear of subject abuse in biomedical experimentation is a point of discussion. Ruth Cowan describes this panic accurately: "One of the reasons why so many people worry about these kinds of technologies is that they seem to be altering out biological and social environments in disconcerting ways" (301). Dr. Marcia Angell, executive editor of *The New England Journal of Medicine*, unearths the concept of "publish or perish" mentality that "may result in human research subjects' rights becoming secondary to the investigator's career advancement" (Annas 170).

It is also disconcerting that "no U.S. court has ever awarded damages to an injured experimental subject, or punished an experimenter, on the basis of a violation of the Code" (170). Many biomedical ethicists worry, and for good cause; parallels may be drawn to modern reports that the Department of Defense has funded research projects on unknowing, and therefore non-consenting, military personnel and civilians. The argument that ethics takes a backseat to expediency in the face of "medical progress" (McNeill 219) is still very much an issue, as we face a future of stem cell modification to regenerate nerves, animal testing of pharmaceuticals, and the ever-changing definitions of psychological disorders. As we proceed with the future of neuroengineering, in the light of cognitive psychology and developing pharmacology, we are faced with a troubling question. With the survival tactics ingrained in our human nature, in situations such as the political and cultural climate of the Nazi era, are we to trust our fellow man, or even ourselves, with making such ethical decisions when facing death?

References

Annas, George J., and Michael A. Grodin, eds. "The Nazi Doctors and the Nuremberg Code." Comp. Kristine M. Severyn. *Journal of Pharmacy & Law*. 4 (1994-1995): 167-70.Http://heinonline.org. HeinOnline. Web. 22 Oct. 2012.

Cowan, Ruth Schwartz. "Biotechnology." *A Social History of American Technology*. New York: Oxford UP, 1997. 301-27. Print.

Lopez-Munoz, Francisco, Cecilio Alamo, Pilar Garcia-Garcia, Juan D. Molina, and Gabriel Rubio. "The Role of Psychopharmacology in the Medical Abuses of the Third Reich: From Euthanasia Programmes to Human Experimentation." *Brain Research Bulletin*77.6 (2008): 388-403. Elsevier. Web. 17 Nov. 2012.

McNeill, Paul M. "A History of Unethical Experimentation on Human Subjects." *The Ethics and Politics of Human Experimentation*. Cambridge: Cambridge UP, 1993. 15-36. Print.

(1) Schwan, Herman, Ph.D. "Oral History: Herman Schwan (1992)." Interview by Frederik Nebeker. *IEEE Global History Network*. Institute of Electrical and Electronics Engineers (IEEE), 1992. Web. 22 Oct. 2012. <http://www.ieeeghn.org/wiki/index. php/Oral-History:Herman_Schwan_(1992)#University_Education_and_ Hardships>.

(2) Schwan, Herman, Ph.D. "Oral History: Herman Schwan (1999)." Interview by Frederik Nebeker. *IEEE Global History Network*. Institute of Electrical and Electronics Engineers (IEEE), 1999. Web. 22 Oct. 2012. < http://www.ieeeghn.org/wiki/index. php/Oral-History:Herman_Schwan_(1999)>.

Spitz, Vivien. *Doctors from Hell: The Horrific Account of Nazi Experiments on Humans.* Boulder, CO: Sentient Publications, 2005. Print.

Caitlin Bubel

Apple 1984

Apple is one of the most powerful brands in today's society, but it was not always that way. Apple advertisement campaigns are seen frequently in commercials and print ads. When Apple first started the company it needed a way to get its name out and show its innovative product. Its first commercial was shown 28 years ago during the Super Bowl. It is recognized as an extremely successful commercial, and has won a handful of awards because of its uniqueness and effectiveness. The purpose of this campaign was to promote and introduce the Apple Macintosh personal computer for the first time. The company used a movie-like commercial with a large cast and crew, along with a sizeable budget, to promote its product successfully and make a lasting impression on society.

The commercial begins with an army of brainwashed men marching and listening to a person called "Big Brother," who is on multiple television screens. Big Brother is a character from George Orwell's novel *Nineteen Eighty-Four*. Big Brother is a mysterious dictator who only appears to the people through television screens. He is controlling and runs a totalitarian society in which everyone is under surveillance by authorities at all times. The people are given no freedom and constantly hear the phrase, "Big Brother is watching you," to scare them and ensure they obey. While these men are marching, a woman is running by them. She is dressed in a white tank top and orange shorts. She has blonde hair and is an attractive and thin young woman. Her appearance is the complete opposite of the marching men, who are almost colorless, wearing gray and looking gloomy. The authorities are chasing the woman as she runs towards the giant screen with Big Brother on it. Just as the authorities catch up to her, she throws a sledgehammer into the screen and it explodes. After the explosion there is a voiceover saying, "On January 24th Apple Computer will introduce Macintosh. And you'll see why 1984 won't be like 1984." The Apple logo, an apple with a bite out of it, appears on the screen and the commercial ends.

The 1984 Apple commercial displays a very dramatic scene with a happy ending. The commercial uses pathos in a unique way. The woman takes over the dictator and puts an end to the drab lifestyle of the imprisoned men. At the end of the commercial, the audience is left wanting to be like the woman. They want to be free and different, and not boring and controlled like the sad gray soldiers. There is an emotional appeal because the viewer is left rooting for the woman, and therefore rooting for Apple products. The commercial is showing the audience that they need to buy the Apple Macintosh computer, otherwise they will be left behind, as a lifeless solider. The woman shows that Apple computers are going to completely change society, because they have the ability to put an end to conformity and control the computer industry for good.

In 1984, the Apple Macintosh commercial aired for the first and only time on television. Although only shown once, it was enough to spark interest in the product by Americans. I have found that many Americans still remember it. My parents suggested looking into this commercial because it was "one of the best commercials," they had ever seen because it was "almost like a movie," and "was clever and like no other commercial at the time" (Bubel). The commercial aired on January 22, 1984, on CBS during the third quarter of Super Bowl XVIII (Friedman 1). The timing of this commercial was perfect. Millions of Americans tune in to watch the Super Bowl each year and many saw Apple's commercial. Apple reached a large amount of its audience, America, by airing the commercial during the Super Bowl. The commercial is strong in ethos and was very successful because it had a Hollywood director and an unheard-of budget of $900,000. Apple hired a reliable and credible director, Ridley Scott, to direct and produce the commercial. Ridley Scott is a well-respected director who is known for his science fiction horror movie, *Alien*. The 1984 Apple commercial has a science fiction theme to it and has an interesting storyline that resulted from Ridley Scott (Friedman 1). Because the commercial was so well made, it strengthened the product's credibility, adding ethos to the campaign.

The 1984 Apple Macintosh personal computer campaign is considered "the biggest single splash in the history of advertisement" due to its interesting use of logos. (Stein 169) The commercial never showed the product and never said to buy the product directly, but through the use of the story it indirectly persuades using logical reasoning to buy the product. The woman in the commercial symbolizes the coming of the computer. The Apple computer will put an end to conformity, just like the woman ends conformity and overtakes the dictator "Big Brother." The audience wants to be on the woman's side, just like they want to be on Apple's side. This is indirectly showing the reason Apple is better. During this time, IBM controlled the computer industry, but Apple wanted to change this. PCs were introduced in the 1970s as tools—utilitarian objects designed to facilitate specific tasks (Friedman 2). Apple's vision was to "create a user-friendly computer with an intuitive interface for the domestic market and to reclaim the dominant position in personal computing" (Stein 177). With a computer that the everyday person could operate, Apple would change the world. The woman symbolizes empowerment, and her demonstration in the commercial shows that Apple will be powerful enough to change society. She is powerful enough to take over a dictator, just like Apple is powerful enough to take over IBM.

The 1984 ad completely altered the advertising world. The Super Bowl became the major advertising event that it is today. People look forward to seeing the commercials during the Super Bowl, because they are supposedly "the best of the best," considering it costs two million dollars for a 30-second time slot (Stein 180). Apple changed the way products are advertised. The 1984 Apple advertisement expressed to consumers that anyone could own and operate a computer. Through the use of ethos, pathos, and logos, Apple effectively captured a large audience and promoted its campaign. This commercial launched Apple computers and it has been successful ever since.

Works Cited

Bubel, Jennifer. Personal Interview. 22. Jan. 2013.

Friedman, Ted. "Apple's 1984: The Introduction of the Macintosh in the Cultural History of Personal Computer." *Apple's 1984*. N.p., n.d. Web. 22 Jan. 2013.

Stein S. "The '1984' Macintosh Ad: Cinematic Icons and Constitutive Rhetoric in the Launch of a New Machine." *Quarterly Journal Of Speech* [serial online]. May 2002; 88(2):169. Available from: Communication & Mass Media Complete, Ipswich, MA. Accessed January 21, 2013.

Jimmy Warren

Midas Touch

Every kid in grade school has heard the story of King Midas's Touch: the greedy king who wished that everything he touched would turn to gold, making him the wealthiest king in all the land. Soon he discovered that gold did not make everything more valuable: his food turned to inedible metal in his mouth, and his loved ones were lost to him in a cold golden embrace. This same curse has long plagued humanity in its crusade to the farthest corners of the globe. From the earliest days of human exploration we have sought to turn our travels into treasures, but have failed to see that our touch is nothing but poison to the lands we reach.

The spread of humankind around the globe over the ages has been measurable in extinctions, a symptom of the disease called *Homo sapiens*. Centuries ago, the first species to fall victim to our influences when we would reach a new land were often the most majestic. For examples, we drove the megafauna of the land from Europe, with the quiet death of the final aurochs, and in Australia, aborigines killed the last of the giant moas for food. As these species disappeared from the Earth, their primordial mysticism went out of the land. Gradually, humanity was eliminating the things that went bump in the night, that had once rested so dominantly at the top of their ecological community that the very idea of their vanishing from the Earth was inconceivable. But vanish they did, and humans replaced them—but human beings are never content with being part of the landscape as these species were, and it was inevitable that once we removed these top species from contention, we would continue to toy with their ecosystems, constantly altering them with our mere presence.

Humans have never limited themselves to eliminating species only through hunting; they bring a regular plague of Biblical proportions down upon whatever ecosystem they happen to invade. We have never been able to travel alone, instead bringing a multitude of pestilential animals with us— rats, cats, snakes, even pigs, which have even fewer inhibitions than we do, and have been known by themselves to wipe species from the Earth, acting as a model of humanity in miniature, destroying all the resources in an area without a thought of conserving them. The casualties of such species are innumerable, ranging from the mighty Pinta Island Tortoise to the smallest, most nondescript birds on tropical islands around the globe.

Once we have a firm foothold in an area, we seek to mold it for our own desires, usually marring the landscape beyond recognition. We cut down trees, divert rivers, and eliminate any species we see as being counterproductive to our own survival. If the environment can be looked at as a delicately balanced machine, we are sure to stomp upon as many of the small, interlocking cogs as possible, twisting and mangling them until they cannot possibly work for their original purpose. Throughout history there have been a multitude of species that vanished from the Earth simply because they were unable to live in a world so dominated by humans. Ivory-Billed Woodpeckers, though overhunted for a century, ultimately vanished under the hack of an ax, not the shot of a gun, as the last lonely female persisted in a tree until it was at finally cut down to make sewing machines. The number of species, both known and unknown, that vanish daily as we let open sunlight shine for the first time on a forest floor, or pave over a marsh to build a shopping mall, is devastating, and certainly justifies referring to the current era as the anthropogenic mass extinction.

Perhaps the most terrifying implication of the terrible damage that humankind has wrought over the millennia is the simple fact that we seem almost totally incapable of learning from our mistakes. In 1848, the last pair of Great Auks were beaten to death by hunters, closing the book on a species that once nested in colonies in the millions, yet almost a century later, the final Passenger Pigeon died in the Cincinnati Zoo, ending the reign of a species that moved in flocks of billions, as possibly the most numerous terrestrial vertebrate on the planet. Even today we continue such practices, continuing to harvest many of the world's most numerous fish populations into oblivion, and poaching the final remnants of much of Africa's big game for bushmeat. This failure is even visible on a global scale, as much of the world continues to deny the existence of a global climate problem, despite the acceptance of this notion by scientists worldwide. This demonstrates the same mentality that drove Passenger Pigeons off the face of the Earth: that we as a species do not believe we can be the cause of a catastrophe until it has already occurred and it is far too late to do anything about it.

As the years go on and our influence on the Earth continues to grow, our past begs a question about our future: will the final species we drive to the brink be our own, as our relentless destruction of our planet's assets eventually and inevitably leads to our own demise? If it does, we will have no one to blame but ourselves, as we cut the ground out from under our own feet, driving our race into the void just as we have done to countless others.

David Nehring

Implementation of Instrumentation

Whether created with the intent of measuring a specific, novel observation or derived from existing equipment to perform novel experiments, instrumentation is generally considered to be one of the most necessary components of "doing science." However, the role of instrumentation is complicated because it is situated in the middle of what one might regard as the "scientific process"—namely, observation, experiment (or experience), and theory, and how this relationship articulates what it means "to know" something in the scientific sense. Furthermore, what it means "to know" something through instrumentation exhibits "intellectual trade-offs" in that the approach to doing science forms a dialectic between empiricism and rationalism. Instrumentation exemplifies a similar dialectic between the creation of new instruments and the use of existing instrumentation to answer new questions and it is this similarity that makes instrumentation a necessary component of doing science.

The relationship between observation, experiment/experience, and theory raises the question of what it means to do science by approaching the relationship from either the forward or reverse direction. For instance, generating observations from experiments and compiling those observations to fit a broad theory defines the empirical approach to "knowing" something. Conversely, if a theory is formed and then experiments are made in order to test the proposed theory, with observations to verify, the approach is considered rational. In the Baconian sense of manipulative experimentation, the "doing" of science takes place with both approaches: observations (empirical) of an experiment are used to form theories (rational), which are further verified by observations. The use of both approaches is used to overcome the "intellectual trade-offs" in doing science from either approach individually. For instance, from a rational viewpoint, if any experiment conceived bears evidence that conflicts with the theory, the entire theory is moot. Similarly, if looking at the empirical evidence, formation of a theory may be too specific to extrapolate to novel experiments.

It is through instrumentation that the bridge between these two approaches is created. This is best exemplified in the creation of new instruments and use of existing instruments in that a theory (or idea) that generates a new experiment may require a new instrument, but also in that existing instrumentation can aid in creating new experiments and generating new theories.

In considering the uses of instruments, it is also essential to understand what an instrument is. In the Newtonian definition, an instrument is merely a means by which to perform observation oneself, or rather to sense the observed phenomena (as vision is not the only way to observe). Spurring from the ideal of empire of observation, the root of empiricism, Newton played a major role in the scientific revolution insofar as he claimed that firsthand witness of an event was essential to "doing science" and that to make such an observation was an integral part in "knowing" something (Dear 1-9). It is from this concept of observation that the relationship between observation, experiment/experience, and theory is formed, and by which instrumentation is necessary.

Consider, for example, the role that instrumentation played for Robert Boyle and the air pump. With his creation of the air pump, Boyle was able to derive his gas laws (*Conversations...*, CHF). In this instance, the former implementation of instrumentation is taken: creating a device to serve a specific function to aid in making repeatable observations. Boyle's air pump was useful for more than just determining gas laws, though. Chemists Antoine Lavoisier and Joseph Priestly later used Boyle's air pump in their independent discoveries of oxygen, thus exhibiting how the use of existing instrumentation can have uses in generating new experiments (Poirier 1996). Consider, also, Robert Hooke who—in trying to discover the small particles that compose matter—had an observation that he wished to make, but lacked the instrumentation. In formalizing the microscope, Hooke was able to observe what he coined as 'cells' (Hooke 1667). It is with the refining of an existing instrument to perform new measurements that Hooke was able to carry out his experiment, and in this way the microscope exhibits qualities of both a new instrument and an existing instrument to perform measurements for a specific experiment while simultaneously generating new experiments.

Instrumentation is not only useful to these manipulative experiments in the Baconian method, but also in the Humboldtian "experiential" method of science despite its typical association with qualitative, natural observations. Furthermore, a critique of the Age of Enlightenment is that the era lacked a common system of scientific units; but at the turn of the 19th century, conversion to a standardized measurement system allowed experiential observations to bear quantifiable data (*Symbols...*, CHF). Between 1790 and 1793, the French Academy began working on an International System of Units (SI) using its existing toise (approximately two meters) to measure the distance between the northern and southern poles and defined the meter as one ten-millionth of said distance (Nelson 1981). Standardization of units, like the meter, allowed scientists like Humboldt, Maskelyne, and Darwin to label observations with quantifiable measurements, such as the estimated height of mountains or area of observed biodiversity. As seen in his 1824 *Journey to the summit of Chimborazo*, Humboldt's measurements are in toises despite the standardization of the meter—understandably so, as the toise was indirectly standardized in its defining the meter. Similarly, the concept of longitude was based on the accepted measurement of 360 degrees in a circle and the use of existing instrumentation like sextants, astronomical charts, and watches allowed Nevil Maskelyne to derive mathematical verifications of precise longitude while sailing to measure the transit of Venus (Wulf 2012). And though his method of calculation was impractical, it bore incredible precision without the need for new instrumentation. Furthermore both of the transits of Venus in the mid-18th century, before measurements were standardized, hinged on one of the few measurements that was standardized: time (Wulf 2012).

The approaches of "doing science" have been introduced as either an empirical or rational approach, or even a combination of the two, but neither identifies the motivation of doing science. Most, if not all, of the aforementioned instrumentation has been for the purpose of doing science for the sake of personal interest or doing science strictly for the sake of science, funded by the Royal Society. However, popularization of some instrumentation is funded not for knowledge or science, but for entertainment. Especially in the case of experimenting with electricity in the late-18th century, scientists like Priestley (the same scientist who, as mentioned before, discovered oxygen) would build devices with the intention of entertaining a small audience by allowing them to participate in the "science" firsthand. In his case, the instrument was the Priestley battery (also known as a Priestley capacitor): an assemblage of Leyden Jars (an existing instrument responsible for generating electricity) in parallel formation (Meyer, CHF). This interactive form of "doing" science predates Priestley by his predecessor, Robert Boyle, who was infamous for his lecturing technique of requiring each student to visually verify the science for himself, spurred by the Newtonian concept of actively participating in science rather than the mere dictation of science (*Conversations...*, CHF; Dear, 1-9).

As suggested above, the motivations of doing science may be for academia, entertainment, or otherwise, and even in the commercialization and industrialization of science, instrumentation still engages the same pivotal requirement: motivation. William Perkin, at the turn of the 20th century, was able to easily produce chemical dyes of colors like purple and blue, which provided a great alternative to other available dye methods, thus revolutionizing the dye industry (*Rivaling...*, CHF). Rather than sitting back and feeling satisfied by his work, Perkin pursued the industrialization of his newly found niche and was able to manufacture purple (an otherwise expensive dye) linens, dresses, and a plethora of other materials. His motivation: monetary gain. However, in order to mass-manufacture his purple dye, he required an instrument that could scale his chemistry to an industrial size, and so he had an experiment which he knew worked, but required a novel instrument to repeat that experiment on a larger scale (*Rivaling...*, CHF). Despite the varying motivations responsible for doing science, each relies heavily on either existing instrumentation or outlining the need for a novel instrument.

It is because of the relationship between existing and new instrumentation that observation, experiment, and theory require instruments to both grant observations of an experiment based on new theory and generate new experiments from observations that will in turn help form a theory. Whether in the Baconian or Humboldtian (manipulative vs. natural) way of "doing science," both forms of science are heavily dependent on instrumentation to quantify observations and exploit the dialectic between rationalism and empiricism. In this regard, instrumentation may very well be the most important necessity in order to perform science, as the accuracy of said instrument determines the usefulness of the observation and how certain one can "know" something. In turn, the accuracy of an instrument is the crux of what it means to "know" something in a scientific sense, regardless of the intellectual trade-offs involved in an empirical or rational approach. As seen in the examples previously mentioned, both existing and new instrumentation is essential to creating novel theories and discovering otherwise un-quantifiable certainties in the observations of science, which in its most basic definition allows one to answer a specific question.

Works Cited

Conversations and Demonstrations: Showing and Telling. Chemical Heritage Foundation, Philadelphia, PA. Exhibit observed 1 March 2013.

Dear, Peter. n.d. *Revolutionizing the Sciences: European Knowledge and Its Ambitions, 1500-1700.* 2nd Ed. pp 1-9. Print. Princeton University Press; Princeton and Oxford.

De Humboldt, Alexander and Bonpland, Aimé. 1814. *Personal Narrative of Travels to the Equinoctial Regions of the New Continent.* Print. Translation by Williams, Helen Maria. London.

---. 1824. *Journey toward the summit of Chimborazo...* Web. Retrieved on 10 March 2013. <http://libweb5.princeton.edu/visual_materials/maps/websites/thematic-maps/humboldt/humboldt-profile-chimborazo-1829.jpg >

Hooke, Robert. 1667. *Micrographia: or some Physiological Descriptions of Minute Bodies made by Magnifying Glasses with Observations and Inquiries thereupon.* Print. London.

Meyer, Michal. n.d. *Sparks and Flashes, Charged and Ready.* Chemical Heritage Foundation, Philadelphia, PA. Exhibit observed 1 March 2013.

Nelson, Robert A. 1981. *Foundations of the International System of Units (SI).* The Physics Teacher. 19(9). 596-600. Print. American Association of Physics Teachers.

Poirier, Jean Pierre. 1996. *Lavoisier: Chemist, Biologist, Economist.* Print. Translation by Balinski, Rebecca. University of Pennsylvania Press, Philadelphia, PA.

Rivaling the Rainbow: The Essence of Color. Chemical Heritage Foundation, Philadelphia, PA. Exhibit observed 1 March 2013.

Symbols of Change. Whatchamacallit. Chemical Heritage Foundation, Philadelphia, PA. Exhibit observed 1 March 2013.

Wulf, Andrea. 2012. *Chasing Venus: The Race to Measure the Heavens.* Print. Knopf.

Week of
Writing

Introduction

Drexel University's eighth annual Week of Writing (WoW) was held in May of 2013. WoW is a weeklong celebration of writing sponsored by the Department of English and Philosophy and the College of Arts and Sciences. This past year's events included such panel discussions as "Pitfall! What Writers and Videogame Designers Need to Know about Each Other," "When Readers and Editors Attack! How to Stand Up for What You Write," and "Strange and Familiar Places in Young Adult Fiction." Once again, at the WoW Reading Marathon, faculty and students read their own original creative writing back-to-back, a new reader every few minutes, as the audience came and went throughout the days.

Each year, the lead-up to the marathon is the WoW Writing Contest, used to determine which students will be invited to read at the event. The faculty judging panels determined the best fiction, poetry, and creative nonfiction submitted by Drexel students in 2013. Those winning students not only read at the WoW marathon and earned prizes, but also now have their writing published in the sixth volume of *The 33rd*.

Creative writing is among the most challenging fields. Even experienced authors who have been writing for years often struggle to find just the right word. As author Gene Fowler famously said, "Writing is easy. All you do is stare at a blank sheet of paper until drops of blood form on your forehead." The writers whose work appears in this section have stared at that blank sheet of paper, or that computer screen. Whether or not blood formed on their foreheads, they have struggled for the right words to touch their readers and bring their vision to life. The Week of Writing will continue to celebrate and reward their efforts.

Marie Ruisard

Hunting the Sun

It was barely night
when we left the runway,
lines of lights passing
like rapid flashbulbs at the windows;
rungs on a ladder into the air.
And as we rose,
so did the sun,
peeking back over the wrong side of sky
as if through flight
we have created time travel,
finally finding a way to watch the sunset
not only twice but also backwards;
grabbing at its fleeing rays
and tugging like children afraid of the dark,
not yet aware that the higher we rise,
the more light will find us
over the shadows of earth.

Hannah Mindl Gittler

Last night (like every other night)

Last night was wonderful, when you came to my steps, your hair dirty and your shoes clean, to see me and only me, and as you walked towards me I felt my skin begin to sweat, a drink in my right hand, your favorite that I had mixed for you (leaving out the ice) hours before you arrived, just to know that you would be thankful for me, and that reminded me of the night you drew me full of dots and lines and arrows, fully nude and made my body look like an ancient map of a mountainside somewhere, somewhere that you probably have dreamed of living, and after you gave it to me, I cried drunk tears and you didn't understand why, but as you laid in my bed last night, in the night light that poured from my open window, you said the moonlight made you sober and I poured you another drink because only gin makes you touch me.

Nahjan Amer Nordin

The Monkey (Homage to Iain Haley Pollock)

The house, bought the year I was born,
Solid wood trunks contrasted against the bustling city of Kuala Lumpur.
The soft rustle of leaves and branches,
Muffled by brick walls, a garden and the open road.

Cracked pavement, overgrown weeds,
My older brother, a fallen hero on the ground, curled on his sides. Sharp pain.
The rope a tangled mess.

The shadows of trees. Banded leaf monkey shadows—furry,
wild, hungry, stark desperation in its eyes—settles on the brick wall.
Wide-eyed, blank stares exchanged. The soft rustling of leaves and branches,
Divided by brick walls, a garden and the open road.

The monkey moves languidly to the tree. Unflinching wide-eyed, blank stares
    exchanged.
My older brother, a fallen hero still on the ground. A purple bruise on his right
    leg.
Naked fear.

The soft rustling of leaves and branches,
Muffled by brick walls, a garden and the open road. The monkey—wild.
Overgrown weed,
moss on the swing, shards of broken flower pots swept to the corner.

Kate Rosenberger

10K

Liz maneuvered into an empty spot a few stores down from the bar and cut the engine. Every time she came back to the old neighborhood she was struck by how everything seemed both familiar and different, an alternate version of the Port Richmond she remembered. Or maybe it was her that was different. She closed her eyes and leaned back against the headrest, listening to a bus lumber by and come to a stop at the corner ahead. A group of boys from the local Catholic high school tumbled out the back door. On the street to her right, a woman stopped to wait for a toddler who was inspecting what appeared to be a crushed beer can on the sidewalk. The woman opened her mouth as if to say something and then closed it again. She looked as tired and hopeless as Liz felt. Liz sometimes wondered what her life would be like if she had stayed in the neighborhood. She used to consider herself fortunate for having been able to leave. Not anymore.

Her Dad had played in the dart league at Daly's when she was growing up. Liz would sit at the big square bar sipping Cokes and watching him play. When she stepped inside, she felt like she had gone back in time twenty years. A group of men were clustered around the dart boards, a smattering of hardcore drinkers sat scattered around the bar, and Harry was leaning against the cash register watching the news on one of the big TVs. Harry was probably in his early sixties, big and stocky. He still wore his hair slicked back, though it was mostly gray now. Liz had always gotten a kick out of Harry. He was always smiling and cheery, loud. In retrospect, Liz realized he was probably a drunk.

Liz sat down at the bar far away from the other customers. Harry came over to take her order. A minute later he returned with her rum and Coke, grinning down at her, "You're Lizzy, Richie's daughter, aren't you?" Liz nodded, smiling for what seemed like the first time in months. Harry leaned over the bar and hugged her. "It's been a long time, Hon! How are you? How're Richie and your mom? I heard you married some lawyer from school and moved out to Montgomery County. How's your husband?" Liz froze, opened her mouth to answer, but tears filled her eyes and her throat tightened. Once she started talking, she told him everything, even showed him some of the bruises. Part of her felt like a dumb cliché, but it felt good to tell someone, and this was Harry. He'd been like an uncle. The concern on his face was real.

Liz downed the rest of her drink and laid her arms and head on the old oak bar like she had when she was little. "I can't take it anymore. I wish he was dead." Liz looked up at Harry. "I want him dead," she whispered. Harry tilted his head back and stared at her.

"You don't mean that, Hon," he said.

"Yes, I do," Liz said, sitting up, "Do you... know anyone?" They stared at each other for what seemed like forever. Harry turned, looked back at Liz, took a half step, and looked back again.

"I might," he said, "Gimme a minute." He went back by the cash register and made a call on his cell phone. He came back and handed her a scrap of cardboard with a name, Patty, and a phone number. "This is my nephew, Pasquale. He might be able to help," said Harry. He reached out as if to rub her head like he had when she was a kid, but patted her hand instead. "Be careful, Lizzy." He hugged her again and gave her a fake smile.

She kept the piece of cardboard tucked in her glove compartment for almost a month. Then one night after Steven was asleep, she crept out to the garage, retrieved the scrap, and dialed the number with sore, shaking hands.

Two days later Liz met him in a pizza shop in Mayfair. It was a little early for lunch and he was the only customer when she stepped inside. He was sitting at a table in the far corner drinking a soda. She had imagined him to be either a wiry Irish guy like Harry's son, or someone out of the cast of *The Sopranos*. He was more like a hybrid of the two. His dark brown hair was buzzed close to his head and dark, serious eyes bored into her. It was barely lunchtime but he had a heavy five o'clock shadow. He looked lean but well built. Tattoos ran up one forearm and peaked out from underneath each sleeve of a black t-shirt. Long, khaki-clad legs were visible under the table, capped off by heavy black shoes. He looked to be in his late thirties.

Liz found herself standing in front of him. Neither of them had said anything. She couldn't read the expression on his face. Suddenly she felt like she was going to faint. She sank into the other side of the booth, pulled her hair off her neck with one hand, and rubbed her forehead with the other. What was she doing? Was this really happening? She could still back out. Couldn't she? She tried to calm herself down, decided to talk to him, see what he had to say, and take it from there. She looked up to find Pat watching her from the corners of his eyes, twiddling a straw wrapper between his long fingers. An image of E.T. popped into her head. *E.T.* had been her favorite movie as a child and she smiled before she could stop herself. He raised his eyebrows.

"Sorry, I just... thought of something. I'm Liz. You're Harry's nephew, right?" She held out her hand.

"Pat," he said, dropping the wrapper and shaking her hand.

"Nice to meet you. Like I said on the phone, Harry told me that you might be able to help with my... problem."

He nodded. "You can tell me what you have in mind while I eat. You hungry? Do you like Hawaiian?" Pat sat up straight and looked behind her. A waitress appeared carrying a steaming hot pizza. Liz hadn't eaten in over a day and her stomach started grumbling.

That was how it went. Pat was as easy to talk to as his uncle. They sat there like a couple of friends, calmly discussing Steven's murder over pizza. He would do it at the mud run in a few weeks. Liz and Steven were signed up for the 10K. The crowd thinned out in the middle part of the race that went through the woods. They had run the same race last year and Liz told Pat about the steep downhill area around this point. A racer had taken a header down it last year and gotten pretty banged up. They'd had to take him off the course in a stretcher.

They would make it look like an accident. It turned out that Pat was a runner. He would enter the race and line up a wave or two ahead of Liz and Steven. He would ambush them in the woods, break Steven's neck and throw him down the hill. Liz had to make sure they were alone by the time they came to the spot. It sounded simple. Liz's nausea had dissipated. They ordered coffee and Pat had a piece of cheesecake.

"So, tell me about yourself," said Pat. Liz hesitated. This seemed like an odd question for him to ask under the circumstances, but what did she know? She'd never done anything like this before and Pat wasn't at all what she'd expected.

"I'm 31. I grew up in Port Richmond. I moved out of the city six years ago when Steven and I got married. I'm a lawyer." Why did she tell him how old she was? Why did she make herself sound so boring? Oh wait, she was.

"You work for your husband's family's firm?" asked Pat.

"Yes," said Liz, "but not because I have to."

Pat raised his eyebrows. "Okay... I was just asking. I didn't mean to imply that you got the job because of your husband. You seem very smart."

"Don't patronize me. You don't know me," Liz said. Did she just snap at a hitman? Oh my God, he probably had a gun on him right now. "Sorry. I just... I guess I'm just sensitive about that. They offered us both jobs there when we graduated. I took the job because his family's firm has such a good reputation. But I worked hard in law school and I'm good at my job. I've had offers to work at other firms..." Liz could see the amusement in Pat's eyes as he looked at her over his coffee cup. Her anger faded and she found herself smiling. When he lowered his coffee cup, he turned his head to the side, but not before she could see that his stoic expression had been replaced by a surprisingly boyish smile. His coppery brown eyes lit up and crinkled at the corners. He was handsome. That night, Liz barely noticed her sore ribs. It was Pat's smile that had her up half of the night.

They met one more time before the race, at a coffee shop not far from the pizza place. He told her to bring the money in a bag and meet him there at 7:30. He was again sitting in the far corner, dressed much the same as he was the last time. Liz ordered a coffee and bagel and joined him at the table. She hooked her purse on the chair and plopped the Sephora bag containing the money on the table. Pat fought off a smile and poked the inside of his cheek with his tongue. "Nice, couldn't find anything more embarrassing?"

"It was either this or Victoria's Secret," said Liz. Pat raised his eyebrows but said nothing. He had a coffee and a jelly doughnut in front of him. They talked as they ate. Pat had grown up in the Italian section of Tacony. They talked about books and TV shows. They talked about growing up in the city and the Mummers. It was almost 9:00 when Pat looked at his watch and said he had to get going. He hesitated before picking up the bag. They shook hands in the parking lot, looked at each other for a minute, then drove off in opposite directions.

*****

That night in his apartment, Pat looked through the manila folder with Liz's name on it again. Her medical records resembled that of a boxer: sprains, fractures, concussions. Most recently, just last month, she had been treated for cracked ribs. There were police reports against Steven that were about five years old. The charges had all been dropped or thrown out. Just another perk of being the son of a well-connected family of lawyers, Pat thought to himself. He looked through her college transcripts, newspaper clippings about her court cases, financial records. She had no criminal record, just a handful of speeding tickets and other traffic violations. He stared at her driver's license picture. It was older, taken about four years ago. It kind of reminded him of a mug shot because her blonde hair was sticking up in several spots, but she had a big grin on her face and he found himself smiling back at her. Almost time for a new picture, he thought. Pat absently jabbed his tongue into his cheek and he wondered if he had made the right decision. Well, it was too late to change his mind at this point. Pat yawned and tossed the folder back onto his desk. In his bedroom, he removed the gun from his hip and placed it on the nightstand. He laid his wallet and badge next to it, stripped down to his boxers, and lay down to go to sleep.

*****

Liz leaned back against the headrest as the X3 barreled down the highway. Steven had the news blaring as usual and she tried to tune it out. She was always nervous before a race, but this morning it felt like her heart was going to explode. This morning it wasn't the race that she was nervous about and she had no second thoughts about her decision. She was worried about getting caught. No, she was worried about Pat getting caught. How stupid was that? Steven angled the car into a handicapped spot at the edge of the park. Droves of people were migrating past from the event parking a mile away. As soon as Steven put the car in park Liz leapt out and trudged along with them as she pinned the bib to her shirt. She didn't care about making him angry anymore. However this went, she knew that she wouldn't be going home with him tonight.

*****

Pat spotted Liz waiting in one of the 10K corrals with her husband. Steven was short but athletic in a somewhat nerdy way. It was mid-July but he was pasty white in a sleeveless top and running shorts. He was wearing a pair of those running shoes with the toes separated. Pat couldn't suppress a small smile as he lost himself in the corral ahead of theirs. He felt out of place among the 10K runners. Most of them were built like skin-covered skeletons and were dressed similarly to Steven. Pat had on an old green t-shirt and loose fitting black mesh shorts that fell to his knees. Pat twisted around under the pretense of stretching and stole a glance back at Liz who was looking nervous but intent. She was standing a good ten yards behind him, but he thought the left side of her face looked yellow. A starter pistol went off ahead. The first wave of 10K runners was on its way. He eyed the tree line just visible in the distance through the early morning fog and sighed. It was definitely too late to change his mind.

*****

A dull ache had settled into Liz's ribs as the race wore on. She had stalled earlier, told Steven that she needed to walk for a minute, in order to separate from the pack. Now they were almost at the top of the hill and no other runners were in sight. They came around the bend and there was Pat, off to the side pretending to tie his shoelace. Liz had managed to get a couple of strides ahead of Steven. As they came abreast of Pat, Liz clutched her side and slammed on the brakes. Steven barreled into her, cursing and knocking her into a small tree. Liz lay there for a minute. She could feel a fresh bump forming on her cheek but seemed fine otherwise. She climbed to her feet.

Both men were on the ground a few yards away. Liz didn't know what to do. She looked around. No one was coming. Thank God, it was almost over. "Do it!" she found herself yelling. An ID and a car key had tumbled out of Pat's pocket. Liz scooped them up, not sure what to do with them. She glanced down at the ID and a sick feeling surged through her. It was a police ID. He was a cop. Pat was a cop. Liz scanned the trees again, waiting to see red and blue lights and a swarm of uniforms. Her life was over.

*****

It was a Monday night and there were no dart tournaments, so Daly's was quiet. A few regulars sat rooted to their usual spots, a guy from one of the dart teams was nursing a beer and getting in a little practice, and a couple sat at a small table next to the bar. Harry sipped his vodka-laced iced tea as he watched the story play on the news again. One of the City's high-profile lawyers had died at the mud run on Saturday morning. It was coming out that he had a long history of abusing his wife. They'd had an argument during the race. Things were starting to get physical when an off-duty cop who was also running stumbled upon them. The lawyer fought with the cop and ended up at the bottom of a rocky hill with a broken neck. Neither the wife nor the cop were speaking to reporters but tons of runners were more than willing to give their two cents.

Harry shook his head and turned his attention back to the bar. The dart player was still nursing his beer and he'd just refilled the regulars. He mixed two more rum and Cokes and brought them to the couple next to the bar. They were talking and holding hands across the table. "Here ya go, Hon, Patty," he said.

"You trying to get us drunk, Uncle Harry?" asked Pat, releasing Liz's hand and leaning back.

"Drunk?! Nah, we can't have you two getting drunk. You might go out and do something crazy," Harry said. Pat raised his eyebrows but didn't say anything. Liz smiled and turned her head. Harry laughed to himself and retreated behind the bar. When he looked back at the couple, they were holding hands again.

Araks Ohanyan

Field Journal

August 17, 2008

8:05 a.m. Sunday morning. Weather is beautiful once again. About 85 degrees, according to my thermometer. A bit of rainfall last night. I discovered a hole in the roof of the tent. Shelly woke up because some water was dripping on her head, and she wouldn't let me sleep until I patched it up. Finally managed to stop the dripping with some chewing gum. I need to walk to Moengo tomorrow and buy patching clay, and some more matches for the stove. The humidity has gone up a bit and my matches are all wet. And we're running low on pork and beans. Shelly doesn't seem to mind the humidity, and hopefully neither will the Morphos! I'm travelling about five miles north of Moengo today, to a little patch of pristine forest on the other side of the hill. Remy told me that some hunters have seen large brown butterflies in that area. I need to go find what they are. Oh, I also need to buy some pecans for Shelly.

10:25 a.m. Finally reached the pristine patch. Shelly decided not to come with me today. I may have ruffled her feathers a little when I gave some of her breakfast to a curious capuchin. She's hated those monkeys ever since one of them snuck up on her from behind and dropped some rotten fruit on her head. No sign of any Morphos yet, but I did see some plants that look like they might be in the pea family. Hoping to find some caterpillars on those. I've taken a sample of the plants to identify later. I spotted some river otters playing in a stream. They vanished as soon as they saw me, so I couldn't get a photo. That reminds me, I also need to buy some tissues from Moengo. This dampness is not good for my lens.

11:10 a.m. Spotted a Morpho floating above the river around 10:40. It didn't sit down, so I couldn't tell what species it was. I wanted to follow it, but an insect landed on my head. I thought it might be a wasp, so I stood very still and waited for it to fly away. I wasn't going to be stung again, especially since they stopped shipping antihistamines to Moengo. I still have nightmares about waking up with my head twice its normal size. Remy told me I looked like Tweety Bird. I told him he should stop watching old cartoons. But back to this morning. I stood still for 25 minutes, but I finally had to move because my foot fell asleep. The insect fumbled around in my hair for a minute, then flew onto my shoulder. It was a dung beetle. I took some pictures of him and placed him in a vial. I'll put it in my collection, just as a reminder of the little incident. I think I need to buy a small pocket mirror as well.

2:35 p.m. Some Morphos at last! I was having lunch by the river when three *M. rhetenor* specimens landed on the muddy banks to have a drink of water. There were two females and a male. I managed to capture one of the females. They are almost too big for my net. And I filled out my first findings report in two weeks! Shelly will be happy when she sees the butterfly, even if it's not one of her favorite bright blue ones. Still no sign of *M. hecuba*, but these blues have definitely lifted my spirits!

5:45 p.m. Spotted a family of capybaras coming up the river. It's amazing how much you can see when you stand in one place for a while. The capys froze suddenly when they saw me, then scuttled away to the other bank of the river. They reminded me so much of Cassie's guinea pigs. They would always freeze when someone walked into the room, then they would dash into their igloo and murmur amongst themselves, probably discussing how big and scary the thing they had just escaped from was. Also found a dead spiny tree rat in the forest. It looked like it might have been caught by a fox, and then dropped. Something must have startled the fox. I thought about taking it back with me to examine, but I just know Shelly wouldn't like it one bit. It's beginning to get dark. I think I'll call it a day.

August 18, 2008

7:45 a.m. Monday morning. Getting ready to walk down to Moengo. It's a balmy 90 degrees this morning. We didn't have any rain last night, so I'm hoping the road won't be too muddy. There was, however, some animal— probably an opossum—scratching at the base of our tent for hours last night. I tried to scare it off, but it just kept coming back. We had a similar encounter last week with a hog-nosed skunk, and with a fox the week before that. I'm beginning to wonder if maybe our tent is seated atop a treasure trove of food that I'm not aware of. But I think Shelly would have let me know a long time ago if that were the case. By the way, Shelly's still not talking to me. She perked up last night when I showed her the Morpho female, but then she went back her morose state after dinner. Hopefully the pecans will cheer her up. I don't like it when she gives me the cold shoulder.

5:30 p.m. A day of misadventures! I managed to buy the pecans, the matches, and the mirror, but the shop was out of pork and beans. And instead of patching clay, they sold me Silly Putty. What am I going to do with that? As if that weren't enough, I had a row with one of the villagers at the local restaurant. Apparently, he's not happy with the fact that I'm taking some of the butterflies out of the forest for my collection. I assured him that I am studying them so that I can better protect them, that what I was doing was for science, but he refused to listen. He called me a thief, an intruder, and several other names I didn't understand. The villagers assured me he meant nothing by it. Apparently, he's their town lunatic. And a fisherman. I was told he sometimes talks to his fish and apologizes for catching them. But all of that is nothing compared to what happened afterwards. I came back to my camp to find Shelly keeled over, making strange noises and tossing her head from side to side. I knew something was very wrong, especially when she wouldn't take the pecans. I quickly called Remy to come and take a look at her. He told me he'd seen symptoms like these before, and that it was probably malaria. I remembered that I had forgotten to spray the camp last week. How could I have been so stupid? Remy gave me some antimalarial drugs for Shelly. He said to put them with her food, and give them to her three times a day. He also gave Shelly a mild sedative to help her sleep. I hope she does. One of us at least should get some rest tonight.

August 19, 2008

10:15 a.m. Tuesday morning. Shelly isn't doing any better. I tried to give her some food, but she's completely lost her appetite. I had to force her to take some antimalarial drugs. It's almost like she doesn't realize she's ill. Remy's going to come take another look at her this evening. I'm postponing this morning's outing until the afternoon. I have to make sure Shelly's okay before I leave her.

5:45 p.m. There's good news and bad news. The good news is, I finally found my *M. hecuba*! It was sitting on the trunk of a tree about three miles northwest of here, and I almost missed it because it was camouflaged so well. What's more, I think this one might be a bilateral gynandromorph. Its left wing is orange, black, and white, and its right wing is brown with large owl spots. It's almost 15 inches long! I couldn't help but be excited when I found him (her?). I've been waiting for one of these to appear for seven months. But now for the bad news. Shelly was asleep at 2:00 when I left for my outing, but she was awake when I got back. She was tossing her head back and forth again, and making very strange gargling noises. She's still not eating, and I'm getting worried. I called Remy, and he assured me that the symptoms are usual. I'm waiting for him to come take a look at her again. I won't be easy until he's told me that everything is all right. I've also asked him to bring some raisins for Shelly. She won't refuse those, I know it.

August 20, 2008

Wednesday morning. I don't know what time it is, and I don't really care. I haven't slept all night. I'm barely able to collect my thoughts. It was all going okay until she began to vomit. Remy told me there was nothing he could do, but that didn't make it any easier for me. I had to watch her suffer until it was all over. Remy said that parrots are sacred in Moengo, so they'll give her a proper ceremony and burial. He's arranged it for tomorrow night. I don't know when I'm going to return to my work. It won't be the same without Shelly around. And her empty cage is making me even more depressed. I think I might sell it to a villager. The *M. hecuba* is still sitting on my desk. I haven't touched it since yesterday afternoon. Maybe tomorrow I'll examine it. Maybe the day after. The opossum visited again last night, but he only stayed for about five minutes. Well, I'm off to Moengo now. Remy has to do the necropsy. I'll just spray the camp real quick and head out.

Marcus Kunkle

The Upper Gauley

After seven hours of driving into the night, we pulled up to that wooded clearing as if Mother Nature had handed it to us herself. Maybe it was the fact that I'd been sitting in the hot, wet stink of neoprene gear for the past seven hours that made the cool mountain air seem so aromatic. Or maybe it was that I'd already been living in Philly for almost an entire year, inhaling the abundant hydrocarbons. My cramped legs took weary steps from the jeep down onto the earth, and with a sigh I slurred, "God damn it, this is close enough."

There were a number of obstacles that prevented us from finding the campsite, but the darkness that shrouded those dusty gravel roads was likely our toughest adversary. We had driven all night, and were now willing to settle for passing out on a blanket thrown over the dirt, rather than in the tent we were just too exhausted to deal with. We pulled our gear from the cluttered jeep and lay face-up on the blanket, listening to the chirping of insects, the rustling of small mammals, and the other unidentifiable noises that together composed the choral music of the night. Starlight peeked through the forest's towering canopy of branches as we drifted from the waking world.

Every September, hundreds of whitewater enthusiasts flock to West Virginia for Gauley Fest, which takes place during a series of six successive weekends in fall. On these weekends, water is released from the dam responsible for regulating water flow from the above Summersville Lake. When enough of this water is released, the levels of the river rise, the rapids get bigger, and, naturally, people start to get excited. Many people come to Gauley Fest for many reasons—food, entertainment, social interaction, spectating, festivities, shopping. But I had come for one: to ride the viciously opaque waters that have spelled the end for countless paddlers. Here's how the end is spelled: The Upper Gauley River. I'd been taking risks with my boating all summer, but they'd been closer to adrenaline glimpses than adrenaline rushes, and they didn't even compare. I awoke anxiously that morning, ready to take a guided tour of death.

We hit the water like wounded penguins, clumsily stumbling down the riverbank to wet our synthetic feathers. Oh wetsuits, the bane of my existence. Whenever I sit wearing a wetsuit for any period of time, the neoprene of the pants inevitably bunches up behind my knees, resulting in a total loss of circulation. But that day, cradled by a beautiful West Virginian canyon, the numbness of my legs didn't even matter. And I could tell by my companions' wandering eyes that they felt the same. Barber, April, Scott, Sean, and I had all grown up in the Poconos, so while mountains weren't exactly unfamiliar to us, the sheer majesty of their pristine slopes certainly was refreshing. As we floated downstream, we couldn't help but gape at the radiant azure sky above us, as well as the surrounding stone walls of swirling tan, brown, and cream.

With each paddle stroke, water spattered up around the tubular frame of the rubber raft, dampening its occupants. The water droplets, as they formed, tumbled between freshly raised goose bumps on their descent back down the sides of my arms. They fell rapidly, only to be temporarily contained by the thin, self-draining, rubber floor of the raft. Barely conscious of the moist chill, I continued to observe the landscape, wishing that I could trade Philly's lifeless skyscrapers for the Gauley's teeming mountains. As we continued into the faster-moving water, however, I needed to restrain myself from gazing in awe so that I could listen to the paddle commands of my raft guide.

When running serious whitewater, it's important to have an extremely experienced river guide captaining the raft. That is, it's crucial to have some scraggly old alcoholic sitting in the back of the raft, steering. Mine's name was Larry, and he is a living, breathing cartoon character. That preceding summer, I had worked for Larry as a whitewater-rafting guide on an entirely different river. We got along well enough, although we often got into arguments when our fragile egos collided.

I was fairly competent on the water and felt that I was ready to regularly guide the Upper and Lower Gorge of the river in my hard plastic kayak (something that most first-year guides aren't typically capable of doing). Larry, of course, insisted that I had no idea what I was doing, and that I wasn't even remotely ready. Our arguments typically centered on this ongoing debate, and Larry, being the boss, was the irrefutably predetermined winner. The truth of the matter is that I was ready, but that I had no right to tell Larry he was wrong about anything whitewater.

Larry was, in his prime, an Upper Gauley raft guide. He was (and still is) known as "Scary Larry," because he had a reputation for purposely taking dangerous routes, flipping rafts, and sending their terrified occupants flying into the rapids—for the cameras. But now Scary Larry was just a shaky old guide manager. On the day preceding our trip, he had almost drowned in a recirculatory hole about nine times his size. There have been multiple occasions on which Larry has experienced the ruthless, unrelenting grip of the Gauley's largest holes. And for this reason, he was more terrified than the rest of us. With his graying dreadlocks and patchy beard, he croaked out tenuous orders in a faded southern accent that's seen far too many Marlboros. This was my guide on one of the most dangerous rivers in the world, which, as one could imagine, was problematic.

"All forward, three strokes!" Larry shouted.

My face lit up as we began plowing through the waves of the larger rapids. With each coming impact, we preemptively wedged our feet under the inflated rubber cross tubes of the raft to prevent ourselves from being jolted into the air to subsequently land in the rapids. While paddling, I imagined what it would be like to fall out of the raft and swim a Class V rapid. The sheer force of thousands of cubic feet per second of water is unfathomable, and in its clutches, I would be nothing more than a piece of debris. It would be like being thrown into the angriest washing machine ever created, curling up into a ball, and praying to some deity that I eventually get flushed out downstream, alive.

"Left forward! Right back!" Larry wailed.

I quickly adjusted my paddle, begging myself not to make any mistakes. A simple misdirected paddle stroke could flip the entire raft, and send us all flying into the ruthlessly churning water. The knowledge that at any second I could end up freezing and fighting for my life was hysterically thrilling, and I laughed the laugh of a crazy man as we continued on.

Water sprayed forth in all directions as the raft continued punching through hydraulic features that could easily swallow a midsized sedan. I observed them from the raft, imagining my unconscious body thrashing about like a helpless ragdoll in the raw power of the bubbling hydraulic upcurrent. The raft buckled on impact, disorienting its passengers who spat out crisp river water almost as quickly as it reentered their mouths. But considering the inherently rough nature of our whitewater ride, our trip had actually been going fairly smoothly. No one had even been close to falling out, or flipping the raft—yet.

But cold water was the least of my worries, because I knew "Sweets Falls" was approaching. The twelve-foot waterfall is a popular spot on the Gauley due to its great potential for carnage. River guides and whitewater enthusiasts have a particularly interesting sense of humor, for in the center of the falls is a rock that they've named "Dildo." Simply put, the rock is called Dildo because "if you hit it, you're fucked." At any given time during Gauley Fest, there are roughly a hundred people standing on the humongous rocks that frame the pool at the foot of the falls. Some of these people sit there for an entire weekend, waiting for some paddler to make a mistake and be caught in the recirculatory hydraulic created by the cascading plumes of water that consistently penetrate the surface of the pool below. For these spectators, a life in danger is equivalent to a good time. Although, given my position, I suppose one could say the same of me.

I had been feeling like a badass all day, but as we approached the infamous waterfall, I could tell by the look on Larry's face that I was about to get a real taste of adrenaline. It wasn't until he threw his only half-smoked cigarette into the water that I fully realized the gravity of the situation.

A guy in a kayak floated past us and, in a southern accent, yelled, "Y'all gonna die!"

We all laughed at the dark potential truth in his words, because for all we knew, he could be right. With the horizon line of the waterfall in sight, we clenched our teeth, as Larry began his paddle commands.

"All forward! Now left back!" he squawked. Reaching the edge, and with all our spectators in view, Larry gave us his commands, but followed them with a quick, "Oh fuck, too far."

Startled, I looked up, only to see us about to smash head-on into Dildo. I repeated Larry's sentiment, then braced for impact. Picture the Titanic hitting its famous iceberg. Now picture it moving roughly thirty-five miles per hour, hitting the iceberg, and flying sideways off a twelve-foot-tall waterfall.

In mid-air, my life did not flash before my eyes. Instead, the adrenaline circulating throughout my bloodstream forced me to laugh hysterically—harder than I ever had before. With death all 'round me, I was so alive. I could feel the raft flipping, and as I looked down, I could see myself hovering over nothing but monstrous explosions of whitewater. I felt Larry's helmet smash into mine as I attempted to throw my body weight back over the drown-proof, rubber safe haven I had once been in. And then we hit the bottom, hard.

When I opened my eyes, I was utterly shocked to realize that everyone had managed to stay in the raft. Before I knew it, we were cheering and cursing like sailors, giving each other the most enthusiastic paddle-fives (which resemble high-fives) I'd ever seen. Grateful that we wouldn't be fishing an unconscious friend from the depths of the Gauley, my companions and I resumed our regular breathing. Well, everyone except for Larry. For as long as I live, I will never forget the humbled grin painted across his face, coupled with the words, "Congratulations Marcus, you're not a pussy anymore."

Marquerita Algorri

Zoloft

The middle drawer of my dresser contains four containers of fruit-scented bubbles, a dilapidated calculator, a hair straightener, an old cell phone, a box of vintage handkerchiefs, a collection of video games, a TV instruction manual, an old journal, and an unopened prescription bottle of Zoloft.

*****

I stare at the wall. It's not quite white. More of an ecru. Beige. Taupe. My parents love that color. Our entire house is painted taupe. It's the color of old soup, the skins of elderly people, sewer rats. It reminds me of decay. Spoilage. I shift my eyes to the left. A calendar labeled "January" with a picture of a scenic snow bank hangs, slightly crooked. It is the end of February. My eyes scan to the right. A poster prompts me to have the doctor check my feet if I'm diabetic and shows a cartoon picture of a fat, bubbly man sitting on a table with his bare foot extended. A similarly fat, bubbly doctor grasps the foot at the ankle and holds a magnifying glass to it. Both the bubble doctor and patient are smiling. It's probably not that way in real life. No magnifying glass and no smiles. Another poster prompts me to stop smoking and depicts a diagram of the respiratory system. The pink lungs of a young boy are exposed. One is cut in half to show the inner workings of the lung. His head tilts to the right. He is not smiling. Maybe he would be happier if he had his feet checked. I stare at both of the posters for a few minutes, reading every visible word. I'm not diabetic and I've only smoked a cigarette once.

I turn my head to stare forward, back at the ecru, beige, taupe. I feel my bare legs sticking to the maroon, leathery table covered in paper. I'm wearing a paper dress designed for someone three-times my size. It wraps all the way around me twice. The dress is essentially a giant paper towel with armholes. What if I wore this to prom? Or on my wedding day? It is white, after all. I stare down at my arms, which are folded in my lap. I examine my arm, raising it to meet eye level. The lighting in the room makes my skin look like meat, bits of anxious red broken up by marbles of white. It's the kind of lighting that makes sick people look sicker, the kind of lighting that makes people in dressing rooms hate themselves.

I shift my body to unstick my legs from the table. The paper rustles and clings to my skin. I think about getting up, but don't, lest the doctor appear. I don't want to be caught off guard, so I stare at the door, much like a hunted animal would stare at its pursuer. A deer and a wolf. This is the worst part of the appointment: waiting, naked and alone. It takes all the self-control I can muster to continue to sit there. I turn my eyes towards my clothes, which are strewn over a chair along with my purse. I hear a rustle. My eyes turn back towards the door, which is made of a mahogany colored faux wood. The rustling noise fades. My sticky legs settle back onto the table. My paper dress crinkles. I stare forward again.

My eyes continue to scan the room, this time focusing on a yellow cabinet. It reminds me of the worktables in the microbiology lab at school. They are the same kind of cold, hard metal and the same design. This time, however, the roles are reversed; I am the specimen, not the examiner. I picture myself as a tiny microbe, being chased by a giant doctor clutching a large, white swab. My flagellated arms squirm around in my petri dish, trying to dodge the swab. "How do you like it?" My microbe peers jeer at me. Voices from outside the door interrupt my thoughts. Three women are talking. I can't understand what they are saying. I hear only segments of words.

"It's..."

"...ah... mm..."

"Good."

"...ahhhk..."

I don't know how much longer I can sit here.

I decide to get up and stroll around the room, swinging my arms at my sides with every step. I check the time. 3:55. My appointment was scheduled for 3:30. Twenty minutes of additional torture. My bare feet feel weird on the scratchy gray carpet. I look down at them and think about how many feet have been on this carpet. The thought bothers me. I don't like feet. I climb back on the table. I think about how many people have sat on the same table. It's a disjointed sense of unity in a sterile, isolated room. My paper dress won't stop gaping open so I cross my arms against my chest. I begin to swing my feet. A nervous habit. I feel more and more like a specimen with each passing minute.

For five more minutes, I continue to stare at the walls, the calendar, the posters, the yellow drawers, until I hear footsteps outside the door. I hear the doctor grab the clipboard pinned to the door. The clipboard clatters against the door as she grabs it. The doorknob turns slowly, and the door makes a soft banging sound as it opens. I become more aware of how sweaty my palms are. It feels as if the corks have been pulled from the necks of a thousand tiny wine bottles, ingrained in the pores of my hands. I close my eyes and try to breathe slowly.

In-out. In-out. In-out.

When I open my eyes, the doctor appears.

"What brings you in today?"

*****

My doctor was quick to prescribe the Zoloft. During a routine physical, I told her about the pervasive sense of worry and unease I feel on a daily basis. She inquired further.

"Are there specific things that you're worried about?"

"No."

"Just a generalized feeling, then?"

"Yes."

"Does it ever interfere with your daily life?"

"Sometimes."

I briefly recalled a period of time when it was difficult to leave my apartment without going through a sequence of light-switch flipping, stove checking, and door locking, repeated continually, until I could gather the courage to step away. This often took upwards of 20 minutes. I was late for everything: class, doctor appointments, birthday dinners, holidays, work, and with a new excuse every time. I told only my mother the truth. She seemed disappointed, asked me to get help, and sighed when I refused.

"Any hallucinations, unreasonable thoughts?"

"No."

She scrolled a few notes on her clipboard. I stared at her. I knew she was going to give me drugs. I wondered if she'd give a diagnosis, though I felt pretty sure I already knew what it was. I elaborated further.

"When I first entered college, three years ago, and even now, to some extent, I had a problem with repeating rituals. Like, I felt like I had to do things a certain way or it would make me very uncomfortable."

She looked up, stared into my eyes, picked up the pen, scribbled. I continued.

"It used to take me forever to leave my house, because I had to check to make sure every appliance was off, and check to see that I had locked the door, until I felt comfortable enough to leave. It used to take me over an hour to wash dishes after dinner, because plates needed to be washed four times, cups twice, and utensils, except for spoons, three times. Taking notes in school was difficult because certain words needed to be erased and rewritten. My notes were covered in scribbles, almost illegible. In the bathroom, I flicked the light switch on and off, again and again, until I could make myself walk away. I still have to step out of the shower with my left foot first, instead of my right. It doesn't feel right otherwise. "

She looked up again and continued with her insincere barrage of questions, which seemed almost rehearsed.

"Do you ever feel depressed?"

"Sometimes."

"Often?"

"Not terribly, not anymore."

"Have you ever harmed yourself?"

"Yes. Not anymore. Sometimes I have panic attacks."

She scribbled again.

"Are you interested in trying medications to help you manage these symptoms?"

I took a moment and pondered this. If this scenario had been happening three years prior, I would have insisted that I could manage the problem myself, and that psychoactive pharmaceuticals would never be an option for me. Seven years ago, when I was 14, I had dated a boy who had been on Prozac. He abruptly stopped taking it, which is strongly advised against, and his personality changed entirely. My mind then drifted to my parents.

My mother's disappointment was a result of my behaviors, which refuted her lifelong thesis: "Mental illness doesn't exist." Ironically, my mother eats fruit loops separated by the color: first red, then blue, green, yellow, and, last, purple. She meticulously arranges her spice rack and stack of cookbooks and becomes upset if something is out of order. She exhibits some of the same behavior patterns I do. Despite this hypocrisy, her words had an affect on me; her mantra of insensitivity had circled my brain for years. Now, however, seven years later and somewhat bored of the mantra, I felt far more apathetic to the suggestion of psychiatric medication. Preserving my mind and sanity seemed like less of a priority. I wanted to try new things. Maybe it would be nice to feel, or not feel, something else.

"Sure," I responded.

"I like to start my patients with Zoloft. Many people have good experiences with it. I'm prescribing Zoloft, for daily use, and Ativan, for use when your anxiety feels overwhelming, or in the event of panic attacks. I'm starting you off with 50 milligrams. We can increase the dosage as necessary."

When she first said, "Zoloft," I thought of the TV commercial. There's a little anthropomorphic circle with a sad face. He's looking around, and notices a rain cloud above him. He moves a bit, and the raincloud follows. A cartoony diagram is shown of the synaptic vesicles and the uneven distribution of serotonin between them. Circles of serotonin molecules bounce between each vesicle and speed up as the commercial continues. After his serotonin levels are adjusted, the circle man's raincloud disappears. He smiles and bounces around. I've never felt as sad as the circle man, though. I never felt the raincloud. But can the circle man leave his house without twisting the doorknob 22 times? No more, no less: 22.

"Zoloft, while it's mainly used for depression, can be used for anxiety, too. It should help quiet your worries, though it could take up to three months to make a noticeable difference."

"What are the side effects?"

"Well, everyone experiences the drug differently, but some of the most common side effects are the ones typical of many medications: nausea, headaches, dry mouth, fatigue, sexual difficulties, weight gain..."

As she listed the symptoms, my mind abruptly changed. She lost me at weight gain and sexual difficulties. Weight gain would only add to my self-perceived psychosis. Sexual difficulties didn't sound fun, either. Zoloft: sucking the pleasure out of your life since 1991. At this point, I was fairly certain I would be throwing the pills into a drawer without ever taking them. I said nothing. The doctor kept talking.

"However, there is a serious side effect to be concerned about. Amongst people of your age group, suicidal ideation is a common side effect of Zoloft and other medications of its kind. If you experience any motivation to harm yourself, go to a hospital. They will help you get your medication adjusted. I recommend scheduling a follow-up appointment with me in two weeks to see how the medication is affecting you."

I nodded in agreement. I knew I wasn't going to take the pills. As a recovered anorexic, weight gain was enough to cast me into a realm of mental instability; I didn't need the drug to guarantee a trip to the psychiatric ward in addition to that. The doctor handed me two slips of blue paper, on which my prescriptions were written illegibly. I redressed and prepared to leave the office. On my way out, the doctor called out to me.

"Would you like to make the follow-up appointment now?"

I politely declined, thanked her, and told her I would make the appointment at another time. When I got into my car, I stared at the blue papers for a few minutes, tracing the outlines of the handwritten letters with my eyes. I drove to the pharmacy. I waited until the prescriptions were ready. I felt like the pharmacists were looking at me differently, knowing that I was prescribed these medications. Kind eyes turned critical. The pharmacy my family utilizes is a small family business. The pharmacists have known me since I was a small child. Fifteen years ago, they were filling prescriptions for antibiotics for my ear infections. Now, they're handling my antidepressants. I felt a sense of shame and defeat. *Life's worn another one down. Kids these days.* I could read the words on their faces. My mother's mantra replayed in my head. *Mental illness doesn't exist.* I stared at an arrangement of hearing aids while I waited.

When I arrived at home, I told my mother about my experience at the doctor's office. She seemed relieved, and congratulated me for finally talking to someone. I shrugged it off and told her I was skeptical about taking the pills, but that I would try it out. I opened my bedroom door and sat down on the bed. I took the pills out of my bag and held them. I was given a month's supply of Zoloft, and ten Ativan. I threw the Zoloft into the middle drawer of my dresser, where it has remained, unopened. I thought about taking it for a while, but the side effects have remained, quite literally, a turn-off. I clutched the bottle of Ativan.

*****

I have used the Ativan twice: once for exam-related anxiety and once because I felt frustrated with my "rituals," the never-ending song and dance within my brain. The first time I took it, I didn't like it much; it made me feel drunk, I couldn't remember things. I fell up the stairs in the main building at school while on Ativan. I dropped all of my books. My limbs felt like noodles. People stared. While I would have normally been mortified, the drug allowed me to feel an overwhelming sense of apathy. Two hazy hours passed. My memory is foggy.

Unfortunately, the second time was better. At least I think it was. All I can remember is an overwhelming sense of calm. My phone tells me that I sent text messages like,

"I'm a sad, anxious bumblebee."

"Oh no, I think I just made a rhino face at someone."

"Like a schrunchy horn face!"

"It's cactus time!"

"Stairs are hard."

I don't know what any of that means, nor do I remember sending any of it. Evidently stairs were a problem again. Later that night, I wrote in my journal:

"To medicate or not to medicate?"

Just like Hamlet, I still can't really answer that.

Six months later, my handbag contains a green compact of concealer, a yellow lighter covered in Hello Kitty stickers, a mechanical pencil, a floral-patterned wallet, a pack of gum, and a prescription bottle of eight Ativan, which I keep with me at all times.

I tell myself it's for panic attacks, but I'm lying to myself. I keep the overwhelming sense of calm at my fingertips at all times, just to know it's there.

Nahjan Amer Nordin

The Elephant in the Room

I was eighteen when I first stood face to face with an Asian elephant.

It was not my first time seeing one, but it was a first in that there were no fences or borders separating us, as it often would be in zoos. It was about twice my height and very likely weighed more than a 10,000 pounds. It should've been menacing, intimidating even, with its large form and occasional loud grunt, its trunk swaying left and right like someone trying to resist sneezing but ending up making a funny face instead. It should've been intimidating, but how could it be? It had the kindest eyes, small and slanted against such a massive figure, blinking slowly. I looked at it long and hard, not turning away despite my beating heart. Following the demonstration by the owner, I raised my hand slowly to its temple, stroking lightly, my hand barely making contact with its wrinkly, rough skin. Despite the coarseness, I was surprised to meet with softness where the small hairs stood. It snorted then and I pulled my hand back in surprise. It simply looked at me, blinking and lifting its front paw ever so slightly, as if it was attempting to shrug. I couldn't resist grinning broadly; I loved it already.

*****

He stood in the center of the group, telling the story. The room was dingy and smelled terrible—musty and damp. Inside, rows of cabinets and cupboards lined against one another, the fluorescent light at the ceiling flickering a dim white light. Next to the door, the wall was full of trophies from big game hunting; the horns of hundreds of deer, antelopes, and plenty of other animals hung freely, taking up any and every space available on the walls. According to the guide, Ned Gilmore, the room housed at least 24,000 mammal specimens dating back from late 19th century to present-day skeletal remains. The stories behind each donation of skeletal remains varied from hunting game trophies to remains of old zoo animals and, mostly, expeditions by brave souls more than a hundred years ago. I stood in between two cabinets and unsuccessfully tried to hold my breath as I listened intently to what he was saying. Unlike the rest of us, he didn't seem bothered by the smell, or by the fact that we were standing in a room full of animal remains. He continued talking, answering questions along the way.

His back was leaning against one of the cabinets and a large skeleton of what looked to be a skull sat on a table next to him. I could see spots on the skull where calcium and other minerals had slowly degraded over time. The skull was mostly yellow, brown at some parts; it had to have been there for a really long time. It took him a while to finally arrive at the story behind it. This here belonged to a circus elephant, he said. Bolivar was its name, a male Asian elephant from Sri Lanka in the 1880s. Bolivar was a star attraction of the Adam Forepaugh's Circus at the time, where he was billed as the largest and heaviest animal in the world. Ned paused then, as if for dramatic effect, before continuing on. Unfortunately, Bolivar was also often thought of as incredibly mean.

*****

The day was sunny, blazing hot, and I was in Chiang Mai, Thailand for a family vacation. Part of the attraction of Chiang Mai was the elephants and in this particular site where acres of wild land surrounded us, it was home to countless Asian elephants like the one standing before me. Not all were large adults, as some baby elephants were seen walking about or shadowing their mothers. The elephants were taken care of and trained for entertainment purposes. The first of two popular activities was the elephant show presented a few times daily, involving a display of tricks and talents such as playing soccer and writing. The second was the elephant ride across a tracked path of the wild forest, including crossing a small river and passing through a small village near the training grounds. We were allowed to pick an elephant by ourselves for the ride and without a second thought, I chose it: the one with the kind eyes.

*****

Bolivar was given up to the zoo because he was deemed too dangerous for the circus. The tale had it that Bolivar was believed to have stomped on a circus lion that tried to escape. As a result, the lion died and Bolivar was thought unsafe to be around. He was forced to retire and was sent to the Philadelphia Zoo where he spent his last 18 years chained in the zoo with limited human contact. After his death in December 1908, Bolivar's remains were donated to the Academy of Natural Sciences. The Academy scientists preserved his hide and displayed it side by side with his skeleton for ten years. However, the skin eventually deteriorated and was subsequently destroyed in 1919. The skeleton, however, remained intact and kept in the basement within the Academy's mammalogy collection, which was exactly where we were.

Ned then moved on to the next skeletal remains, a killer whale from New Jersey. I lingered near Bolivar's skull, the smell of mothballs no longer a bother. Small, illustrated posters of Bolivar the circus elephant were pasted on the wall behind it with engaging captions like "Bolivar, the largest animal in the world!" and "See the original Asian elephant from Sri Lanka!" The year was scribbled at the end of one of the posters: 1880. I tried to imagine Bolivar at his height of fame and felt a pang at the cold reality of what took place after, including his last 18 years spent chained, possibly poorly cared for, too. His eyes, how must they have looked then?

*****

Southeast Asia is unique for its open, continual struggle against modernization, almost like a butterfly with two separate, different patterns on each wing. The untainted terrain of lush open forest and flowing river provided an interesting dichotomy against the stone-walled houses sprawling sporadically in the open field, just across the river. I loved the paradox because it translated so well even to the people; I still find myself debating between sticking to local cultures versus Western paradigms.

Just then, I laughed aloud, trying to mask my nervousness as the elephant moved languidly forward, hardly bothered by the three humans sitting on its mount: the owner sitting with his legs spread wide, leaning behind the elephant's enormous ears and directly behind him, my eldest sister and I sitting in the makeshift bamboo seats, decorated with gaudy hand-woven drapery. Occasionally, my sister would stroke the elephant's back, as if trying to display affection and appreciation for the mile-long ride it was giving us. I soaked in the sun, the view, and the sometimes bumpy ride, feeling the elephant's every muscle and sinew as it tread through the river and then onto solid ground again. Just in front of us, another elephant carrying my father and second sister continued its leisurely pace, equally as hardly bothered as mine was.

A mile later, the track ended and we readied ourselves to hop off. The owner asked if we would like to feed it some treats and I gladly took up the offer, taking the bananas from his hands. Once again, the owner demonstrated how to stroke the elephant; I followed suit. My sister did the same until no more bananas were left. It was time to say goodbye.

I stepped forward to it, stroking its temple lightly. My eyes met its soft, kind eyes. I whispered a thank you to it, quietly and somewhat embarrassedly. It seemed to understand my words as it lifted its right front paw, as if wanting to shake hands.

*****

I thought of the elephant I encountered at eighteen. Where it roamed mostly free and was allowed human contact, Bolivar's life went on a different trajectory and ended so tragically. I paused, trying to imagine what it must have been like, those last years of his life.

I thought again of the elephant from Thailand. If its end had taken place since my one and only encounter with it, I sincerely hoped it did not suffer, that it died quietly and peacefully. I put in a small prayer for it as I moved to where the group was standing. Ned was once more in the center, engaging my classmates with the story behind the remains of the last surviving Eastern elk, dating back to 1853. Directly behind me, Bolivar's massive skull sat proudly on the table, unobtrusive and unsuspecting.

Faculty
Writing

Introduction

Writers render their perceptions from far off places and times; rarely do they live close to us, and rarer still do we know them or have the opportunity to know them, if only because they have died. They're almost always strangers with disembodied voices to whom we have no easy access. This can be a source of frustration to anyone who has wanted to ask a writer to elaborate on a particular point or share his or her experiences with the nuts and bolts, from conception to execution, of a written subject.

In the following section, examples of the work by Drexel faculty have been included in *The 33rd* as representations of professional, creative, and scholarly writing. The authors are alive and kicking and on campus; some may be your teachers now or in the future. You can see from the pieces that the approaches range from original works of poetry and personal essay to blog posts and scholarly articles. You can assume that each subject and genre presented particular challenges that the authors had to grapple with in the same way that all writers must, including, of course, those in a composition class.

Ron Bishop

Tankya, Spike Jones

Charles Delfino and I were two of seven tenors in Maplewood Junior High School's chorus in the mid-1970s. We hatched detailed plans to start the first, and what I'm guessing was the last, impressionists club in school history. Not the art kind of impressionist—the Rich Little kind of impressionist. Thanks to his many *Tonight Show* appearances and riffs on Dean Martin Roasts, Little had made doing impressions cool, at least to Delfino and me.

Charles, or "Chas" as he signed his name in my 1976 MJHS yearbook, was short and stocky with a premature mustache that I envied as mine struggled (and still struggles) to emerge, despite my shaving a lot to highlight my few organized hairs. It requires a mini-exercise in powerful anachronism, but Chas looked like Rob Falcone, the talented actor who's appeared the last couple of years in Target back-to-school ads (in one, he sings the tagline "Shawn White hoodies and *de*-nim").

During the 1974-75 school year, we had chorus after school on Mondays and Wednesdays under the direction of G. Davidson Kendrick, a diligent and enthusiastic educator who doubled as my (and Chas's) third-period music teacher. Every Friday, G. Davidson allowed us to bring in our favorite albums to spin for the class on a boxy beige Emerson player. These sessions often turned into group therapy; Kendrick was a lovely combination of good listener and confidant. Nothing left the room—not Amy DiMaria professing she could absolutely tell when the government had contaminated her marijuana with paraquat or Glenn Dorsey regaling us with the tale of how he lost his virginity to Peggy Willis while parked in his mom's Impala at South Mountain Reservation on a windy, unseasonably warm April evening. Glenn was 14 at the time and barely tall enough to see over the steering wheel. The Friday after Glenn's revelation, I brought in George Carlin's classic comedy album *Toledo Window Box*. Despite the lack of music and its many hilarious references to smoking weed and being stoned for extended periods, G. Davidson was okay with it. If my son decides someday to replicate my act, we all will surely be arrested, or at least brought before the overzealous members of the Needlessly Instill America's Families With Fear Council to watch and discuss *Reefer Madness*. G. Davidson could be earnest, but not in the ersatz and suffocating way experts and commentators suggest is the only hope for students attending our unfairly derided public schools. He was also quite corny, an underrated attribute that may disappear from the cultural scene if we're not careful.

After some lobbying from us about not limiting our repertoire to creaky standards, G. Davidson agreed that we could sing Simon and Garfunkel's "The

Sound of Silence" to open our ninth grade concert—but we'd do it as a march. He would have none of the former Tom and Jerry's sensitive folk ethereality.

"We have to grab them, gang—grab them!" he shouted repeatedly during a Thursday rehearsal, his massive balding head dripping with sweat. G. Davidson always wore a thick wool vest—knitted by his wife, Barbara—over his dress shirt and tie, no matter what the temperature was.

"Silence like a cancer grows," the tenors, baritones, and Phil Jellinek, our lone real bass, sang expectantly.

"...*like a cancer grows!*" brashly answered the sopranos and altos in descending harmony. John Philip Sousa would have been proud. Chas and I thought G. Davidson's interpretation more accurately resembled a polka; we would dance accordingly during breaks in the action, using music and steps gleaned from late night Jimmy Sturr TV ads.

One of our first orders of club business was to rule that *everyone* did President Nixon; it was a cliché, especially since the President had resigned the previous summer. It was like putting on training wheels, passé and bordering on outdated. Thrust your arms straight at 45-degree angles above your head in the shape of a V, duck your head, and waggle two peace signs. Consider it terrain well traveled. We could build on Nixon, but we had to go further. Rich Little would no doubt congratulate us today for having such a well-developed sense of craft at a young age.

"We need to pick about a half-dozen and really get good at them," Chas announced, going down a list of about 20 names he'd written on a piece of loose-leaf paper. He then proposed that we spend at least a half-hour a day practicing. Hold on there, Sparky, I said. I was a charter member of the get-sort-of-good-at-something-then-procrastinate-and-move-on school. Chas was just a little too serious for a brand new two-person club. It sounded like he would soon want us to chase gigs at the local comedy clubs. I just liked ripping Nixon, mainly because I was finally playing a minor role in my being ridiculed by peers, but also because I was thrilled (yes, as a teenager) that he was out of office. I had watched the Watergate hearings, sometimes with my mom, a couple of years earlier, and ended up going to journalism school because of *All The President's Men*—and *Lou Grant*, starring Ed Asner as a hard-charging doppleganger of Mary Tyler Moore's former boss.

"Counting Nixon?" I asked. I tapped with a pen at my own sheet of paper, which was blank.

Sensing he might be losing me, Chas gave in.

"Yes, counting Nixon," he said, shaking his head. I quickly jotted down a few names as G. Davidson arrived, already sweaty but always enthusiastic, to start practice.

Lawrence Welk was my first post-Tricky Dick excursion. His show was a favorite in our northern New Jersey household, right up there with *Adam-12*, *Emergency*, and *The Waltons*. Nearly every Sunday evening, we watched on WPIX-TV (Channel 11) as Welk put Guy and Ralna, Norma Zimmer (shot through at least 14 layers of gauze, my father repeatedly noted), and the lovely Bobby and Cissy through their Perma-Press paces.

I nailed the Welk impression after only a few tries on the same day Mark Kaufmann threw one of those chair-desk combos out of G. Davidson's second-floor classroom window because he was pissed at a math teacher who was torturing him in class. As a matter of fact, my first really good Welk came just as he grabbed the chair and rushed toward the open six-foot-high window.

"Fuck you Wagner—you dick!" he shouted, chair above his head.

Mark must have laid the throw out on paper using a slide rule; the chair didn't even graze the window frame as it passed through. The crash was impressive, like furiously whacking the bass strings of a piano with a hammer. The injured chair then bounded down the hill, its desk part flapping nervously, and landed on the sidewalk adjoining Baker Street.

Like Nixon, Welk was easy. Don't think so? I'll teach you. His accordionist's name was Myron Floren. Got it? Okay—now imagine what an extremely nasal German duck would sound like saying Myron Floren. Give it a try. As Robert Reed so many times reassuringly concluded as father to *The Brady Bunch*, "There you are."

I stood up from my own chair/desk combo, ran to the podium in the center of the room and grabbed G. Davidson's baton. I held my right arm in my left as if I were waiting for the guy with the splints. I tried to slightly rotate the top half of my body for emphasis. I pasted on a big smile and forced my tongue to the roof of my mouth.

"Tankya boyce-um. And-a-now, the talented-a Myron-a Floren-um."

I looked at Chas for approval. He was seated on his hands on the sill in front of the still unrepaired window. He pushed off, jumped down, and rushed toward me like I was a revered relative meeting him at the airport.

"Killer, man—that kicks ass," he shouted.

Chas was being kind. He was much, much better than I was—and he really worked at it. If I couldn't get an impression after three tries, I was done. Impressions came easy for me or not at all—which come to think of it also sums up my athletic exploits. I was only able to add Gerald Ford and Jimmy Stewart to my repertoire. Years later, I would come up with a decent Poppa Bush and President Clinton to spice up lectures for my students, but I knew that day I'd be a career minor leaguer.

My father heard my Welk for the first time on a Sunday evening in November 1975, a week or so before Thanksgiving. Mom wanted to watch *The Wonderful World of Disney*. But Dad, who when he was home dictated our viewing schedule—and what we ate for pretty much every meal—wanted to watch Welk. He was on the road a lot, either at meetings selling pipe organs, or maintaining one of the more than 100 whose churches and synagogues (and one Ethical Culture society) in the tri-state area sought his services. I was watching the New York football Giants tangle with the Washington Redskins in a close game on Channel 2. On the strength of a Craig Morton 36-yard TD pass to Ron Johnson and a George Hunt 22-yard field goal, the Giants were up 13-7 in the third quarter. The Redskins responded with a 1-yard touchdown run by Larry Brown and were driving for the go-ahead score. But the game had run long. About three seconds to 7 p.m., Dad practically leapt from his recliner and began turning the dial. It took nine clicks and a pastiche of hissing channel-flipping sounds we don't hear today to get to Channel 11.

"Well Tankya fucking boyce-um," I said angrily as I got up from my standard viewing position (lying on the floor with my legs up in the air, resting almost parallel to the fireplace wall). As I got to my feet, the show came on. Bob Warren, Welk's longtime announcer, chimed in as the orchestra performed the overture.

"And now, our musical host, maestro Lawrence Welk!" The maestro himself strutted out on stage, bubbles wafting everywhere. Does anyone actually own a mustard-colored leisure suit anymore?

Dad completely missed my profanity, which was never a big deal in our house, and my anger—but loved the impression.

"That's really good, Ronnie—really good," he said as the orchestra began its first number. As I headed toward the kitchen to grab some Ring-Dings, he actually mussed my hair for emphasis—quite a feat, since I was already a couple of inches taller than he was. Dad practically ran past me to the kitchen to tell my mom, on the phone with Gloria, the woman who sold us our cats and convinced mom to sell Tupperware, about what he had just heard. It was as if we had returned from a Little League game I had won with a walk-off home run. I stopped and stood about five feet from the TV, blank stare on my face, watching Welk. All things California was the theme for the night. The orchestra pivoted nimbly from Welk's intro into a rousing rendition of *California Here I Come*, with vocals by the lovely Lennon Sisters.

I was stunned. Dad had a thing for seeing every last millisecond of his favorite shows. On those few occasions when mom, my brother, and I outvoted him and gained control of the Admiral, he would repair to my parents' bedroom to partake on a tiny Sony black and white set that rested on a flimsy chrome stand that looked like it should be holding dental instruments. It occurred to me only recently that we might have been thinking the same thing: finally, a tiny still-to-be-tilled patch of common ground. I tried to see it from his point of view: Thanks to Woodward and Bernstein and to Lou Grant, I was planning on a career as a journalist. And my favorite season was fall—late October specifically, because all four major sports were in season, on television a lot, and therefore occupied the top four spots on my agenda. Since my dad was 13, he wanted to be a pipe organ builder and tuner, albeit in the body of an impresario. He fancied himself the Sol Hurok of the organ business, always on the lookout for new talent that he could plug in to jobs at churches around the tri-state area. A sports-loving muckraker-wannabe must have frustrated the shit out of him.

In the ensuing days Dad and I felt closer. But my amazement at his reaction that night prevented me from seeing my initial assessment was a little bit off. He was cooking up a new role for me: opening act. Soon, I was doing Welk at his urging for everyone—Dad's employees, visiting organists, organists we'd see on jobs, even our neighbors.

I did Welk for the Sweeneys, my parents' friends from around the corner. Dad was convinced Jack Sweeney was somehow connected to the Mafia. He drove a New York City bus on Staten Island and was active in the drivers' union. That and the Cadillacs owned by Jack's friends parked in front of their house every Saturday afternoon was all the evidence Dad needed to sketch out his own suburban version of *The Godfather*. As for me, I was content to imitate Evel Knievel with Jack's sons, Tommy and Connor, on our modified bikes and lust pointlessly after their older sister, Linda. She's now a federal judge, but back then all my pubescent brain could focus on were her smile and beautiful legs, which she enhanced by wearing miniskirts and stockings or tights, a la Marcia Brady.

Special command performances of Welk came during Dad's sales calls. Where previously I'd either wait in the car, or read in the chapel, he'd ask me to do a short bit before he pitched an instrument to the organist and music committee. I should have charged a cover. Dad liked my Nixon and thought my Stewart was passable, but he told me they came to hear Welk. On the way home in the car, he'd pass on their critiques. Go a little slower. Clap some more. Raise the imaginary baton higher. Can you sound more nasal? As we cavorted about the northeast, I started to accumulate a little bit of fame. When I'd go back years later to work on the organs Dad had sold, organists and committee members would remember hearing the impression, and ask me to reprise it.

But during my junior year in high school, I decided to retire from the "biz." Thank you and thanks for the memories, "tankya boyce-um." I knew when to get out—not like some professional athletes, whose farewell tours last nearly as long as their careers. But retirement didn't cause me to lose my affinity for unsophisticated comedy. I was already a diehard Mel Brooks fan and *Airplane* would soon come out, destroying any chance that I would attempt to understand Woody Allen. The first few seasons of M*A*S*H were a little more cerebral—and I still love them—but I still can't comprehend Woody, or maybe just his appeal.

The same could not be said, however, of Lindley Armstrong "Spike" Jones and his orchestra, the City Slickers. How to explain Spike Jones to a younger audience—let's see... he was sort of like "Weird Al" Yankovic with a hell of a lot more musicians and sound effects, but perhaps just as many copyright permission hassles. He relentlessly and hilariously parodied hits of the 1940s and 1950s. His renditions would begin quite seriously before descending into a manic cacophony of hiccups, whistles, bells, and gunshots. Boomers out there will no doubt remember a Spike Jones reference in the classic The Band tune "Up on Cripple Creek": "Me and my mate were back at the shack; we had Spike Jones on the box. She said, 'I can't take the way he sings, but I love to hear him talk.'" Hearing this song usually sends me to YouTube to find videos posted by Jones aficionados—after a The Band medley, of course. I defy you to not laugh when the City Slickers launch into the second verse of "Cocktails for Two." It's so earnest, so lush, so beautifully performed to that point—and then all hell breaks loose. I learned about Spike one night during my sophomore year, when I caught a late night TV ad for an RCA collection of his hits. Other than the Mets yearbook, ordered annually with grandma's subsidy, I was never so excited to get something in the mail. I love getting mail, period—it's that feeling of expectancy, of maybe hearing from a long lost friend, of order possibly being disturbed by the contents and begging to be restored, that I'm only starting to get from e-mail.

I was out on our front porch flipping through a *Sporting News* Major League Baseball preview issue when our angular Mormon mail carrier, Karl Taylor, arrived with the package. I thanked him and snatched it from his hand, forgetting that my parents also had mail coming to them. I ran inside, dropped *The American Organist*, a Lillian Vernon catalog, and some bills on the hall table, and ran upstairs to my room. I had a surprisingly easy time freeing the cassette from its cellophane. I was prepared to observe my ritual of carefully reading liner notes before even thinking about playing the cassette—my beautiful wife now calls it "marinating"—but finding none, I popped open the player on my table-sized stereo receiver, shoved Spike in, slammed the door shut, and pushed play.

I had found my comedy sweet spot; I laughed for days—heartily, fervently, violently—at Spike's musical stylings. I played that cassette until the tape pulled away from spindles. As with all of the albums that we old folks used to buy back in the day, there were a couple of clunkers. The fine folks at iTunes purport to end the need to grade albums (how many out of 10 or 12 songs did I really like?), but in general Spike was a comedy tour de force, on a glorious par with Mel Brooks and *Airplane*. "Cocktails for Two"? A classic. "You Always Hurt The One You Love"? So true. "Der Fuerher's Face"? Raspberries, like farts, are fashionable—and always funny, and can diminish the seriousness of Nazism. Soon I was playing the cassette more often than the work of the other performers in my slowly growing music collection (we were drifting away from our local Christian Science church, whose leaders wanted the devout youth to listen only to Christian Science singers—now *there's* a niche). I was also sharing Spike's music and story with friends, to mixed and often confused reaction. He was a bit of a non sequitur when the Lester Bangs of northern New Jersey would converse about Led Zeppelin and the Stones, but I persevered.

About two weeks before the start of my senior year, I was in my room on a Thursday night doing bicep curls with my mom's pale blue weights in a misbegotten attempt to make my high school's football team. I would end my quest after just three days of practice, laying on the couch in our living room, moaning under a half-dozen ice packs. Spike Jones was indeed on my box as I curled. From the front edge of my bed, I spotted Dad—his white t-shirt first—on the landing, making the 90-degree turn to complete the trip upstairs to his TV, when he heard "Hawaiian War Chant" coming from the three-foot high speakers on either side of my always-unmade bed. Does anyone out there use speakers as end tables anymore?

Dad veered to the right and headed toward my room.

"Where the hell did you get that?" he asked with a growing smile on his square but handsome face. The sound of Spike even caused him to stop picking at his cuticles. It was his chief coping mechanism, and gave him time to think.

I told Dad about buying the cassette with money I earned helping him and explained how Spike fit into my sort of expanding comedy tastes, how I tried hard to go more sophisticated, and how it just didn't work. Dad told me about hearing Spike on the radio as a kid and then watching Spike and his Musical Depreciation Revue on both NBC and CBS in the mid to late 1950s. He tried to explain Spike's appeal as he stood in my doorway, tapping his foot to the rhythm laid down by the City Slickers. I thought he might launch into a diatribe about how you just don't hear comedy like Spike's anymore. A deconstruction of Spike that included deflating the pomposity of the classics maybe. "That Yankovic fellow has talent, but he still can't match Spike's lunacy"—something.

"It's just... funny," he said. "So damned funny. They'd be running around the set, chirping, yelling, burping, screaming. Bells, whistles, guns. They'd all be going off at once."

It wouldn't have earned him a column in *The New Yorker*, but it was honest. By now, Dad had breached the border of my room and was sitting on my bed, sky blue John Blair pants a little short for him, poring over the tiny type on the cassette liner notes. As Spike and the band moved into "Der Fuerher's Face," I flashed back to Welk, to Chas, the sales meetings, to Sol Hurok. And there it was—or there you are: I wasn't as pissed that Dad was really into my Welk impression, and certainly wasn't as pissed that he brimmed with pride when I crushed a performance before a pitch meeting. I just wished that he hadn't treated me as if he were my agent. I sat down next to him on the bed and put my hand on his t-shirt covered shoulder. Remember when I said raspberries, like farts, are always fashionable and funny? Check it out: "When Der Fuehrer says we is the master race, we Heil! (thhhp!) Heil! (thhhp!)...right in Der Fuehrer's face!!" Timeless.

For the first time, Dad and I were laughing. Together. Enthusiastically and loud. *At* something. Tears rolled down my cheeks as I fell back on the unmade bed. My ribs hurt. I struggled to catch my breath. Dad's laugh always started with a loud "ha!" as if he were an auctioneer beginning to manage the bidding on an item. He settled into a Barney Rubble rhythm, though at a note or two lower than Barney's. He dabbed at his eyes under his glasses with the handkerchief he always kept in his left hand pants pocket. When I was imitating Welk for prospective clients in narthexes and naves across the northeastern U.S., he laughed at me in kind of a mercenary way. He was gauging their reactions, contemplating how much mileage he could get out of me. It was like Elvis and Colonel Tom Parker. But that night, sitting there on my bed listening to the City Slickers, we were, for a few minutes at least, father and son, not a stage parent urging his charge to muster the courage to try out for *American Idol*.

Dad died this past April of aggressive liver cancer. After nearly coming to blows on our front porch about my decision in the mid 1980s to run off and get married to a person I had only dated for three months—I had the sense eight years later to divorce that person and find the true love of my life—our relationship had become quite warm. We didn't share a lot or go too deep, but we talked at length by phone, usually about the organs he had started working on again and about the celebrities with whom he had come in contact in the past. He was an Olympic-caliber name-dropper. He still talked a lot more about the other important Ph.D. in his life, a theater organ aficionado who teaches at a college in Michigan, than about me, my classes, or my research—but even that didn't piss me off anymore. I'm sure he told me he was proud of me, but sometimes you hold so eagerly to the stories you tell yourself that you don't hear the stuff that challenges the story's cohesion—or at least that's what I tell my students. I even did Welk now and then for Dad, usually when our calls coincided with an airing of the show on PBS and we could sync up the broadcasts of our member stations. But neither one of us brought up the sales meetings, the command performances, the post-game critiques in the car. My Welk now made him—not music committee members from across the northeast—laugh, and that made me happy.

About a month ago, I was driving home from class on I-95 southbound just past Philadelphia's airport. Stuck in traffic, I was, I hate to admit, scrolling absentmindedly through the playlists on my iPod as the cars crept along. I meant to cue up a tune by Squeeze—"Black Coffee in Bed," I think—but what I got instead was "Cocktails for Two." Soon, I was laughing as hard as I had years ago that night with Dad in my room. Still gaining only a few feet at a time, I moved on to "Der Fuerher's Face," "Laura," "Hawaiian War Chant," and for good measure "You Always Hurt The One You Love." As my amazing and gorgeous wife will attest, I grieve in an odd way. I artificially smile (for evidence, I direct you to the photos taken when we interred Dad's ashes where Mom and I look we had just won the Powerball jackpot as our friends sobbed), joke around, comfort others when needed—and then break down about three months later. That day in the car, on my way home, I held true to form.

Paula Marantz Cohen

"For Truth, Justice, and the American Way":
A Close Reading of an American Sonnet

Faster than a speeding bullet—
More powerful than a locomotive—
Able to leap tall buildings in a single bound—
Look! Up in the sky!
It's a bird! It's a plane! It's Superman!
Yes, it's Superman—
Strange visitor from another planet
Who came to Earth with powers and abilities far beyond those of mortal men—
Superman—who can change the course of mighty rivers,
Bend steel in his bare hands,
And who—disguised as Clark Kent,
Mild-mannered reporter for a great metropolitan newspaper—
Fights a never-ending battle
For Truth, Justice, and the American Way.

I have arranged this "opening signature," as enthusiasts call the introduction to the adventures of this most famous of superheroes, in what I feel best represents its poetic form. For I believe this is a poem—the first poem that many Americans growing up in the 1940s and '50s were exposed to. The lines above were originally conceived to introduce a figure with a voice (on radio) and, later, a body (in animated cartoons and, subsequently, live action TV shows and movies), but for me, the Superman poem (as I shall hereafter refer to it) works best as a stand-alone piece: words arranged on a page, with no sound or image to complete them.

Taken this way, the Superman poem lends itself to a certain kind of critical interpretation that I associate with my youth. I was born in 1953, the year after *The Adventures of Superman* came to television, and as I made my way through primary and secondary school in the late 1950s and '60s, a method of literary criticism called the New Criticism had become popular in the academy. When I reached college, the method was established (i.e., no longer "new"), and it had become outmoded by the time I entered graduate school in the mid-1970s.

The New Criticism operated under the assumption that a poem refers only to itself and that context and intention are irrelevant to its meaning. Yale critic Cleanth Brooks's 1947 *The Well-Wrought Urn: Studies in the Structure of Poetry* helped solidify the method. Brooks's title alludes to John Keats's "Ode on a Grecian Urn" that ends with the famous lines spoken to the urn: "*Beauty*

is truth, truth beauty," —that is all | Ye know on earth, and all ye need to know.
A poem, according to Brooks, was like that urn—a well-crafted, self-contained artifact—and the critic's job was to explore its form so as to comprehend its content, to plumb its *beauty* in order to reveal its *truth.*

In the 1970s, the New Criticism had begun to be eclipsed by other methods of interpretation more in keeping with the ethos of the time. Eventually, these newer methods were grouped under the title of Postmodern Criticism, an approach expressly directed at dismantling, or deconstructing, assumptions about universal meaning and coherence. According to the Postmodern perspective, cultural artifacts are formed—and, more often, *de*formed—by the ideological context in which they are made.

It is easy to critique Superman in Postmodern terms. The hero becomes a "hero," emblematic of patriarchal authority and American imperialism. And the poem becomes inseparable from the commercial contexts of radio and movie production that used it.

But to take this approach seems to me wrong-headed. It does violence to the poem's uplifting message; it ignores the beauty of its form; and, finally, because such objections can easily be countered by Postmodernists as regressive or reactionary, it doesn't jibe with the way the poem makes me *feel*. Feeling may be subject to deconstruction, too, I know, but I hold to it as essential to a poem—a variation on what lyricist "Yip" Harburg called the function of a song: "[it] makes you feel a thought." If you jettison the validity of feeling in poetry, you might as well jettison poetry itself. And so, determined to respect my visceral response, I will attempt to analyze the poem through a New Critical lens.

Since the Superman poem was written to be read aloud, my presentation of it on the page is subjective. It reflects how I hear the poem inside my head, and some readers are sure to take issue with this. Still, I hope to show that the form I have chosen makes sense. If it is not the only form possible, it is one that conforms well to the meanings I derive from it, and these strike me as fundamental to its ability to move me.

As I have transcribed the poem, there is no regular pattern to the lines, but there is a *logic* to the irregularity that suggests a trying on of different combinations of verse lengths and meters. The drive, I would suggest, is toward *iambic pentameter*, the consummate English poetic meter. The Superman poem doesn't conform to it: overshooting the number of feet in many places, pulling back on that number in others, shifting stress throughout. Nonetheless, the classic form seems to shadow the poem and is achieved in the last line:

For Truth, Jus-tice, and the A-mer-ican Way.

This is iambic pentameter with two slight deviations: *Just-ice* has the first, rather than the second, syllable stressed, and *A-mer-ican* has the two-syllable *i-can* collapsed into a single-syllable *ican*. Both these deviations are fitting: Superman is *just* at the same time that he promotes *Justice*; and he is fast and America is, too. In short, the poem invokes the classic poetic form of America's progenitor culture, but in a way that is distinctively American. Note my sense that the poem should be amply supplied with exclamation points and dashes—punctuation favored by our two greatest American poets: Walt Whitman (the exclamation point) and Emily Dickinson (the dash). Since my transcription is 14 lines, sonnet-length, I claim it as an American sonnet.

Poems that move us always carry in them the mystery of their making. When we review earlier drafts, we see the necessary emerge out of the contingent—the many infelicities and false starts yielding to the "perfect" final result. The Superman poem reflects this in an especially interesting way. It was carved out of trite, unpoetical material, undergoing change as it moved from radio to animated cartoon, with both forms subsequently borrowing from each other. The poem emerged, one could say, in Homeric fashion out of a collective, albeit commercial, will.

Superman was first introduced in DC Comics by Jerry Siegel and Joe Schuster in 1938. In 1939, DC decided to adapt the comic books to radio, and the company's press agent, Allen Ducovny, and staff writer, Robert Maxwell, prepared the following narrative opening for the radio audition tapes:

> Faster than an airplane, more powerful than a locomotive,
> impervious to bullets. 'Up in the sky—look!' 'It's a giant bird.' 'It's a
> plane.' 'It's SUPERMAN!' And now, Superman—A being no larger
> than an ordinary man but possessed of powers and abilities never
> before realized on Earth: able to leap into the air an eighth of a
> mile at a single bound, hurdle a 20-story building with ease, race a
> high-powered bullet to its target, lift tremendous weights and rend
> solid steel in his bare hands as though it were paper. Superman—a
> strange visitor from a distant planet: champion of the oppressed,
> physical marvel extraordinary who has sworn to devote his
> existence on Earth to helping those in need.

Pieces of this narrative would make their way into the final poem, but how entirely different in form and feel this early draft is from that end result. Not only is there a syntactical stiltedness and pomposity to the word choice at this juncture, but there seems to be little discrimination with regard to the sorts of elements that ought to represent the hero or the words that ought to describe him. What does it matter that Superman can "jump an eighth of a mile" and "hurdle a 20-story building"; or that the bullet he can outrace is "high-powered"? How superfluous and empty the adjectives affixed to the basic nouns—*giant* bird, *ordinary* man, *tremendous* weights, *solid* steel, *physical* marvel. And how annoyingly didactic the overall tone: do we need to be told that Superman is a "champion of the oppressed" and "has sworn to devote his existence on Earth to helping those in need"? By no stretch is this a poem or even a decent piece of prose. And yet from this block of verbiage, the poem would be carved.

In 1941, Fleischer Studios and Paramount Pictures launched a series of cartoons based on the radio serial: 17 animated shorts designed for viewing before the main features in movie theaters. In the first cartoon (and only in the first), the writers inserted the following narrative riff:

In the endless reaches of the universe there once existed a planet known as Krypton, a planet that burned like a green star in the distant heavens. There, civilization was far advanced and it brought forth a race of supermen, whose mental and physical powers were developed to the absolute peak of human perfection. But, there came a day when giant quakes threatened to destroy Krypton forever. One of the planet's leading scientists, sensing the approach of doom, placed his infant son in a small rocket ship and sent it hurtling in the direction of the Earth just as Krypton exploded! The rocket ship sped through star-studded space, landing safely on Earth with its precious burden, Krypton's sole survivor. A passing motorist found the uninjured child and took it to an orphanage. As the years went by and the child grew to maturity he found himself possessed of amazing physical powers.

Faster than a speeding bullet—More powerful than a locomotive—Able to leap tall buildings in a single bound—the infant of Krypton is now the man of steel, Superman! To best be in a position to use his amazing powers in a never-ending battle for truth and justice, Superman has assumed the disguise of Clark Kent, mild-mannered reporter for a great metropolitan newspaper.

By the second cartoon short, the first paragraph of this opening had been dropped and the second streamlined. The triad of lines (*Faster than a speeding bullet—More powerful than a locomotive—Able to leap tall buildings in a single bound—*), amended from the earlier radio draft and which occur here at the beginning of the second paragraph, were placed earlier, but these lines oscillated among two other combinations, as though the writers were trying on different possibilities for the opening. The following three groups were used, with no particular rationale, in different episodes of the series:

Faster than a speeding bullet—More powerful than a locomotive—

Able to leap tall buildings in a single bound—
(used in cartoons 1,2,3,4,5,6,7)

Faster than a speeding bullet—More powerful than a locomotive—
Able to soar higher than any plane—
(used in cartoons 8,9,10)

Faster than a streak of lightning—More powerful than the pounding
surf—Mightier than a roaring hurricane—
(used in cartoons 11,12,13,14,15,16,17)

The first (and original) triad seems clearly the best, but this was not apparent early on. Only when the poem had found its final form—when nature and technology would be partitioned in a certain way, images doled out so as not to repeat each other, and issues of scansion made more insistent—did the rightness of these lines become obvious.

Following this triad, the new draft for the cartoon opening included the onlookers' exclamations, present in the original radio draft. This was followed by a somewhat streamlined version of the second paragraph of the first cartoon introduction:

Up in the sky! Look! It's a bird! It's a plane! It's Superman! This amazing stranger from the planet Krypton, The Man of Steel: Superman!

Possessing remarkable physical strength, Superman fights a never-ending battle for truth and justice, disguised as a mild-mannered newspaper reporter, Clark Kent.

Some of the core vocabulary has begun to emerge, but the effect remains bulky and un-poetical.

Meanwhile, the weekday, 15-minute radio serial had also altered its opening, changing several times in the course of its run and borrowing from the cartoon series. By 1943, the radio introduction reads as follows:

Up in the sky! Look!
It's a bird!
It's a plane!
It's Superman!
Yes, it's Superman—
Strange visitor from the planet Krypton
Who came to Earth with powers and abilities far beyond those of mortal men.

Superman, who can leap tall buildings in a single bound,
Race a speeding bullet to its target,
Bend steel in his bare hands,
And who—disguised as Clark Kent,
Mild-mannered reporter for a great Metropolitan newspaper—
Fights a never-ending battle
For Truth and Justice.

The poem—for now, I would argue, it is one—has a definite pace and dramatic vocabulary. But it still seems truncated and stilted in places, and it lacks a strong opening in the triad that the cartoon shorts included.

Returning again to the cartoon series a year or so later, we see that the poem has now achieved its final form by borrowing and improving on the radio narrative. Stripped of ungainly and unnecessary adjectives and of unmelodious and pretentious verbiage, its metaphors are simple, logically consistent, and eloquent. It now seems impossible to imagine altering a word.

Given the way the poem evolved, it might seem hard to assign authorship, yet the animator Jay Morton has traditionally been given this credit, and rightly, in my opinion. All good poets are, after all, editors, sifting through the language bequeathed to them, editing what came before. The critic Harold Bloom refers to all great poets as "misreaders" of the past. No doubt Morton's experience using simple graphics to produce cartoon characters and creating animated images out of static ones allowed him to see how certain words needed to be changed and certain lines streamlined or rearranged to produce the best possible effect.

I opened this paper with the poem as we know it. Here it is again, to be read as the end point of a lengthy, revisionary process:

Faster than a speeding bullet—
More powerful than a locomotive—
Able to leap tall buildings in a single bound—
Look! Up in the sky!
It's a bird!
It's a plane!
It's Superman!
Yes, it's Superman—
Strange visitor from another planet,
Who came to Earth with powers and abilities far beyond those of mortal men—
Superman—who can change the course of mighty rivers,
Bend steel in his bare hands,
And who—disguised as Clark Kent,

Mild-mannered reporter for a great metropolitan newspaper—
Fights a never-ending battle
For Truth, Justice, and The American Way.

Note how much better *Faster than a speeding bullet* is than earlier alternatives: *Faster than an airplane* doesn't scan well, and the change to *speeding bullet* frees up the reference to a plane to be used by the onlookers in their sighting of Superman in the next passage. *A streak of lightning* lacks the syllabic sharpness of a *speeding bullet* and introduces nature in a context where technology makes for a stronger comparison. We also see how *Faster than a speeding bullet* was revised out of, first, the ungainly: *race a high-powered bullet to its target* and, then, *race a speeding bullet*. *Faster than* is better than *race*, because the bullet is rendered irrelevant. Superman doesn't care about racing a bullet; he is faster without trying.

More powerful than a locomotive is an especially wonderful second line. *Powerful* and *locomotive* complement each other as multi-syllabic words (*powerful*, like the later *Amer-ican*, reduced to two syllables for the sake of the line's meter, adds speed to power), while *faster*, *speeding*, and *bullet* are inherently faster as di-syllabic words. The word *locomotive* also has a quaint quality—at least to a reader today. It seems a throwback to an earlier industrial age when machines were still a source of wonder. But the reference to *locomotive* doesn't so much date the poem as give it a relationship to historical process. Superman is of the past, but also of the present and future. The locomotive invokes another age but also seems a metaphor for the kind of powerful, lumbering mechanism that we must nonetheless take care to keep under human control.

The third line—*Able to leap tall buildings in a single bound*—completes the triad of the opening, so that the lines move from the comparative (*faster*, *more powerful*) to the singular (*able to*). While *faster than a speeding bullet* and *more powerful than a locomotive* make it possible to place Superman with respect to things we know, nothing we know *can leap tall buildings in a single bound*. *Single* is a resonant term in this context as well. We have started with comparatives and moved to a singularity.

All three lines involve Superman's ability to surpass or surmount technology: the bullet, the locomotive, the tall building (i.e. skyscraper). In this way, he both draws attention to technological achievement and renders it negligible in the face of his *powers and abilities*. This prepares us for the everyman voices to follow. From the wonder of technological achievement, which Superman can surmount, we shift to the wonder of ordinary people at the sight of Superman.

In this final version, the sequence of the line has been reversed: from *Up in the sky! Look!* to *Look! Up in the sky!* The shift to a single syllable imperative for the first word is more dramatic but also more logical: it mobilizes the eyes before directing them upward to a particular place, then focuses them on something in particular through a series of graded references: from *bird* to *plane* to *Superman*. This series of perceptions mimics how the eyes adjust to a strange sight—extrapolating from what is common to what is uncommon and, in this case, from animal to manmade artifact to extraordinary human being. Superman is an amalgam of nature and technology—a fabulous synthesis of both. The ultimate recognition of Superman by the onlookers also makes clear that, unlike a bird or a plane, of which there are many such things, Superman is, again, a singularity, here to do good and to be welcomed. He is a special but also an acknowledged friend.

The final portion of the poem remains almost the same as in its previous version, but a number of seemingly minor changes make a great difference in the effect. The phrase, *Yes, it's Superman*, strikes me as hugely important in establishing the poem's narrator as an authority, but a low-key, "mild-mannered" one. The onlookers make an initial surmise which the narrator quietly confirms. This narrator has access to information that the casual onlooker doesn't. He bridges the gap between the world we know and the world we don't. In this sense, he is a kind of Superman in the realm of information—a Super-reporter: Clark Kent raised to a higher power, which is to say, Clark Kent not as superhero but as super-authority.

The reader may ask questions at this point: *Who is this authoritative narrator? How has his authority manipulated us into believing him? What is this authority trying to gain through this manipulation?* The literary critic Fredric Jameson referred to Postmodernism, whose advent could be placed during this period, which also marked the end of the "Silver Age" of comic book heroes, as an "incredulity towards meta-narratives"—an unwillingness to believe, in other words, in *Truth, Justice, and the American Way*. The certainty with which the Superman poem incorporates the authority of the narrator makes it vulnerable to Postmodern critique. But the poem seems to me to have the power to deflect this critique even as it invites it. For it creates a desire for what it describes. The voice of the poem—encapsulated in the simple confirmation: *Yes, it's Superman* —puts one in mind of a news anchor of the sort that the networks are still seeking and audiences still crave. (The popular success of *Good Night and Good Luck*, about the 1950s anchor Edward R. Murrow, is evidence of this.) The authority that we seek does not have to be omniscient, just trustworthy, informed, and mild-mannered (the human incarnation, one could say, of *Truth, Justice, and the American Way*).

The authoritative voice of the poem now goes on to tell us about Superman through a number of simple adjectives and nouns:

> Strange visitor from another planet,
> Who came to earth with powers and abilities beyond that of mortal men.

One of the crucial changes in this final version of the poem involves the revision of "the planet Krypton" to "another planet." The change places the three adjective-and-noun combinations—*strange visitor, another planet, mortal men*—on the same generalized plane. It also engages us more directly in its meaning. We are all, upon reflection, *from another planet*—the mysterious place from which we emerged into life and the weird place that is our families and cultures (an earlier version had referred to a *distant planet*, which not only scans less well but also separates Superman more literally from us in our quest to identify with him). It is a neat reversal, moreover, to have Superman inserted into a super-conventional family in the back story of the comic book, an antidote to his super-weird biological family, when for most of us, the reverse is true—we hanker for a conventional family but live in a weird one. This line of the poem forces us to connect Superman both to our own strangeness and idiosyncrasy and to our humanity. As much as we may feel ourselves to be like Superman, this line also brings us down to earth. The counterpoint to Superman, it should be noted, is not *ordinary* man, but *mortal* man. No matter how Nietzschean our aspirations, we cannot deny our mortality. By reminding us of this, the poem places us on the side of the observers, even as it connects us metaphorically to the hero in the sky.

The reference to *powers and abilities* is also evocative. These words are not about simple strength or athleticism. It is "powers" not "power," and "abilities," an even more elusive idea. What are *abilities* exactly—what are ours? Superman has these *beyond those of mortal men*, but still, one is led to wonder, what *powers and abilities* do we have that might be unrealized, held in check, disguised?

Pausing here as we consider the qualities in Superman—in us—that might, with courage and insight, be plumbed, the poem now provides specific examples of superhuman power:

> Superman—who can change the course of mighty rivers,
> Bend steel with his bare hands

The apostrophe—*Superman*—that begins this pair of lines is masterful. It brings us back again to the subject of the poem: *This is Superman we're talking about, in case you forgot.* It underlines the name for a second time. The first,

Yes, it's Superman, was a deceptively chatty sort of affirmation, but this second reference is more serious, more assertive of the difference between him and us. It is followed by two very specific examples of Superman's powers. One is lifted from an earlier draft—*Bend steel with his bare hands*, while the other that precedes it, is new, the most evocative example of power in the poem: *who can change the course of mighty rivers*. As in the observations of the onlookers near the beginning, these two lines together move us from nature to technology: from rivers to steel. Significantly, however, to *change the course of mighty rivers* is different. Bending steel is superhuman, but in degree not kind, and has no obvious effect on the eco-system. Changing rivers is another order of power and it does affect nature in a holistic way. However, though Superman *can* change the course of mighty rivers, we are not told that he *will*. Superman's *modus operandi*, as I deduce it from this line, is to use his power judiciously, not exert it willfully, and, if required to change nature, to put things back after he achieves the necessary end.

After making us think both practically and philosophically about Superman's physical powers—what he might do and what he might refrain from doing—we shift into a different register:

And who—

How wonderful this "And who—". The poem refuses to come to a stop, but continues on in a new direction, affixing a surprising clause:

And who—disguised as Clark Kent

The clause links Superman and his wondrous powers intimately, which is to say, syntactically, to his alter-ego.

And who—disguised as a Clark Kent,
Mild-mannered reporter for a great metropolitan newspaper—
Fights a never-ending battle
For Truth, Justice, and The American Way.

The disguise is economically explained here—incorporated into the larger whole of *powers and abilities, changing, and bending*. And it mimics the doubleness of outside and inside in the adjective used for Superman in disguise: *mild-mannered*, which I have already commandeered to describe the voice of the narrator who quietly assures us: *Yes, it's Superman.*

Mild-mannered, a compound adjective, seems to have been coined for the purpose of representing Clark Kent. It suggests both an inner temperament and an outer presentation. Here is a man who can melt into the background, which makes him unlike what men are conventionally supposed to be: cocky, aggressive, in-your-face. The connection of mild-mannered and milquetoast (the latter, an old-fashioned term, the former, timeless) is there, but the two are very different. To be a milquetoast is to be a wimp (Clark Kent may be understood as such by people who lack sensitivity and insight), but to be mild-mannered is to be unobtrusive and considerate—not timid and weak but secure and lacking in egotistical swagger. This makes sense. Knowing one is Superman would tend to build confidence and make showy presentation unnecessary.

The combination of names, *Clark Kent,* is itself a metonym for the idea of Superman's mild-manneredness. The names, monosyllabic and reversible, begin with letters that look different but sound the same. This, one could say, is the case for Clark Kent and Superman—or for us, in our ordinary guise and in our secret, more powerful selves. We too are both conventional and unique, negligible and important (if only to ourselves and our loved ones).

By the same token, the distinction being drawn between Superman and Clark Kent is that of a man alone versus a man in society. Superman acts without help; Clark Kent is part of an institution, employed by *a great metropolitan newspaper.* If Superman possesses superhuman "powers and abilities," Clark Kent is a mortal man whose greatness comes from working with other mortal men. The *great metropolitan newspaper* is the means by which individuals can surmount their negligibility.

The pathos of the phrase, *a great metropolitan newspaper,* is not lost on those of us who have seen newspapers die in the last two decades. Those newspapers that remain are now few and, having radically changed their form in pursuit of a dwindling market, may no longer be *great.* Does this mean that individuals now have a harder time surmounting their negligibility? Or is it that they can no longer derive power from institutions but must find it, like Superman, in themselves? We can take the meaning either way—or both ways, as the spirit moves us.

The final lines of the poem are incomparable. That the battle that Superman wages is "never-ending" is important. It makes possible, of course, the continued adventures of Superman in the various venues in which they are dramatized, but it also speaks to the absurdity of the human condition, its Promethean aspect (Superman as the modern-day Prometheus reduces, in interesting but heroic ways, his superhero status). There will always be something to fight. Eternal vigilance is always necessary.

Finally, there is the crucial addition of seven syllables to the last line of the earlier draft of the poem: *and the American Way.* The addition makes a difference on the level of both form and content. Without those seven syllables the line does not scan—it is not in iambic pentameter—or in the approximation to iambic pentameter that is, to my mind, uniquely American. *With* those seven syllables, the poem can both bring us home ("The American Way" is *our* way) *and* take us to a higher place. The crescendo of the line, moving from the one-syllable *Truth*, to the two-syllable *Jus-tice*, and culminating in the multi-syllable, the *A-mer-ican Way* is magisterial but also rousing. If we compare this to the last lines of Keats' poem, cited earlier: *"Beauty is truth, truth beauty,"* —*that is all | Ye know on earth, and all ye need to know*, we see how the idea of *Truth* has undergone change. It is not a static circularity, a feedback loop with beauty, but the first variable in a vital forward motion that takes us from *Truth* to *Justice* to the *American Way*. The American Way turns a generalized poem into a poem about us as Americans, while opening it to something greater that we can never fully or definitively explain.

For what is the *American Way*? At the time the line originated (it seems to have been inserted by 1943), it was perhaps simpler to answer this question. America was then nearing the end of the Second World War, where it was being lauded as a savior, in Superman fashion, of the Western world. This Golden Age of Superman's adventures, and much of the subsequent Silver Age (that included my childhood), coincided with an America at the height of its power (and of its more ineffable *powers and abilities*). Since that time, the notion of what exactly *the American Way* is is less clear.

But the poem keeps the idea of *the American Way* alive. Just as Superman's battle is *never-ending*, so *the American Way*, though it changes over time, endures. I am not a flag-waving American, but *the American Way*, as it is represented in the Superman poem, always incites a feeling of pride and patriotism in me. As represented through the figure of Superman (not the physical image, but the idea put forward in the poem), it seems precisely the sort of idea I can stand behind: of being prepared to take responsibility without taking credit, of being mild-mannered most of the time but steadfast and courageous when it is necessary. The vision of Superman, as expressed in the poem, not least because the poem uses language with such simplicity and grace, makes me feel good about what can be done in the lives of mortal men (and women). It is mass culture deleted of its lowest, meanest elements and raised to the level of art and possibility.

Leonard Finegold

Is Death Valley the Hottest Place on Earth?

When teaching elementary physics, we often have textbook problems like, "The hottest place on earth is in Libya (1922); convert the temperature from 58°C to degrees F." I told students that the Libya report had to be a mistake, and that Death Valley really holds the record. I wrote to the textbook authors about this; they duly took no notice. My reasons for assuming an error were:

• I love Death Valley, and I wanted it to hold the record

• There were no records of outstandingly high temperatures in Libya before or after the claimed one, so the attribution to Libya had to be a Rosie Ruiz effect. Rosie Ruiz is famous for, despite the absence of several recorded fast marathon times, finishing as the fastest woman in the 1980 Boston Marathon. She also missed the many check-points en route, which makes her an astounding outlier (note the last e could be an a). It appears she was aided by the local subways. A Rosie Ruiz Run was scheduled in her honor, where people were invited to run the last 26.2 meters from the finish line. But then, I digress.

• In 1922, Libya had recently become an Italian colony. The US had not been a colony for some time. So the stable US seemed more reliable for weather records.

Fast forward to 2012. Lo and behold, and I quote entirely from *Science* magazine: "56.7°C—Hottest official temperature on Earth, recorded in Death Valley in 1913. In a 13 September announcement, the World Meteorological Organization (WMO) stripped Libya of its 90-year claim to the title after a WMO investigation concluded that the country's chart-topping 58°C temperature had been recorded incorrectly." So I'm vindicated. The full WMO announcement (mentioned below) lists five problems with the Libya claim, including the Rosie Ruiz effect. The announcement has more than a dozen authors from more than a dozen institutions, from all over, including one from my favorite site *Weather Underground*. It is noteworthy that the first author is from the Libyan National Meteorological Center, and that the study was done during the recent revolution. Hence this study nails once and for all the Libya claim, and now the World Meteorological Association says "...the official highest recorded surface temperature of 56.7°C (134°F) was measured on 10 July 1913 at Greenland Ranch (Death Valley), California, USA." Google

Maps has a picture placing the spot on the other side of Highway 190 from the Furnace Creek Ranch entrance. (I vaguely recall a weather station near the—now old—visitor center... can anyone help here?). So Death Valley wins... or does it?

This is a tale of twists and turns. A nice article in *Eos*, by Mildrexer, Zhao and Running, explains that the hottest temperatures are found at the surface of the earth, which is *not* the same as the air temperature higher up. On a 90° F day, I got burn blisters on my leg from touching the Astroturf in the middle of my local jogging track, even though the air was cool enough to run. And try to walk barefoot in hot noon summer sand. (I tried to find real evidence for frying an egg on hot pavements/sidewalks; alas, it seems to be an urban legend.) The air temperature even a few feet above the ground is much cooler. (This is why some people prefer camp beds in the desert, and some desert creatures have long legs.) Hence the standard weather stations are in cute white shaded louvred boxes, at approximately eye level, wind-protected, and there are other requirements—all to measure the true *air* temperature, which is what the weather people report. The *Eos* experimenters used satellites to measure the temperature at the very *surface* of the whole Earth (i.e. from a dark dry surface in the full sun), which can be quite different from the air temperatures. Basically, they used the fact that hot items glow bluer (this is how kid ear thermometers work, and how we know the temperatures of distant stars). They found that the hottest ground temperatures on earth vary from year to year, and from continent to continent. NASA has good maps illustrating their work.

And now Death Valley does not look like being the hottest from ground temperatures, alas, since the satellite (ground surface) measurements should be related to the air temperatures. One should establish "ground truth" by setting up weather stations to measure the air temperature at the places that the satellites predict (from ground temperatures) are the hottest. I propose that the stations be operated remotely, so no one need be there at the hottest times. Moreover, I humbly volunteer to help set up such stations (much preferably in winter). I eagerly await the call.

To read further:

Rosie Ruiz... see Wikipedia

Science 21 September 2012 p. 1439

WMO... browse WMO Death Valley Libya

Mildrexler, D. J., M. Zhang, and S. W. Running (2006), "Where are the hottest spots on Earth?," *Eos Trans.* AGU, 87(43), 461.

http://earthobservatory.nasa.gov/Features/HottestSpot/

I am grateful to Steve Running for e-mail and to Jon Burton for the Rosie Ruiz Run reference (St. Petersburg Times—May 15, 1980, page 2c).

Valerie Fox

Memo Regarding your Future

Let me start off by admitting that the world can be a coarse and harrowing experience for any of us, even me.

Let's be frank and honest here.

When you were on the seventeenth floor, Randy, over last weekend did you notice the splattered microwave or the unlocked window, several inches ajar, because, well, somebody else did and they have complained and they also saw various and previously mentioned (and documented by Legal) items in your desk and corner area.

By the way, this is for your own good. You will get even more notification mailed to you.

So, lo and behold, more than one person in there saw and became aware of this. Now I must ask you to consult your manual. Just to clarify we are not dialoguing here concerning the matter of your hair.

Of course, we're not literally speaking, but I hope that there is an element of communication in what is happening here as in there is an idea or what I like to call an "image" and it is projected on a screen in my brain and it then miraculously appears, the very same, in someone else's—yours I mean.

We, I really am talking now about me, walk about the halls well after ten o'clock in the evening many an evening and come across people, those who are quite devoted to this their job. They are still working, assessing and reducing costs. They too have opinions including about why you were in the office over the weekend and they have written a report with an overwhelming (in my view) and disastrous (well, not for me) conclusion, and something they like to call the denouement—and here it comes, Randy.

Randy. Planning ahead is not a dirty word. It is what some people call the Way the Truth and the Light.

Valerie Fox

One constant, in the background (Shostakovich #5)

> *When at night I await the beloved guest,*
> *Life seems to hang by a thread.*
> *—from Anna Akhmatova, "The Muse"*

There have been days like this my whole life
when Shostakovich #5 is as likely to
bring me to tears as remind me of Bugs Bunny
being stalked by Elmer Fudd.
Bugs is always in charge. The true secret meaning
 depends upon if you have the ears to hear.
 Our interest in white noise seldom wanes
and a name said once.

This fluty part laps like an unnamed river
that is being traversed by unborn persons
feverishly paddling, just on the one chance in a million
another sentient being might be listening in. Or
that the epithet chosen by these
unborn will become a lasting key
that will unlock an opening, a gray portal
to a new idea, one that is not
encumbered by doubt.

Where will all this lead? How can we all go on?
Seven is a fine age to begin the life
of your art-form. Watching a filmed confession
more than once might help to answer salient questions,
never far from being asked,
seemingly at rest, under the tongue.
Thing is, you have to wait for another to ask.

There is a lot of room on the large screen
for painterly scenes and antics,
for a single grand piano—trilling and serious.
Mistakes lead to false retaliations and relationships
with death. Someone hands someone a cigarette,
a cup of coffee.

I thought I learned this today—to align

the radically material with the violent boots
of pogrom memory. But there are only six
minutes left to decide. A loudspeaker says all that
and more. It may not be enough.
Still sighing, suggesting a hymn,
this solo helps me to connect
with the full force of truth
and lamentation. One kind of happy.

Maria Hnaraki and Evangelia Papoutsaki

Dakos: An Island Bread

O dákos tu delikaní miázi tu kopeliári,
pu ke sklerós ke tryferós éhi peréssa hári.

The dakos of the prideful, handsome man looks like a charming lad;
Whether he's tough or tender, excessive is his grace.

—*Mandinada*: Traditional Cretan rhyming distich, by
Anna Skandalaki

Dakos is my name. Born and raised on the Mediterranean, Greek island of Crete, today I deliver my miraculous dietary secret all over the world. I am no longer considered as a staple food only at home; yet I remain an islander at heart: harsh, tough, independent, but full of substance: a true Zorba!

My texture and shape are best described by my distant relatives, *takos* or *takaki* (from the Italian *taco*), namely pieces of wood wedged under a table to stop it wobbling; or a wooden, round lid used to cover and drain fresh cheese. In ancient Greece, Hippocrates and Aristotle—who, by the way, would highly recommend me as part of the daily diet—would refer to me as *dipyros* or *dipyritos artos*, literally "twice-fired bread" (namely, dough that was baked, sliced, and then returned to the warm oven to dry out completely). When various flours (such as wheat, barley, corn, whole wheat, or rye) are milled into my body, I am called *migadi*, bastard.

Depending on which part of the island of Crete you meet me, my name may also vary. For example, in the Iraklio area, I would be called *dagos*; whereas, in Rethymno, because of the way I look, particularly when dressed, I would be called *koukouvagia* (owl). I can be long and round, with a hole in the middle, in which case I might be called kouloura; or else round without a hole in the middle, and called *tabakiera*. In the Lasithi area, I carry the names *ladopsomo* (olive-oil bread), *ladouristo* (bread soaked in olive oil) or *kouloukopsomo* (dog's bread, as locals used me soaked in olive oil to feed their lucky dogs). In addition, when round, I am separated into two shells, the upper and crispier reserved for guests, and the lower and more compact shared by one's immediate family. But, if you find yourself at a Cretan bakery and you ask for *dakos*, you will most likely be given the square looking slabs (*paximadia*).

Speaking of family, there is no other place within Greece where I am considered more fundamental than Crete. To give you an idea of what I'm talking about, when a youngster loses a baby tooth, it is not placed under a pillow to get picked up by the tooth fairy. Instead, it is placed in a hole in a stone wall, while wishing that "a mouse will take it and give back an iron one"—so that the youngster can chew me! Note that a meal without bread is simply inconceivable to a Greek. The poet Hesiod and the historian Herodotus both spoke of "wheat-eaters": a polished and cultured people, versed in farming as well as in preparing bread—not like the savage and uncouth "meat-eaters." Moreover, the Greeks were the first to show how mixing various flours produces better tastes. They added grains and nuts to their breads, along with such other ingredients as cheese, honey and olives. Today, over 50 kinds of bread exist in Greece, made by a variety of flours but mainly using wheat, barley and rye.

I taste wonderful on my own, but I also enjoy partnering with others. When partnered, especially with a non-Greek, I am usually referred to as "Greek pizza," "Greek bruschetta" or "Greek salad sandwich." For sure, when single, I can last forever in good shape. Because I am easy to use and inexpensive, you can store me or carry me anywhere. I can be eaten dry whereas eating me "wet" is usually associated with weaker characters (or older people). In either case, I am so essential, so staple, that I have been branded as "The Manna" by the Tsatsaronakis bakery in Chania, Crete, that enjoys playing with my texture and imaging, and makes me available all over the world as an organic, kosher, halal, green, sustainable product.

My personality has been a source of literary inspiration throughout the ages. Anna Skandalaki, a Cretan folk poet, wrote a couple of *mandinades* in my honor where she illustrates how "you only need to grasp two of us along with some olives and good wine to enjoy a wholesome lunch, as the Cretans of old used to do." After all, a popular approach to preparing a meal in Greece is *vale oti vris* (throwing in whatever is available).

My fellow Cretans are tough like me and always rise above all difficulties, solid as a rock. They are quite an independent bunch, their motto being "why fix something that is not broken?" This is also true of the Cretan diet, an interesting mix of simple food, with plain seasonal fresh ingredients that are lightly cooked so that one can still taste the original ingredients. Cretan ingenuity transforms me and a bunch of wild greens into the most delicious dish with the simple addition of olive oil, salt and fresh lemon juice. Most senior Cretans today would recognize wild edible greens, having foraged for them in times past when the land was a local supermarket. That knowledge comes from a lean upbringing, a consequence of both poverty and a strong connection to "Mana-Mother Earth" for feeding.

I am often considered the epitome of Cretan food as I contain its core ingredients (grains, olive oil, oregano, tomatoes and cheese): simple but nutritious. My main dressing ingredient is olive oil, the island's main agricultural product since Minoan times, well known for its very low acidity. If the Mediterranean is the world's olive grove, then Crete marks its heart. Regardless of where they live, many Cretans grow their own olive trees for their own olive oil consumption and generous use in their cooking.

Although I am often eaten with feta cheese, Cretans will consume me like the mountain shepherds of old days, with any local cheese, including the soft, sweet-smelling *myzithra* or *anthotyro(s)* (a ricotta type of cheese), *xinomyzithra* (tangy salted white cheese), the homemade intense flavored *tyrozouli* (hard goat cheese), and the island's best export, *graviera* (a full-fat *gruyère* type of cheese made from sheep's milk). The combination of crunchy, creamy and juicy is guaranteed to arouse the palate and never fails to please.

My family also includes sweet cousins: delicately scented with anise, cinnamon, almonds, coriander seeds, orange juice, currants or just plain decorous white slices or rough-hewn barley bricks studded with bran, all usually accompanied by the drinking of Greek coffee. I am also an indispensable part of the Greek Orthodox tradition. In times of fasting, I am eaten just soaked with olive oil, tomatoes and herbs; or else I accompany *orfana* (orphans), the meatless versions of such dishes as stuffed vegetables (*gemista*) or vine leaves (*dolmades*).

Although traditionally a farmer's lunch, I am now an indispensable dish at restaurants all over Crete, Greece and several parts of the world. In a taverna or a *kafenio* (local coffee place), I accompany as *boukies* (bites) the *tsikoudia* or *raki* (the Cretan version of grappa) or the wine with the several local *mezedes* (tapas). As time passed, I have been diluted and have become more popular in a softer version (with more non-whole grains ingredients and yeast). But, it is in my island nature to continuously adapt to changing circumstances while still maintaining that core of my Cretan identity: tough but wholesome and definitely... *nostimos* (tasty), evoking to all who savor me a Ulyssean *nostalgia*—what Homer called "the journey home."

Further Reading

Deftereos, A. (2000) *Bread at Greek customs: Its symbolic and magic use by modern Greeks*. Athens: Legato.

Farr, D. L. (2009) '*Paximadia*: Cretan twice baked bread', *Art of Eating* 82 (1): 29-33.

Hnaraki, M. (2006) 'Greece', in *The Ethnomusicologist's Cookbook*. New York: Routledge, pp. 240-245.

Hnaraki. M. (2010) 'Baked realities: big fat Greek breads', *Petis Propos Culinaires*, 89 (1): 35-66.

Psilakis, M. and Psilakis, N. (2001) *The bread of the Greeks and the confectioneries of our folk tradition: A folklore, gastronomic and historic passage based on Cretan fermentations (and 450 recipes)*. Iraklion, Crete: Karmanor.

Valamoti, S. M. and Anastasaki, S. (2007) 'A daily bread—prepared but once a year', *Petits Propos Culinaires*, 84 (1): 75-100.

Rebecca Ingalls

The Student as Witness: Cultivating Creativity in the Yogic Body of Research

Cooling the "Mind-stuff": Finding Freedom in the Vastness of the Body

My yoga practice began a decade ago, on the top floor of an independent bookstore just off the campus of the university where I was doing my Doctoral work. On cold Midwestern mornings once per week, a few of us would gather in the early hours to follow the gentle direction of one of the bookstore's managers as she led us from standing, to seated, and slowly to a Savasana meditation. While we practiced, I could almost hear our collective minds buzzing from *asana* to *asana*, that is, from one yogic posture to another, with the assorted anxieties of trying hard to get them right, comparing ourselves to one another, worrying about coursework, hoping we would make candidacy, sensing the distant nervousness of dissertating to come, and wondering if tenure-track jobs would await us.

This mind chatter was bound to come up, for *asana* breeds a quiet in the body that leaves audible the more subtle body action of the breath, the tremblings of muscles, the noise of thoughts, and the soulful connections we humans share. *Asana* means "seat," and it asks the practitioner to hold a posture for several breaths, and to be acutely present in that stillness. The second of the Yoga Sutras of Patanjali (Satchidananda,1990: 3) is *Yogas citta vrtti nirodhah*, which means "The restraint of the modifications of the mind-stuff is yoga." This mind-stuff includes the chaotic brain activity of what we see as our reality: memory, fear, love, pain, imagination, environment, sensory awareness. *Vinyasa*, or breath-led movement, is what stabilizes the body's move from asana to asana as the brain slowly (over years) begins to descend into the heart, leaving the mind open and receptive to peace. As the practitioner tries to still the mind, thoughts flood back in, and thus the brain's descent is an ever-calibrating process of letting go without judging. All the while, the body is using breath to extend and soften, utilizing large muscles for strength, and then opening space by relaxing them into each posture. Ultimately, working within the confined space of the body can lead to an opening of the joints; more importantly, it leads to an opening of the heart and mind, and a sense of oneness with each other and with the universe.

The transfer of skills from my yogic practice into my teaching and research has astonished me. In my early years as a teacher, I stood in front of my composition students with an ideological dilemma: wanting to see them grow in creative, empowering directions, knowing full well the constraints of academic discourse and institutional expectations, and battling my own fledgling efforts to carve out creative intellectual spaces in the academy and in my research while playing by all of the rules. How could I help my students to cultivate creative intellectual freedom when I was still learning to cultivate it myself? Then, I spent most of the time burdened by the anxiety of needing to publish, and by the additional layers of pressure about where and how to publish, and which publications "counted." It was a paradox: I was in a tenure-track job, fascinated by writing and rhetoric, and brewing some passionate ideas for creative, rigorous projects in the back of my mind; but I couldn't shake the nagging feeling of constraint, much as I wanted to. I couldn't believe that such anxiety had to be a part of the job I wanted to love so much.

These days—now a decade into my teaching career and in my fourth year of a dedicated *Ashtanga* yoga practice—when I stand in front of students, I have only a few hours before stood on my head, or on my hands, or on my sitz bones with legs folded around my head and *then* on my hands. (I have also done many of these things with a baby in my belly; Figure 1.) Seemingly fixed, nonnegotiable elements of the body many years ago are now anatomical components that usually collaborate peacefully in bends and twists, in spaces opened between joints. In journeying deep inside the contained space of the physical body, I have worked intensively with the breath to cultivate openness not only between vertebrae, but also in the spaces of my mind. Through practice, I have come to discover that the obstacles of writing and research were, for the most part, perpetuated by me. Indeed, I came by my perception of constraint quite

Figure 1: The author in Pincha Mayurasana, eight months pregnant

honestly: the discourse of academia can be harshly confining (as our students know very well). But it was not until I started to deepen my awareness of the yawning spaces in the body and mind that I could begin to imagine that my own research, my life work, could breathe.

I am daily inspired to think about what these bodily negotiations lend to writing pedagogy. I have witnessed in the last few years an ease in my research anxiety, which has opened space for creativity to flow. With this ease has come bravery, as I seek to cultivate new ground in rhetoric and writing pedagogy, experimenting with hybrid journals that open spaces for creative research on media and culture to both academic and public audiences, and collaborating with colleagues in a peer-reviewed bricolage of perspectives on plagiarism, students' rights, and originality. I doubt that I would have found the courage to navigate the obstacles of academic anxiety and cultivate innovation in my work if I hadn't journeyed deeply into the practice of yoga.

Sutra 29 in Book One (Satchidananda, 1990: 49) states, *Tatah pratyak cetanadhigamopyantarayabhavas ca*: "From this practice all the obstacles disappear and simultaneously dawns knowledge of the inner Self." For the present discussion, I focus on one, complex obstacle that my students and I share. As I have witnessed the impact of my practice on my work as a scholar, it has inspired me to think deeply about how yogic theory might offer a useful lens to think about how students can negotiate one of the more challenging aspects of their composition practices: freely setting out into the realm of creative, original research while working within the constraints of their academic writing. Using yogic philosophy and practice to theorize writing bodily—characterized in particular by varying degrees of flexibility— has helped me to understand how students might creatively navigate the flexibility of the "body" of their own researched writing practices. Whether a student has simply been told to construct a researched, written argument about *something* or has been given more detailed directions, I discuss here how we can help students to engage authentic exploration in these projects while they deal with the reality of constraints. To be sure, students will find themselves navigating these and other writing constraints way beyond their academic years—in their professions, in their personal lives, in their lives as public citizens. Using their academic writing to plot and re-plot their way through these constraints is its own form of yoga.

Opening the "Container" of Composition Through Contemplative Practice

One of the beautiful and often harrowing challenges of writing is the ongoing negotiation of physical and mental space that it involves. Composing asks us to measure pages and margins, and to evaluate what we know about the constraints of a writing task as we imagine what we can meaningfully say in that space within those constraints. What's more, a text is constrained not only by the rules of the task, but also by the heuristics for writing that we've been given over the years. In the brew of formulaic writing, fears of plagiarism, and the visible and invisible limits of genre and audience, students—whether they are first-year writers or graduate students—often find themselves heavily focused on writing according to what they think is and isn't "allowed" in an assignment.

In conversations about writing pedagogy, such "contained" rules for writing have been under scrutiny for years. In the construction of an assignment, Bowden (1993: 367) has suggested, an instructor constitutes an assigned piece of writing as a "bounded space within which elements can be located" or strategically placed, often specifically cordoned off according to page length, paragraph structure, word count and font size. These boundaries are rhetorical, for "when things fit properly, the paper is well organized" (*ibid.*). If the paper is not filled correctly an instructor may tell a student, "'There are gaps in your argument'" or "'Your paper is full of holes'" (Bowden, 1993: 370). Comments like these aim to help students imagine their compositions in tangible ways. But Bowden and others (e.g. Reddy, 1993; Slack, Miller, and Doak, 1993) have also argued that such "contained" perceptions of writing can also significantly *inhibit* communication because they suggest that the meaning in a text comes prepackaged and sent along certain channels in specific vessels with guaranteed delivery confirmation, and that if we either don't package it correctly or receive it correctly, we are to blame. In the composition classroom, this idea of "fault" can be problematic. Students' perceptions of the "fixity" of texts, argues Bowden (1993: 373), are connected to their perceptions of the mind as a vessel for knowledge that is "static and decontextualized." If they challenge or manipulate the container—the genre, the assignment—too much, they are likely to pay a penalty for it (a poor grade, lack of understanding, or being told that they are "wrong" about their interpretations or writing choices). Moreover, the presence or absence of correct information in a composition can suggest to students that they know nothing at all.

Archibald's (2009) more recent exploration of the history and ideology of the essay form in the composition classroom offers one explanation for why fixed perceptions of research writing, in particular, may persist over those that embrace a more open-ended, even creative approach. She traces an intriguing contrast between the writing traditions of Michel de Montaigne and Francis Bacon, arguing that many school systems today continue to reproduce an ideology of the essay and student writer that aligns more with Bacon's philosophy. She explains: "Montaigne's writing needed a form capable of representing the fluidity of self-identity and his fluctuating opinions on the changing world around him" (Archibald, 2009: 26), a perspective that both contemplative pedagogy and yogic philosophy would embrace. However, explains Archibald, institutionalized education today—and the textbooks that tout institutional principles—continue to follow more of a Baconian approach, which maintains its focus on " 'objective' observation and control" (*ibid*). A holdover from this approach is the construction of the student as a "unified locus of consciousness" (p. 19), one that privileges the "facts" over the unique, socially constructed identity of the student writer and her/his "imperfect human passions" (p. 26). What is lost behind that scientific objectivity, that containment of form and content, Archibald (2009: 27) suggests, is "the mind at work"—in all its uniqueness—that Montaigne sought to make visible.

In the last fifteen years, research in writing and pedagogy has continued to explore the local and global benefits of analyzing and expanding this notion of the "container" of awareness or knowledge. Genre theorists (e.g. Bawarshi, 2003; Bawarshi and Reiff, 2010; Bazerman, 1997; Devitt, 2004; Devitt, Reiff, and Bawarshi, 2004) have examined how generic constraints of composition assignments can stifle a student's agency in cultivating a rhetorical understanding about what those compositions are meant to do. In researched writing, a student's constrained view of the composition process—which often involves the boundaries of page length, number and genre of sources, format, style, and the contained identities of "student" and "expert" researcher—can frame the assignment as if it had fixed walls. Add to this framing the rhetoric of plagiarism, and students can see a researched writing task as a potential prison. *Writing & Pedagogy* (from which this article has been reprinted) devoted an entire issue to the problem of plagiarism in student writing in 2010, and Pennington's (2010: 150) editorial introduction to the issue illustrates the academic constraints that continue to fuel this dilemma. As Pennington describes, plagiarism reigns as a serious issue because students face both the limitations of their knowledge and the limitations of the generic restrictions of academic writing. Such containment can inhibit the student from being experimental or creative, can squelch alternative views on source gathering (which I will discuss later), and can place so much responsibility on the student to put the right stuff "in" that the student loses focus on the spirit of inquiry and the innovation of creating a new conversation about a topic. Indeed, class discussions with students every fall term for the last decade have revealed to me that they still feel afraid of plagiarism and also disempowered and stifled by what they have come to know as the genre of "research paper."

This tension students negotiate between access and lack of access, between knowing something and knowing nothing, Reynolds (2004) points out, extends even beyond the boundaried space of the page; it is part of a larger culture of containment in academia. She reminds us that the classroom acts as a transitory space that may hinder students' connection to the work they do there; and she cautions us that those texts that seem to block out readers because of their form or content "result in many readers turning away" rather than exploring the "many routes through a text" which challenge "containerized ways of reading" (Reynolds, 2004: 166). Reynolds argues that students' connections to learning involve "learning to dwell" in the physical and discursive spaces of the institution. This "learning to dwell"—in the discourse of the institution, in the academic tasks that our courses ask students to tackle—involves a critical, mindful attention to discursive constraints, a contemplation that is central to yogic practice.

In fact, the echoes of yogic philosophy may be found in more current and progressive educational philosophies that seek to integrate contemplative pedagogies into academic work (e.g. Baurain, 2011; Dencev and Collister, 2010; Hall and Archibald, 2008; Kirsch, 2008–2009). Physicist Zajonc (2006) has worked to combine the realms of student research practices, the culture of the academy, and global peace-making efforts in order to lead a critical discussion about the "container" of epistemology and our individual and collective roles in making change in the world. Zajonc addresses the role of critical research in education, speaking to all of us, when he asserts that our ability to process information meaningfully, rather than as "simple 'input-output'" (*ibid.*), will require that "we must turn our attention toward the hidden container" that structures the ways in which we understand our world. Education itself, Zajonc urges us, "will need to transform the very container of consciousness, make it more supple and complex" (*ibid.*). To address a step toward this transformation, Zajonc proposes "a view of the human being in which the individual develops the capacity to move among worldviews, transcending particular identities while simultaneously honoring each of them" (*ibid.*). And yet, he claims, the individual must become aware that this ability to "move among" is only made possible "when we find peace among the component parts of our own psyche" (p. 1).

That uncertain, even precarious landscape of the mind and its "component parts," which Montaigne wanted to uncover, can be a space for students to discover and make visible—not just to their readers, but also to themselves in their research practices. The key to creating a sense of peace between these parts of the mind, Zajonc argues (2006: 2), is *contemplative practice*, whose definition reflects the core of yogic philosophy: "Contemplative practice works on the human psyche to shape attention into a far suppler instrument, one that can appreciate a wide range of worldviews and even sustain the paradoxes of life, ultimately drawing life's complexity into a gentle, non-judgmental awareness." Indeed, this intellectual work of negotiating worldviews and ideological contradictions without judgment, so central to the challenging, meditative work of *asana*, is also at the heart of meaningful, creative research. To understand, process, and contribute to the diversity of voices in a complex discussion about an issue—whether face-to-face in the classroom or on the pages of their compositions—students must be able to negotiate and respect difference, and to acknowledge others' views accurately, while seeking to carve out innovative perspectives. Yoga teaches us that, while the body may be very familiar territory, there is a vast landscape to learn and discover within it and around it—through the stumbling, the grace, and the rigor of postures—that is new, unfamiliar, and inspiring. So, too, is research-based writing a matter of students' navigating familiar practices of gathering and analyzing data amid the unfamiliar territory of being asked to arrange and deliver that data in an innovative way, even when the constraints of body, mind, and context are present. Yogic philosophy illuminates the creative power of this ability to meaningfully and mindfully engage in the research process.

The Yogic Body

Yoga gives us two critical concepts that can be mapped onto students' experience negotiating research in their writing: the convergence of mind, body, and context as a discursive, embodied space; and the concept of a universal creative force and the Seer who watches it all happen. The human physical form as a discursive subject is at the heart of yogic philosophy. The *Bhagavad-Gita* (Prabhavananda and Isherwood, 2002), one of the fundamental Hindu scriptures and a text that I will offer as a primary lens for my discussion, is part of a 100,000-verse epic poem known as the *Mahabharata*. The 700 verses of the *Gita* unfold a conversation on the battlefield between Arjuna, a Brahmin who must do battle with his relations, and Lord Krishna, the God figure, who reveals to Arjuna the wisdom of yogic philosophy and its connection to Arjuna's role as a human, as a Brahmin, and as a man who is about to go to war. In Lord Krishna's teachings to Arjuna (Prabhavananda and Isherwood, 2002: 44–45), the complex role of the human form is central: to dwell in the body, its senses, and the imprisonment of worldly desires and perceptions, is to be sinfully attached; and yet, the body has its role in the world that has to be fulfilled. The key, argues Lord Krishna, is to engage the activity of the body with "self control." Only with the calming of the mind can a human fulfill his bodily responsibility and still be on the path to heaven.

The body as a discursive space is illustrated poignantly in Chapter 13 of the *Gita*, "The Field and Its Knower." The chapter opens with Arjuna's question, "And now, Krishna, I wish to learn about Prakriti [nature of the universe] and Brahman, the field and the knower of the field. What is knowledge? What is it that has to be known?" Lord Krishna responds: "This body is called the Field, because a man sows seeds of action in it, and reaps their fruits. Wise men say that the Knower of the Field is he who watches what takes place within the body." He goes on to list the components of the body or bodily-ness—the "cosmos," "intellect" and "ego," nature and its elements, the senses, "consciousness"— and to emphasize the critical importance of a human's detachment from those bodily elements that keep her/him from seeing universal mortality for what it is (Prabhavananda and Isherwood, 2002: 100–102). Knowledge, argues Lord Krishna, may be found in the Brahman's total acceptance of the fact that he is "beginningless, transcendent, eternal." That is, it is not until a human can fully grasp the truth of mortality and the boundlessness of that which inhabits the body, that s/he can begin to know universal oneness with God (Prabhavananda and Isherwood, 2002: 102–103). Lord Krishna clarifies:

> The supreme Brahman in this body is also known as
> the Witness. It makes all our actions possible, and, as it
> were, sanctions them, experiencing all our experiences....
> (Prabhavananda and Isherwood, 2002: 103)

The Witness in the body, argues Lord Krishna, is the consciousness that watches. In the Yoga Sutras, this Witness is known as the Seer, as described in Book One, Sutra 3 (Satchidananda, 1990: 6): *Tada drastuh svarupe 'vasthanam*: "Then the Seer [Self] abides in his own nature." Sri Swami Satchidananda explains:

> You are not the body nor the mind. You are the Knower
> or Seer. You always see your mind and body acting in
> front of you. You know that the mind creates thoughts; it
> distinguishes and desires.
>
> But to understand that eternal peaceful You, the mind
> must be quiet; otherwise, it seems to distort the truth.
> (Satchidananda, 1990: 6)

In yoga, practitioners strive to acknowledge that the body and its desires are temporary. Critical to this endeavor, however, is the body itself: without it, we cannot recognize that it is a temporary container for the Self, or supreme consciousness, and find ultimate freedom from earthly constraints. To experience what it is to be the Seer, one must be aware of the body and mind, and learn to navigate both, in order to draw quietly away from both.

The concept of *prakriti*, the universal creative force, as referenced in Lord Krishna's discussion of The Field, is also critical to my discussion, for *prakriti* is the ether of creativity. Yoga master Richard Freeman offers an accessible definition for *prakriti*: "The universal creative energy that forms any object of awareness no matter how subtle. [It] is not conscious, and its products are always impermanent" (Freeman, 2010: 230). Freeman offers an explanation of concepts *purusa* and *prakriti*: purusa is "pure consciousness," equated with the Seer, Self, and Witness discussed above; *prakriti* is "the object of awareness" (p. 77). Freeman explains further that *prakriti* is "the object—be it a cloud in the sky, a thought, an emotion, a physical sensation, or an everyday object like a teakettle" (p. 77). *Prakriti* is all that is created, including our ideas about our realities, while *purusa* is the Seer who is able to examine even the inner workings of the mind as creations. It is coming to a peaceful place of resolving *purusa* and *prakriti*—beginning to understand the Seer and the seen for what they really are—that is the ultimate goal of yoga. For the yogi, it is a long journey through asana and meditation. In this discussion, the notion of prakriti works as an apt comparison to help us imagine students' tapping into a kind of creativity that doesn't seek to escape boundaries, but rather recognizes them, works with them, channels them as part of *prakriti*, creative energy.

Embodiment of Students' Researched Writing

How can yogic theory of the body help us to see more clearly the struggle of a writer within the confines of researched writing? Even more, how does a yogic view of the body help us to appreciate those constraints as opportunities for creativity? First, we might recognize a natural instinct to "contain" texts and writing processes, and see that we are actually working with an organic heuristic. In *Metaphors We Live By*, Lakoff and Johnson (1980: 29) observe, "We are physical beings, bounded and set off from the rest of the world by the surface of our skins, and we experience the rest of the world as outside us. Each of us is a container, with a bounding surface and an in-out orientation." Such "surfaces" include texts both as physical and as abstract notions. Bowden further articulates our intimate connection to body, and thus our tendency to view texts in terms of containment:

> Our concept of the body as a vessel, capable of holding,
> transporting, carrying elements within it, becomes a
> prototype for perceiving other kinds of experiences,
> especially those that are so mysterious and vague as to
> be difficult to talk about using conventional discourse. It
> becomes an organizational tool with which to categorize a
> range of enigmatic experiences. (Bowden, 1993: 366)

Consequently, writing, one of those "mysterious and vague" practices that can be challenging to explain, to teach, and to do, becomes all the more conceivable when we imagine it in terms that we can most basically understand, via the container metaphor.

While there are numerous reasons to doubt and challenge containment as a heuristic in writing, the fundamental argument of the *Gita*—that we can find freedom only in recognizing the body itself—has inspired me to approach creativity in research writing from a perspective that honors the material body, both in terms of its limits and in terms of its vastness. Stenberg's (2002) theorization of the "embodied classroom" is helpful in theorizing this materiality. She cautions teachers against the "postmodern tendency to textualize the body [and create a] conflation of 'freedom' with disembodiment" (Stenberg, 2002: 46). In pedagogy, she points out, the use of technologies in online and hybrid classrooms tends to revere the disconnected student voice and the constructed identity it (re)creates from its body, suggesting that more freedom of expression comes from that disconnection (pp. 47–48). She urges teachers, rather, to see the importance of the "body situated in space, time, and material boundaries" (p. 47). Although Stenberg recognizes that the disembodiment of the student has its benefits, she is invested in an *embodiment* that "approach[es] the body as a material site of political struggle, one that has been written on by a history of pedagogies...that both enable and deny subjects' authority" (p. 48). Her conception, I argue, is similar to Krishna's conception of the Field. Drawing upon notions of space, Stenberg compels us as teachers to ask how we can make "an opening for students...to make visible for themselves (and potentially, for others) the complicated contexts that surround their embodiment, to consider the 'myths' present in our local culture" (p. 58). To Stenberg's (2002) discussion I add Kazan's (2005: 383) notion of the "embodied pedagogical act," which she describes as a nexus of "discursive and corporeal texts." Working with this embodiment, these theorists suggest, means staying put in our bodies—an act rather like *asana*—locating them in the contested spaces of cultural construction, and letting those analyses teach us about how we read ourselves, one another, and the tasks at hand (p. 59). And so, I would like to think about how we as teachers can invite students to witness researched writing as a kind of "embodied pedagogical act," and to negotiate the mythologies and the rhetorical realities of researched writing as writers, as students, as creators.

I use here the yogic body as a metaphor for the "embodied pedagogical act" of researched writing. *Kapotasana* (Figure 2) is a pose in the Intermediate Series of Ashtanga that I (and many other practitioners) battle daily. And yet, in striving toward even deeper clarity of mind with this pose, I negotiate the challenges of the mind-chatter, which is constructed by the body, the memory, my senses, my environment, and the intellectual sense-making that I am doing as I journey

Figure 2: The author in Kapotasana.

toward the pose. Like Arjuna on the battlefield, I engage in this embodied experience, which is composed of so much more than the physical body itself, in order to see even the smallest glimpse of what it means to quiet the mind or experience *prakriti*. In working toward this quiet (day after day, year after year), I have had to cultivate and defend a certain creativity in getting into this pose. While the way "in" may look quite similar among practitioners, I have had to innovate around my shoulders, my upper back, and the "mind-stuff." Every iteration of this pose is, for me, an act of originality, though it is built upon a pose that has been done for centuries. And yet, without those material realities of the individual body—those "instruments"—there is no path, no creativity at all.

When we talk about students' cultivation of creativity in their researched writing, we are talking about their freedom to express new ideas, to find voice, to explore style, and to add something innovative to an intellectual conversation. As in yogic practice, the discursive constraints of researched writing, too, can become instruments, the material conditions that embody and are embodied by the process. I want to suggest that a student may find originality by negotiating, and learning to control, the instruments that are at work in the rhetorical situation of the researched writing assignment. Although the assignment may contain and be contained by constraints, we can help to empower students toward finding their own way into the research and the composition that reflects that research.

Praxis: Opening Creativity Through Embodied Research

> *The yogi never neglects or mortifies the body or the mind,*
> *but cherishes both. To him the body is not an impediment to*
> *his spiritual liberation nor is it the cause of its fall, but is an*
> *instrument of attainment. (Iyengar, 1979: 42)*

Contemplating a Way out of the "Research Paper" and into Research Process

As yogic meditation asks the practitioner to be present and observant even amid the distractions of a challenging posture, so do scholars of contemplative pedagogy recommend reflective writing practice as a way to open space in students' thinking so that they may focus, relax, and build confidence and community in the midst of challenging writing tasks (Hall and Archibald, 2008:10–12) and at the same time "bear witness" (p. 14) to their own and others' practices. I have found that sharing the writing scholarship—our scholarship— with students has helped to open their minds and foster contemplation, to feel more a part of the critical conversation, to become a "witness" to the ways in which they have been the subject of scholars' discussions about the problematic nature of this genre. To jumpstart their contemplation about what research writing means, I ask my first-year writing students to read some of the contemporary scholarship on plagiarism (I like to use Devoss and Rosati, 2002), as well as older scholarship on research writing. Students read scholars like Larson, who argues that "the generic term 'research paper' is for practical purposes meaningless" (Larson, 1982: 813) and that, although instructors try to teach it as a genre, it is only pretending to be one. They discuss independently and then together in our online discussion board Larson's argument that research should be an "activity," not a subject, whose "fruits" can emerge from a wide range of places and forms. I have found that students' reflective writing about these perspectives on research—their narratives of their own experiences, and their responses to each other's experiences—helps them to focus on the goals and their anxieties about the researched assignment they face. Even *inquiring* about issues like "research" seems to give them permission to begin to think more creatively about how they research, what "counts" as primary and secondary research (beyond what they can find in the university databases), and helps them to relax into it. It also encourages them to see themselves as intellectuals and writers, not just among other students, but also among other scholars who do research *on* research. There is an important sense of oneness to be found in that community-building; as Hall and Archibald (2008: 12) illustrate, shared reflections can help students to see that they may also share "the same struggle and that there [are] ways to gain sustenance from their individual visions as well as their collaborative work."

Revealing Creative Intentions: Collaborative Reflection of Teacher and Student in Conference

This practice of reflection, in which students become a witness to their own process, can also happen in the one-on-one conference between student and teacher. Indeed, helping students to cultivate creativity in their research involves the teacher's listening and guidance as the teacher and student engage in discussion, and as the student begins to witness creativity both existent and emerging. *The Svetasvatara Upanishad* (Prabhavananda and Manchester, 2002: 121) offers a parallel to this mentoring as it defines the yogi: "The yogi experiences directly the truth of Brahman by realizing the light of the Self within." I do not know whether Donald Murray, one of the prominent voices of the process movement, engaged in *asana*, but I do know that the cultivation of reflection (e.g. through conference, peer review, and revision) and of being a witness to one's action was the crux of his argument thirty years ago in "Teaching the Other Self: The Writer's First Reader":

> The act of writing might be described as a conversation between two workmen muttering to each other at the workbench. The self speaks, the other self listens and responds. The self proposes, the other self considers. The self makes, the other self evaluates. The two selves collaborate: a problem is spotted, discussed, defined; solutions suggested, attempted, tested, discarded, accepted. (Murray, 1982: 140)

It is this "other self" that Murray (1982: 141) wants teachers to try to channel in their students, for the "other self," he argues, is the "reader" of a text who is most aware of what a text is doing, of what it is trying to do, and of how it can be revised so that it can fulfill its purpose. Murray's description of the "other self" is eerily similar to Lord Krishna's discussion of the Witness (see Prabhavananda and Manchester, 2002: 103). Similarly, the relationship between *purusa* and *prakriti* works as a parallel: in Murray's model, the other self may be compared to *purusa*, the Seer, while the creation of the text and the text itself may be compared to *prakriti*, the creative force. Murray's other self is not pure consciousness, but that does not matter here; in this discussion it is enough to note that beginning to know the other self involves, for both teacher and student, a special kind of tuning in. Murray's discussion offers teachers an approach to collaborative reflection that guides students toward a consciousness about writing that they don't know exists (yet). As with the yogi and the teacher, who is meant to guide a novice toward independence and self-practice, so, too, does Murray suggest the teacher as a guide who listens "aggressively" to a student talk through her/his larger intensions in a composition. And, as with the yogi, the student is meant to cultivate an ability to hear the voice of the other self: "The teacher helps the student find the other self, get to know the other self, learn to work with the other self, and then the teacher walks away to deal with another Ronald in another course who does not know there is another self" (Murray, 1982: 147). In this guidance, the teacher helps the student to evolve into a writer who can be a witness to her/his own process and intentions.

Asana of Arrangement: Support in the Creative Navigation of Obstacles

Likewise, the teacher assists students in cultivating a mental stillness that can stream the *prakriti* and help them identify a problem or inquiry that they can explore in their research, and so move toward innovation as they cultivate a unique contribution to the discussion of their topic. In the act of problem finding, students explore and invite other bodies as they craft discussions and possible solutions, and we call this research. But to help them get past the static, rhetorically vapid task of integrating sources just for the sake of doing so, and toward the *creativity* of making a new conversation with other writers and readers happen, we as teachers can do our own letting go in order to allow students to challenge the obstacles of the researched writing task. The *Gita's* notion of the body as The Field offers a perspective on a student's composition process. As the Field is where "a man sows seeds of action in it, and reaps their fruits" (Prabhavananda and Isherwood, 2002: 100) the Field is both cultivated by the body and is the body itself. In researched writing, the Field is an often-contained discursive space made up of material impediments that students must deal with as they plant and sows the "fruits" (as Larson, 1982, suggests) of research findings. Conversely, the Field, both in yogic practice and in writing, is also limitless in that the revelations it presents to the practitioner know no bounds. Additionally important in the context of the *Gita* is the fact that the conversation between Arjuna and Lord Krishna takes place on a battlefield, soon to be populated with men who are negotiating their own embodiment. Not only must Arjuna tackle the material conditions of his own body and environment; he must also do so in the company of others, colliding and allying with them, as he journeys toward clarity of mind. So, too, is the student faced with the necessity of collaboration—of integrating and conversing with sources—to clarify ideas. Writing teachers can help students to see "sources" not just as pieces of texts and citations, but as invaluable obstacles through which they must carve their own paths.

In yoga, each practitioner must find a way through each individual *asana*, and through the sequence of *asanas*. There is technique, but it is not blanket pedagogy, for bodies and contexts are always shifting. As I have discussed, each yogi must negotiate the "best practices" of doing *asana* with a creative, multifaceted outlook that is required to work with the realities of body and its context. Freeman (2010: 172) teaches his students: "...when we come to an obstacle in yoga we are able to approach it from many different points of view—from its physiological angles, its psychological viewpoints, and its philosophical perspectives." Freeman might well use the phrases, "the rhetorical situation of yoga" or "problem finding, in place of "an obstacle in yoga." Moreover, in this "embodied pedagogical act" of practice, innovation is not an option; it is imperative.

Just as the yogi may find innovation in navigating the obstacles between and in *asana*, so, too, may students use obstacles as instruments of creativity in the process of problem finding and in the *arrangement* of sources on The Field of their research writing. Brauer (2009: 21) uses the language of containment to invite teachers to open enough space in their expectations of student research and writing to "reconsider disciplinary boundaries." He advises us to guide students' genre awareness into the creativity of source gathering and arrangement, offering this vision for teachers:

> Assignments might call the student writer to deploy
> overtly multiple genres in a single piece of writing....
> Instead of finding themselves treading the familiar ground
> of the formal academic essay, students may challenge
> generic boundaries, blending persuasion with narrative
> and analysis with figurative language. Simply asking
> students to use a central metaphor or analogy in creating
> an argumentative essay will cause their writing to meet
> divergent rhetorical exigencies, in this case, to please
> and to persuade their audience. As students fold use
> value [the intended utility for readers and other writers]
> into aesthetic value in their writing, they will increase
> their awareness of genre conventions as well as how
> the breaking of conventions can lead to writing that is
> multivalent in its rhetorical purposes and aesthetic effects.
> (Brauer, 2009: 21)

Rather than depart from the confines of a contained research project—confines that are actually the *reality* of authentic research—I think a creative approach to arrangement can come face-to-face with its constraints. So, for instance, in my own research writing assignments, I regularly establish (and explain) constraints: deadlines, numbers and kinds of sources, numbers of drafts, product length, even occasionally a particular form of argument (e.g. deductive or inductive). At the same time, I invite students to imagine their own rhetorical situations, and to integrate a diversity of sources and rhetorical strategies that best suit their audience and purpose: scholarly sources, primary research, music, images, film clips, poetry, experimental design, humor. To bring these rhetorical decisions—these instruments—into focus, I ask them to reflect on the choices they have made in written rhetorical analyses. In yogic terms, the creative arrangement of sources invites students to tune in to and negotiate form with freedom, constraint with creativity. Thus, we might also call this arrangement into written form *asana*.

The Pause: Creating Meaningful Silence

Just as we create obstacles in our researched writing assignments, so, too, can we create supports to help students navigate those obstacles. It's up to us to challenge ourselves to find a balance in the artful crafting of the genres of our assignments, to explain the constraints we do use so that our students can cultivate a rhetorical awareness of why those constraints are the way they are, to make room for them to move within those constraints, and to offer them creative possibilities for discovery and innovation (that might even challenge those constraints). Both yogic philosophy and contemplative pedagogy privilege the power of silence in opening space for discovery. As with the physical practice of yoga, one of the fundamental principles of contemplative practice in education is to "quiet the chaos and distractions inherent in a modern life in the name of the best teaching and learning" (Hall and Archibald, 2008: 2). But this kind of silence can be productive specifically because it is not in fact silent at all. As yogic philosophy makes clear to us, the chatter of our internal landscape is its own kind of noise: we strive to quiet it, but first we must recognize it. Sitting, as in *asana*, is the practice of staying physically still and refraining from speech, but stillness and listening are not necessarily the same as silence; listening involves an intentionality in silence. To listen, one may be receptive to the sound of the breath, to the messages our minds are telling us, to the attentiveness of the Witness that is observing all.

So, too, in the classroom, Baurain (2011: 91) suggests, there is invaluable power in a "generative silence" that can "speak and give others a freedom to speak." This freedom, I argue, is key to opening space for creativity among the obstacles of researched writing. As I have discussed, awareness and learning can grow out of the generative silence of reflective writing. Critical to creating spaces for these opportunities in the classroom is a slowing down, a pause in the action of an assignment's progress from beginning to end. In her work on contemplative practice, Kirsch (2008–2009: 8) argues: "The importance of silence, of pausing, of standing still, of attending to the moment, of being fully present, of listening deeply cannot be overstated in this day and age, and especially for a generation of students who are always wired, always multitasking." To be sure, we see more and more people flocking to the practice of yoga to undo some of the chaos that today's culture can bring to the mind, which may alone make a strong case for weaving its principles into the complex, rigorous practice of writing pedagogy and critical thinking development.

This critical pause to acknowledge the present moment, I have found, can happen in at least two important places, and each is informed by the philosophy and practice of yoga: first, it can accompany each stage of the process of a researched writing assignment, and second, it can be reflected in the relationship between the amount of product and the amount of process we expect. With respect to the first instance, I draw from the power of contemplation in asana when I invite students to pause and become aware of the now, to ask themselves, in writing: Which stage of the process am I in (composing the proposal, evaluating sources, writing the annotated bibliography, etc.)? What challenges me about this stage? What did I not expect? I like to use the online discussion board for this kind of reflection because, as with our collaborative discussions about research on research, students can utilize the silence of this kind of writing to ask each other questions about their experiences with stages in the research process. Despite the fact that students are not physically present with one another and that the students' voices might be perceived as "disembodied," as Stenberg (2011) cautions, I consider this practice to be a form of *embodied* pedagogy because (a) students are bringing their intellectual and physical experiences with writing to the shared discussion, and (b) the bodies of students' texts are physically present and integral to these discussions. As the collaborative reflection builds, students tend to support one another by expressing shared anxieties and exchanging sources and ideas. This reflection becomes creatively generative because, given our discussions about rethinking processes and forms of research, it opens up students' projects to the creative suggestions of their professor and peers.

With respect to the second instance, which we might call the *product-process ratio*, I again draw from my own yogic practice of *Ashtanga*, which privileges quality of practice over the quantity of poses: the practitioner and teacher engage in a mindful balancing of the number of poses a practitioner can manage given strength, time, and experience. To underscore this emphasis on quality and to make room for students' creativity with sources and ideas, I have over the years become more focused on how much I am expecting from students at each stage of the research process. So that students can slow down, strengthen their reading and analysis skills, and focus deeply on their own innovative contributions to a conversation, I have decreased the number of required sources in a researched composition, increased the variety of possibilities (as I discuss above), and emphasized more the drafting of the [shorter] annotated bibliography, which is an important reading and reflective practice. Indeed, there are assignments in which I want students to put scholarly sources in dialogue with one another, or in which I insist that they use more than one form of primary research; but I also open the door to sources found in popular media, both to honor them as sources and to give students the opportunity to integrate sources they might be able to process more readily. So that they may engage more deeply in collaborative discussion, I have decreased the number of students in a peer review group to 2–3, increased my expectations of the time they should take to reflect on one another's drafts, and asked students to address one another via peer review letters. While I see many benefits of face-to-face peer review as embodied pedagogy, I use the online discussion board for peer review, taking advantage of the medium and of the silence of this writing practice to embody as discursive subjects the students' drafts, the students' peer review letters, the students' posts in response to peer review letters, and also the virtual student bodies that are present as the authors and subjects of peer review letters and posts. In this practice, the Field—the students, their texts, and their materials conditions—come into view for observation, negotiation, and innovation.

Samsaya: Sitting in Doubt

But even with the Field in view, we must still acknowledge one of the greatest challenges in the praxis of both yoga and researched writing: the student's ability to accept not finding the answer, even if that's uncomfortable. Known in yogic texts as *samsaya*, doubt is, as Freeman (2010: 161) explains, "one of the major obstacles to yoga practice, and many, many practitioners give up because of [it]." He argues that "resolving doubt…means being able to accept the paradox of a situation without contracting so that you can draw your actions out of the very core of your being rather than having to act superficially according to a set belief or a dogma" (Freeman, 2010: 161). This idea of accepting paradox hearkens back to Zajonc's (2006: 2) fundamental description of contemplative practice: developing an ability to sit with contradiction so that the mind might become a "far suppler instrument." Those of us who write and teach writing know that writers come face-to-face with doubt. What if a student writer reaches the limits of the project in terms of ability, time, space, resources, or other conditions embodied in the process? What does the student writer make of this lack of resolution, this uncertainty, and the doubt (about process, product, identity) that are likely to arise? This doubt can further stifle the flow of creativity.

MacKenzie (2010: 1126) explores the ways in which yogic philosophy can shed light on uncertainty in the research process, acknowledging that "knowledge has long been the treasure at the end of the researching quest," which makes the lack of it feel rather like a failure. But yoga tells us that attachment to anything—things, people, knowledge itself—will hold us back from peace, and from *prakriti*, because we can forget which is which. Indeed, says Lord Krishna in the Gita (Prabhavananda and Isherwood, 2002: 103), the yogi who "mistakenly identifie[s]" *prakriti* and Brahman has got it all wrong. For it is in the acceptance that all is discourse, all is created, and all can thus be ever changing and temporary, that we begin to find our way to freedom. In research, MacKenzie (2010: 1131) calls this ability to sit comfortably in uncertainty a yogic "unknowing" that can breed growth:

> Pedagogical spaces are created when I admit that my work
> arises from my own attachment to those experiences of
> struggle or delight that have shaped my understanding of
> mysel(f)es.... It is likely through the release of attachment,
> that I may become lost; however loss is not something
> to be mourned, rather through loss I might discover and
> create open spaces.

Indeed, here in this discursive space of being or feeling lost, creativity may be found.

I argue that this uncertainty does not necessarily mean that a student should abandon a project or a topic. While I think Kirsch (2008–2009: 11) makes a salient point when she asserts that "our culture does not encourage... change of plan: we are taught to fight, carry on, pursue a goal single-mindedly, even if the process comes close to destroying us," and while obviously destruction of ourselves is not what we want, it can be valuable to ask students to sit and reflect for some time on the obstacles and doubt they are facing. In guiding them through this reflection, we might encourage them not to abandon their explorations once they hit the kind of silence (meaning, no new ideas come right away) that scares them, but rather to allow that silence to generate new inquiry and unfolding answers. The same "listen and wait" (p. 11) strategy that Kirsch advocates can be invaluable as we guide students toward a breakthrough in what might seem like stagnation.

In yoga, a practitioner often reaches a point in the practicing of a posture that seems to suggest there is no more progress to be made. For these moments, according to many Ashtangis who have traveled to Mysore, India, to practice, Ashtanga guru Sri K. Pattabhi Jois had these words: "Practice, and all is coming." These words can resonate for all writing teachers and students who are able to find the *asana*, the stillness, and wait for the breath to create more space and the tiniest spark of innovation that opens the mind and body just a bit more. In students' researched writing, we as teachers—whether we practice *asana* or not—can help students to navigate the boundedness and boundlessness of their minds, to draw creatively from the inside and the outside, and to synthesize what they uncover into new knowledge, only then to discover that they still come face-to-face with uncertainty. The uncertainty doesn't mean that they haven't learned anything, that they haven't properly filled the container of the assignment's body, or that they have researched or written inadequately. Rather, by engaging in an embodied practice of research, which includes the condition of not-knowing, they have cultivated creativity in opening an opportunity for others to ask questions, to continue the quest which they themselves have then joined. This opening of inquiry is, at its heart, yogic.

References

Archibald, O. (2009) Representation, ideology, and the form of the essay. *Writing & Pedagogy* 1: 11–36.

Baurain, B. (2011) Teaching, listening, and generative silence. *Journal of Curriculum Theorizing* 27(3): 89–101.

Bawarshi, A. (2003) *Genre and the Invention of the Writer: Reconsidering the Place of Invention in Composition.* Logan, Utah: Utah State University Press.

Bawarshi, A. and Reiff, M.J. (2010) *Genre: An Introduction to History, Theory, Research, and Pedagogy.* West Lafayette, Indiana: Parlor Press.

Bazerman, C. (1997) The life of genre, the life of the classroom. In W. Bishop and H. Ostrom (eds.) *Genre and Writing: Issues, Arguments, Alternatives* 19–26. Portsmouth, New Hampshire: Boynton/Cook, Heinemann.

Bowden, D. (1993) The limits of containment: Text-as-container in composition studies. *College Composition and Communication* 44: 364–379.

Brauer, D. (2009) Canon as palimpsest: Composition studies, genre theory, and the discourses of the humanities. *Composition Studies* 37: 9–30.

Dencev, H. and Collister, R. (2010) Authentic ways of knowing, authentic ways of being: Nurturing a professional community of learning and praxis. *Journal of Transformative Education* 8: 178–96.

Devitt, A. (2004) *Writing Genres.* Carbondale, Illinois: Southern Illinois University Press.

Devitt, A., Reiff, M. J. and Bawarshi, A. (2004) *Scenes of Writing: Strategies for Composing with Genres*. New York: Pearson/Longman.

Devoss, D. and Rosati, A. C. (2002) It wasn't me, was it? Plagiarism and the web. *Computers and Composition* 19(2): 191–203.

Freeman, R. (2010) *The Mirror of Yoga: Awakening the Intelligence of Body and Mind*. Boston: Shambhala.

Hall, M. and Archibald, O. (2008) Investigating contemplative practice in creative writing and education classes: A play (of practice and theory) in three acts. *International Journal for the Scholarship of Teaching and Learning* 2(1): 1–18.

Iyengar, B. K. S. (1979) *Light on Yoga*. New York: Schocken Books.

Kazan, T. S. (2005) Dancing bodies in the classroom: Moving toward an embodied pedagogy. *Pedagogy* 5: 379–408.

Kirsch, G. E. (2008–2009) Creating spaces for listening, learning, and sustaining the inner lives of students. *Journal of the Assembly for Expanded Perspectives on Learning* 14 (Winter 2008–2009): 56–67.

Lakoff, G. and Johnson, M. (1980) *Metaphors We Live By*. Chicago: The University of Chicago Press.

Larson, R. L. (1982) The "research paper" in the writing course: A non-form of writing. *College English* 44: 811–816.

MacKenzie, S. (2010) Disciplined (un)knowing: The pedagogical possibilities of yogic research as praxis. *The Qualitative Report* 15: 1124–1144.

Murray, D. (1982) Teaching the other self: The writer's first reader. *College Composition and Communication* 33: 140–147.

Pennington, M. (2010) Plagiarism in the academy: Towards a proactive pedagogy. *Writing & Pedagogy* 2: 147–162.

Prabhavananda, S. and Isherwood, C. (trans.) (2002) *Bhagavad-Gita: The Song of God*. New York: Penguin Group.

Prabhavananda, S. and Manchester, F. (trans.) (2002) *The Upanishads: Breath of the Eternal*. New York: Penguin Group.

Reddy, M. J. (1993) The conduit metaphor: A case of frame conflict in our language. In A. Ortony (ed.) *Metaphor and Thought* 164–201. New York: Cambridge University Press.

Reynolds, N. (2004) *Geographies of Writing: Inhabiting Places and Encountering Difference*. Carbondale, Illinois: Southern Illinois University Press.

Satchidananda, S. S. (trans.) (1990) *The Yoga Sutras of Patanjali*. Buckingham, Virginia: Integral Yoga Publications.

Slack, J. D., Miller, D. J. and Doak, J. (1993) The technical communicator as author: Meaning, power, authority. *Journal of Business and Technical Communication* 7: 12–36.

Stenberg, S. J. (2002) Embodied classrooms, embodied knowledges: Re-thinking the mind/body split. *Composition Studies* 30: 43–60.

Zajonc, A. (2006) Contemplative and transformative pedagogy. *Kosmos Journal* 1 (Fall/ Winter 2006): 1-3.

Henry Israeli

SWING

Once you pushed your daughter on this swing. Then
she learned to push herself. Then the urge to swing
diminished—you both stopped pushing.
Now when you push the swing, emptiness
pushes back. The child she once was, a ghost child.
Your own childhood, a ghost childhood.
Your mother never pushed a swing. It wasn't her style
to push a child in any way. With every blast
of radiation therapy, she retreated more deeply into
the ghost of herself. Once childhood is shed,
a long slow skinning that aches the way a phantom limb aches,
it can drive you to lunacy, the echo of colors
bleeding out to gray. This swing swings,
pushed by no one. Laughter brined
in autumn's breeze stopped years ago
although it took you this long to know.

Dawn Kane

Africa and a Sister School Journey

In Africa your senses open wide. From the swirl of language and vividness of color to the smell of animals, diesel, spice, roasting meat, and earth—there is no place like it. It all combines to create a sense of immediacy, which is very different from most of our everyday experiences. When you are there you can feel that it is a place not fully tamed.

Many have described Africa as a continent of extremes. On one hand, there is beauty; but on the other hand, there is grinding poverty. It seems unfair to just go for the former, and not do anything about the latter.

Still, it is hard to embrace an entire continent. One can begin with a community. If you go back to a place, it is not just an exotic faraway land that you got to see once, but also a community whose people you are connected to. You can reach out and touch that community—try to heal parts of it, and in turn, it heals parts of you. So, there is this little town in Kenya where I went back.

The beauty of Nanyuki, Kenya is that it is small enough to embrace. You can go there to climb Mt. Kenya, to safari in the Ol Pejeta Conservancy, to live and work, or to do some good. In this place it feels like one's efforts have some effect. They don't just get swallowed up. You can say, 'there, I did that one thing, and it helped.'

I went to Kenya the first time to participate in an Earthwatch expedition, Saving Kenya's Black Rhinos. Although I am a teacher, I went for the animals, not the people. The idea of tramping around to see the animals and not being confined to a jeep appealed to me. So I went for selfish reasons.

Then we arrived at Ol Pejeta. The bus turned into the conservancy, and the animals were everywhere. Zebra, giraffes, elephants, gazelles—they seem to be coming out of the woodwork. Although I had been nervous, in this place I relaxed and breathed in the air.

The Ol Pejeta Conservancy sits on 90,000 acres, or slightly more land than the Philadelphia area where I live. It is a protected place with a mission to safeguard endangered animals. However, the management has also embraced the idea that healthy communities are better able to participate in the conservation of animals.

I had a great time, and I only worried about the animals—until our outing on Community Day. This was the day that they packed all of the EW volunteers into a matatu, a minivan of sorts, and drove us around to visit people in the villages surrounding the conservancy. It was a chilly morning and we were tired from working on the black rhino project. Our first stop, Njoguini Primary School, brought the human reality back in a rush.

The sight of a rickety wood building with holes in the walls and a rusty tin roof brought me up short. Was this really a school? Inside this building we found full classrooms and children with inadequate clothing for the morning chill—a lot of children. The reading materials were old and yellowed with the edges curled up from use and time. I felt the return of that familiar feeling—the one that shouts in your ear, 'You must do something for these kids!'

We returned to the research camp having seen other schools that were happier and had more modern facilities, but I could not get Njoguini out of my mind. Nanyuki is at an elevation of over 6,500 feet and it gets quite cool at times. How could the students learn if they were cold? The vision of an uneven cracked dirt floor in a classroom where not every child had shoes wouldn't leave me.

I recalled a meeting where we had learned about the partnership between Ol Pejeta and Project Kenya Sister Schools, PKSS. Other schools that we had visited had real floors and libraries. These were PKSS schools and had a sister school in North America. I decided that I would present the idea at my school, Stephen Girard Elementary, in Philadelphia. If we could adopt Njoguini perhaps we could improve things for these students.

Upon my return I spoke to my principal, Mr. Thomas Koger, and he agreed immediately. After all, it is not hard to be a sister school. The staff of the sister school only had to send one cultural exchange project, such as friendly letters, and hold one fundraiser.

The journey for me was not only what happened in Africa, but also what happened in Philadelphia. My school in the city is a fairly large K-4 with more than 600 at-risk students. They are the ones normally on the receiving end of charity. Mr. Koger and I both thought that this was a chance for our kids to be the givers and we hoped that it would be an empowering experience for them, as well as a chance to learn about another culture.

The environment at Girard is fast-paced and sometimes chaotic. How was I going to get anyone's attention for this project? I tried a coin collection before the holidays. When I came around in the middle of a reading lesson looking for money, more than one staff member might have wanted to strangle me.

Still, the 3rd grade students and teachers were a great support in writing friendly letters to the children in Kenya. We had raised a few hundred dollars in the coin drive, but most of that was from teachers. We had fulfilled our obligation, but it seemed to me that something was missing—that is, until the dancers from a Canadian sister school visited Girard.

The students from the Langley School of Fine Arts were mostly tall, lithe dancers with ready smiles for our kids. Our students were convinced that they were Kenyan—we worked on some geography lessons later. The Langley dancers wowed our students and staff with their gorgeous dances and kindness.

Before they arrived, our computer teacher, Maria Yanga, designed and printed big posters to hang around the building proclaiming that we were a PKSS sister school. After their visit, while the buzz was still flowing through our building, another teacher, Domenick Maiorano, shared a basketball fundraising idea he had read about in the newspaper. Paulette Nichols, another 3rd grade teacher, had her students donate their self-published stories. Suddenly things were moving.

Things culminated with our late spring fundraiser, Helping Hoops for our Sister School. Our gym teacher, Jed Bordner, helped plan and manage age-appropriate basketball and hula-hoop activities for our students. Third graders created African-inspired art that they donated to an art sale. The students from the entire building raised money to participate in the helping hoops event. Tracy Teal's kindergarten classroom alone raised more than $165. We combined the art and bake sale with the hoops activities in a one-day blast. It seemed that everyone got involved and our little inner-city school raised nearly $800 on that day.

I knew that $800 goes a long way in Africa, so I was excited to return that summer to see what was happening at Njoguini Primary, and to meet the Canadian organizers of the PKSS program.

I arrived to Ol Pejeta one July day to find the volunteers were out. I waited in Pelican House, a beautiful country cottage with a thatched roof where the volunteers stay. The house overlooks a lake where birds roost and elephants come to drink. Hakuna Matata—no problem!

Elizabeth and Helen, who took care of us during our stay, put out a lovely lunch of fresh bread, cheese, tomatoes, and tea. To tell the truth, I wasn't 100% sure how I was going to be useful, so I was happy to be ignored for a while.

Later that evening the PKSS gang arrived. I had actually given them up for dead, but the PKSS days are long, as I was soon to find out. I immediately felt comfortable with the entire crew. Silvia Knittel sings to everyone she meets, and back home she teaches creative writing. Alison Stuart is the other half of this leadership duo. She's a wildlife biologist, vice principal, and science teacher. The others included Heather Hall, Sheridan Tochkin, Brittany Wallace, and Madeleine De Little, and that was just the volunteers at this house. There was another group of young volunteers staying in town who gave their time to the Nanyuki Orphanage.

The dinner that evening was typical, I would soon learn. There was a lot of food on a big long creaky wooden table. People were talking, eating, having a glass of this or that, and occasionally someone would get up and open the door so the bats could fly back outside where they allegedly belonged.

I quickly found that I would not really be working at my sister school and helping teachers as I had earlier imagined. The primary things on the PKSS to-do list involving visiting schools to interview students, teachers, and administrators about PKSS-funded projects, taking photographs and video that will illustrate what's been done, and finding out what still needs to be done.

There are other things that happen along the way; like going to buy cows for schools so they can make bio-gas for the science labs and provide milk for the students; and going to the secondhand market to buy shoes and coats for students and their families—not to mention beans, maize, and furniture.

I found that I basically would go along with everyone to visit all of the schools in the community. I took notes and pictures, and later wrote some stories about PKSS and the sister schools. It had been a while since I had done reporting work, and it felt good to dust off those old skills.

The highlight of my time with PKSS came, of course, when we visited Girard's sister school, Njoguini Primary School. I felt a little nervous as the car pulled into the yard. This, after all, was my reason for being here. As the children spilled out of the woodwork, I looked around in wonder. Was this the same place I had visited only the previous year? A whole new wing of classrooms was being built. There were greenhouses and water tanks, but more importantly there was a liveliness about the school that had seemed lacking on that last visit.

Surrounded by laughing children and friendly teachers, we toured the classrooms, old and new. We were treated to little ones showing off their English counting skills. We saw the trophy that the school had won for the most improved in the district, and finally we sang and we danced. It was a celebration that was joy-filled. I felt honored to be a part of it.

In reflecting back on my time working with the PKSS team, I recall the work, love, and compassion in the project, and also the laughter and fun. There are several memories that I add into my mental scrapbook alongside the Njoguini visits.

One of those was the day that Silvia announced that it was going to be an easy Sunday. We were only going to have lunch with one of our family's teachers and then visit Grandma Mary. Well, between the time Silvia said that in the morning and the time we got back to Pelican House, after 7 p.m. that evening, the PKSS crew had thought of 22 other urgent things we needed to do to further the program or just help someone out. That became the running joke. Oh, we don't have that much to do today! And everyone would roll their eyes.

On one occasion, we were driving to a school and passed a manyatta, or Samburu settlement. We saw a really beautiful young man and child. We chatted with them through our PKSS coordinator, Sylvester Loimaso, who happened to a Samburu himself. We made a plan to visit the next day and meet the family. One thing led to another and we made friends with the tribe, which led to a day of singing and dancing with them. Definitely, Kenya has its own brand of trail magic!

Other memories remind me of the work still to be done in this community, such as my first visit to Joel's house. Joel is a student who came to his principal at Sweetwaters Secondary School for help because he was having trouble studying at home. School administrators followed up with a home visit and promptly contacted PKSS.

It was not a wonder that Joel couldn't study. The family's mud and thatch house was small and partially destroyed by fire. A previous home had been blown in by a storm. There were 9 children and two adults trying to make do with this inadequate shelter. It was cold on that first visit. PKSS had contracted for a simple new house of corrugated tin, which was going up alongside the old house. Joel introduced his brothers and sisters, many barefoot and shivering in the cool air. The older children seemed excited to have visitors, while some of the younger ones hid behind Joel and his mother. After this visit, Silvia and Alison agreed that it was time to make a trip to the secondhand market.

The secondhand market is another vivid slice of Africa. This colorful place extended outside of town and into neighboring fields. Even on a weekday afternoon the place was busy with people circulating through simple wooden stalls to purchase everything from blankets to shoes and socks. The shoe sellers mostly spread their wares out on tarpaulins in the fields. I was amazed by the sheer quantity of stuff. I understand now why many charitable organizations, when responding to a crisis, don't want our clothes. It seems that our old clothes are already there.

All of these memories are part of the reason that I plan to return again. Africa and its wilds thrill, but it is more than that. It's a chance to be my best self. I am a part of the PKSS team, and my senses are awake to a new world. Sometimes it is discouraging when we cannot fix everything, but to be able to make a difference in a faraway corner of Kenya is not bad.

Lynn Levin

The Ask Sandwich

The TSA lady at Newark Airport had a nice touch, and Josie enjoyed the pat down. The blue gloves slid under her arms, along her sides, down one leg, then the other. They searched, discerned. They pleased with just the right amount of pressure. Josie thanked the TSA lady, who nodded back with very professional brown eyes.

In bed last night in Robert's apartment, it was their sixth time together, Josie had attempted the "ask sandwich," something she'd read about in a woman's magazine. First she told him how nice his cologne smelled and trailed her fingers playfully down his arm. That was the first slice of bread. Then she said she'd really love it if he rubbed her back. That was the sandwich filling. She would have praised him and reciprocated generously, which would have been the other slice of bread.

Instead he said, "You're really bossy, aren't you?"

Sheesh. She'd only done what the magazine had instructed. Josie curled away from Robert, then on his hard mattress, she recovered a little backbone. "I don't consider that so bossy."

"Well, I do." The atmosphere in the room wadded up like paper.

Pulling her carry-on bag, striding in beige pumps, Josie made her way to her gate. She tried to wall off the Robert fiasco and focus on the nursing conference in Atlanta. She was looking forward to presenting her paper on pressure sores but hoped her seatmate would not inquire about her work. She'd about had it with folks who squinted and scrunched their faces when she told them about her field. Oh, you mean bedsores, they'd say using the old term. Didn't know they were that important. Well, they can be fatal, she'd retort. She would educate them a little about patients who were stuck in bed, about reduced blood supply, friction, cell death, complications. And that pretty much ended the conversation.

At first, she'd seen a future with Robert. They agreed on politics and comedians, hated remakes of classic films, and pork pie hats.

Maybe she should try being old school, passive. What was she anyway, a thirty-three-year-old sensualist who only thought of touch? And she wasn't exactly a winner in the dating game—one six-month relationship and a lot of first dates with few follow-ups. Was it her or Match.com?

On the way to her gate, Josie passed a Hudson News. An array of cover girls beckoned her, fringed by come-on headlines: *Drive him wild tonight. Ten types of sex to try at least once. Better orgasms now.* Did everything have to be about the sack? Well, she would like to have some great sex before she died. Addicted to the promises on the cover, she bought a copy of *Cosmopolitan.*

Josie's seatmate was a fortyish man in a blue short-sleeved shirt and Phillies baseball cap who said his name was Solly.

Josie said her name was Mimi.

Solly smelled freshly showered and had a dimple in his chin. They chatted about the weather and airplane coffee. When he asked her what she did for a living, she told him she booked models for fashion ads. With a light heart, she fibbed her way through a conversation about beauty, dieting, and divas. She'd met the famous Kate Upton. Yes, Karlie Kloss really was that skinny.

Solly said he didn't know who those women were, but he complimented Josie on her big career.

"Sometimes those girls are so beautiful and sexy they're unreal," said Josie.

"I like the real type," said Solly with a playful grin. "Real gals, like you." As he sipped his airplane coffee, Josie spied no wedding ring. The two laughed a lot. Each time she said something he found fetching, he touched her shoulder. He had a big paw, but his touch was gentle and warm. It would have been nice to get to know him better. When it turned out they were both from central Jersey, Solly asked if he could have her phone number. Could he call her sometime?

This Josie now desperately wanted, but her wardrobe of lies made it impossible. She gulped and rubbed her nose. She almost knocked her coffee off the little depression in her tray table. "I guess with your schedule that would be hard to arrange," he said.

"I do travel a lot." Solly opened his laptop and began to study some documents. Josie paged through her *Cosmo.* Her head felt hot. She was very cross with herself, whoever she was.

Joanna Lyskowicz

Grass Should be Equally Green on the Other Side of the Fence—Improve your Translating Skills

While I doubt that you ultimately want to be a translator, I am sure that if you have taken a language class, or at least tried to impress someone with a foreign language, you had to write something and you used a dictionary. I can bet that it was one of those online dictionaries that you can access anywhere, even from your phone. From your phone? I wouldn't be surprised if your grandma wouldn't get what you were saying while trying to explain to her what type of dictionary you had used to look up the word. It's unbelievable how we do things in the 21st century.

From my experience, most students don't own a hardcover dictionary but they are best friends with Google translator. It is an abusive relationship. Today's student tends to reject the paper dictionary that, when found on the shelf, looks abandoned, forgotten, often very dusty, with yellowed-due-to-age pages. It might have never been used by anyone and spent its entire life sitting on the shelf. Although it is not the case in my house, sadly in today's high-tech world, the paper language dictionary is disappearing. The Internet changed everything and I'm not sure it's for the better.

The Internet has become an automatic library for all the language learners. When you need to look up a word in a foreign language, you go online. You can look up the same word in many languages within seconds and without any cost to you. You don't even need to lift your arm to reach a book from the shelf. Right at your fingers, at any time and place, your online dictionary is waiting to be used. But be wary! Such a resource can feel like water for someone stranded in the desert, but it may actually be more harmful than useful for the naïve and inexperienced language student.

Writing in a foreign language is more than just copying your thoughts from your native language. There is a long list of things that you need to check before the text created in the foreign language will be a reflection of what you meant to write. To detach from your own language while writing in a foreign one can be a daunting task. If you are aware of the differences between your native tongue and the target language, you will be able to make the appropriate modifications and, in the end, you will get what your intention was. The translator (here I mean a novice writing in a foreign language) has to be aware that not everything can be translated literally. Different languages have different structures. In order to bring the same sense into another language, you sometimes have to flip the sentence upside-down. Idioms, proverbs, regional dialects, and slang cannot be translated without making an effort and looking deeper into the context. When translating these types of words and phrases, you cannot just look one up in the dictionary. One word can have several meanings and translations. A dictionary is only a tool. You are the manager who needs to know how to work the sentence. You must use all you know about the target language.

Let's see how it works with this simple example.

It's 5 o'clock.

In Spanish: *Son las 5 cinco.* In French: *Il est 5 (cinq) heures.* In Portugues: *São 5 (cinco).* In Italian: *Sono le 5 (cinque).* In German: *Es ist 5 (fünf)* Uhr. In Russian: 5 часоb *(5 chasov).* In Greek: Είναι πέντε ώρα. *(einei pente ora).*

Notice that while in English, French, Portuguese, German, and Greek, we tell time using a singular verb "to be," it is, in Spanish and Italian, the verb in its plural form: they are. It will change and look alike in other languages at 1 o'clock: Es la 1(una) in Spanish and É l'una in Italian. In Russian, however, the verb is not even part of the phrase.

Have you also noticed that in Spanish and Italian before the number stating the hour, there is a plural feminine definite article? It's a long name for something so short, but it is a part of this structure and cannot be omitted.

Making little notes of this kind while you are navigating between languages will make you a better language learner. There is no automatic translator and your friend Google will disappoint you big time.

The bigger the difference between two languages, the bigger mistakes can arise from literal translation. In case you already know one of the languages with the same roots, I suggest translating from that language into the new one that you are learning instead of English. You'll be less likely to make a mistake. Learn to not assume anything and do your research carefully.

I will never forget one of the first compositions that I read after I began working as a Spanish professor. The topic of the composition was "Music in My Life." As much as I was familiar with all styles of music, I got stuck because I had never heard of the music genre that in Spanish sounded like "el salto de la cadera." I felt ignorant not knowing that style until my Mexican friend came to the rescue and enlightened me. The student had literally translated Hip Hop as "jump of the hip." It gave us a good laugh and an anecdote to share, but there is a lesson for you to learn from this. Don't translate internationally recognized names of anything: jazz, soul, tango, salsa, or even pizza will sound the same in any language. It should remain in its original language and everyone will comprehend it.

As I mentioned before, the list of corrections to check is long, but here is one last easy thing to remember. As a Drexel student, you often want to share the fact that you are part of the co-op program. While in this community everyone knows what you mean, some people definitely won't, especially foreigners. If you want to use an acronym or abbreviation, you have to realize that whatever it stands for may have its own equivalent in the foreign language, or you will have to explain in full words the meaning of it. For examples, UN (United Nations) has its acronym as ONU in Romance languages and GPA (Grade Point Average) should be explained as *Promedio de calculaciones* or *Promedio Escolar* as, in Spanish, there is no such acronym to refer to a grade average. Co-op translates as *cooperativa*, but even better would be to explain that it is *una profesional experiencia cooperativa* and this way it will be clear what program your university offers that others don't.

Writing in a foreign language can be a challenge, but if you take your time it could be fun and pay off with all the knowledge you gain in the process. There is a Spanish proverb, *Lo que de prisa se escribe, lento se lee,* which means that what was written in hurry, requires time to be comprehended. My advice it is to stay away from online dictionaries until you have learned some crucial rules of the target language. Also, maybe dust off one of those forgotten dictionaries on your grandma's shelf.

Harriet Levin Millan

Hang up

A thin bent rod comes out of the frame.
There is no painting
in the frame,
just space penned in,
scarce and hardly there,
which is our awareness of it,
      white-knuckled, narrow, concealed. There must be something else there—
        some current visible in a more electric realm of filling
    lungs
with big gulps of air to withstand the rising shock.
                             An inside
out world of drenched skin
the full length of the whitewater,
the viewpoint both emptiness and "dependence upon the support."
The crumbling schist at the confluence of rich salt springs,
where the artist,
abandoned,
knows deeply the demands of her work,
stretches her frames to over life-size,
      winds cloth over wood and steel
to wrap them
in the configurement
of mind
where the materials accrete.
Not a bench,
    just a couple
of slats of wood
nailed
    into a rusted girder.

Not a drawing, just lines
without shape
beribboning a page.
Not a self, just gradations of light and dark
derived from the combinations.
The quiver in your voice
over the line
      as I lean in
hearing it, not hearing it

into my ear—beating of the drum,
oscillation of the hairs,
ridged from having held it.

Harriet Levin Millan

Urban Myth

A projection straight from my roiling mind's swamp:
at an intersection in Palm Beach Gardens, a fourteen foot long alligator
stops traffic, its tail swinging out from behind its body
not thrashing so much as flat-bottomed squiggling,

viewed through windshields—accelerated, mechanized.
I cannot deny it. No longer paranoia but a real
reeling monster equipped with a toothy smile
and tender oscillating eyes.

Before my encounter I was flipping through pages,
seeing whose address I'd come to by chance.
A gentle wisp could proffer a shortcut
to sainthood, build a nest of a name pinpricked with light.

You said we should talk. A lot of things get said over the phone,
but never in person, the cord buckling.
Is *hi, how are you?* truly preferable to that surge
of sweet dark Ghirardelli cut into squares,

confection infiltrating our defenses?
Garish, cartoonish, festooned in scales, claws, and teeth—.
ours, salient. This is what saturates the sky at sunset,
a twinge's blood red hue. Prowess merges

with the throttle of diesels, my stop and go attempt
at wrestling an instinct only to tie rope around its jaw
and trap it back into its cage—still reeling from the impact,
it brought me to my knees.

Anne-Marie Obajtek-Kirkwood

Pat, Dave and the others ... by Hélèna Villovitch

We owe Hélèna Villovitch, a multifaceted artist whose output encompasses painting, photography, graphic design, experimental cinema, literary criticism for the magazine Elle, children's books, short texts in several collections (L'Entreprise, Naissances, Plumes et dentelles[1]), a documentary essay: Le bonheur par le shopping[2], and a literary work characterized by fragmentation. It starts with Je pense à toi tous les jours[3] (1998), a series of twelve short, autofictional texts where Villovitch sometimes poses in very humorous photographs; Pat, Dave et moi[4] (2000), a novel portraying trendy youths of the eighties; Petites soupes froides[5] (2003), a collection of thirteen short stories on job insecurity and the difficulty of succeeding as an artist; Dans la vraie vie[6] (2005), another collection of eight short-stories centered on professional difficulties; and finally L'Immobilier[7] (2013), a collection of short stories in which housing reflects precarious success or deep dissatisfaction

Recurring themes can be spotted in these six texts ranging from 1998 to 2013, such as the art world of exhibitions, or avant-garde artists who cannot prevail and often drift into company work. This leads Villovitch to write funny stories and scenes in which she practices in turn amused irony, self-deprecating and fierce humor, accompanied by a critique of widespread social cynicism. School graduates or students in search of a job in Pat, Dave et moi or Parisians in their thirties or forties combining professional and personal insecurity in Petites soupes froides, Dans la vraie vie et L'Immobilier, all inspired by current events, and Villovitch's own life, form a contemporary social fresco where the allegedly autonomous individual is the victim of a relentless market society. Such are some of the leitmotivs that the study of Villovitch's writings will attempt to identify, showing that behind the humor pierces a real disenchantment.

Le Bonheur par le shopping, with its ironic title, is a collection of short stories of contemporary society or fragments of mercantile culture driven

---

1 None of Villovitch's books have been published in English. The titles of these collections, if translated, are: The Firm, Births, Feathers and Lace.
2 Happiness Through Shopping.
3 I think about you every day.
4 Pat, Dave, and I.
5 Small Cold Soups.
6 In Real Life.
7 Real Estate.

by the pleasure Villovitch experiences observing and describing customers' behavior in a Parisian department store. Consumerism expresses itself in diverse cultural styles, but also a copycat attitude, which Villovitch satirizes. In Convertibles an argument thus arises between a man and his partner: "If you love this stuff, it means that our relationship is based on a terrible misunderstanding"[8] says one of them (11). Villovitch points out in turn to a generation-conflict for torn jeans (17), opposite reactions--the "ultimate punishment" of finding the Do-It-Yourself department in the store-basement (27), or unmatched euphoria in the high tech one (83-84, 87, 88, 91-92), feelings of body shame (17) or other distress when a customer gets excited over a lilac-colored pullover and then feels anxious about not finding a skirt and matching shoes. Many do not know what to buy despite a spouse's advice given over a cell phone (27-30). Some are poorly served like the lady who was sold twenty-eight door-handles with no screws to fix them on the eve of a weekend (31-33). At the health and beauty department, Villovitch laughingly wonders whether it is "better to be beautiful and rebellious, than ugly and super ugly? Be Catherine Deneuve rather than a second-hand Catherine Deneuve?"[9] (37). Following trends generates fascination for hair products in a customer who instantly swallows the advertising message in the product description: "I'm terribly broke but I must absolutely buy a special nutritional intense repair pre-shampoo for brittle and damaged hair, a bigger hair-volume treatment, a vitamin detangling spray, a color enhancer, and a styling mousse which makes hair smooth while providing exceptional shine for a natural effect," she says (39-40). Close enough to this mocking style exercise, the text on "nutraceuticals" justifies food purchases for their therapeutic properties. What follows is a list of purchases with three pompous and therefore amusing examples: "I buy garlic because it reduces cholesterol. (...) I buy black radishes because it is low in calories and against arthritis and rheumatism. I buy eggs as animal protein is very well assimilated by our body" (68). For the purchase of a CD, Villovitch describes with robotic precision all the subsequent actions that lead to the purchase: " I look at the CDs, I choose a CD, I look for a salesman, I find a salesman, he gives me a ticket, etc." (83). This maniacal juxtaposition of subject, verb, and direct object makes the list hilarious and the purchase a disaster. The computer, so useful to Villovitch for screen shots, layouts, corrections and editions of texts, writing of articles, filmic and literary creations, is praised by her as a driven customer but she is aware of being the victim of a vicious circle because, she writes: "The harder I work, the more equipment I buy, the more equipment I have, the more I work," and also, "My short film wins an award at the Bochum festival, and I use some of the money

8 All translations of Villovitch's excerpts are mine.
9 A very famous actress of French cinema.

to buy a new memory card to increase the autonomy of my camera (which I also use as a movie camera)" (89).

According to Villovitch, happiness is generally not to be found on the shelves of a store because, for lack of time, she goes through it very hurriedly and often pays a high price for "clothes that are not much fun" (21). When she was young, she and her friends "would spend whole days" (21) buying for fun "incredible and ridiculous clothes" (20), and "for very cheap" (21) at the Flea Markets of Montreuil,[10] Boulevard Barbès,[11] the Emmaus Companions,[12] or the Salvation Army. To look psychedelic or pop "was a lot of work," she adds. "I would tease my hair, wear red mini-skirts, white boots and little jackets with gold buttons" (20).

In the art and culture department, "keen on encouraging an author full of talent but still not known well enough," she claims to have moved "a few copies of her works onto the table of the best selling books, covering that way books by Christine Angot and Virginia Despentes"[13] and having purchased Portraits crachés[14] by Yves Pagès to steal some ideas (52).

With Le Bonheur par le shopping, Villovitch makes fun of and disparages the "belly of Paris,"[15] where the market economy levels people and lifestyles and goods flow. Villovitch's short stories and novel discredit labor organization in postindustrial society that has been affecting large masses of people for decades.

Pat, Dave et moi narrates Villovitch's years of depression (from 19 to 20 years old) (19) following an emotional breakdown and an admission refusal to the Ecole nationale supérieure des Arts Décoratifs, due to her rude and provocative dossier proving by A plus B that "Everybody fucks everybody else." As a result of this double failure, Villovitch begins "to watch herself (...) in the mirror" (21), announcing the main theme of her films and many of her short stories, self-portrait reaffirming an identity subject to the laws of the instantaneous and the precarious. Having come back from Paris to live in the suburbs with her father, "the exact opposite of David Bowie" (51), she

---

10 A city in the suburbs of Paris.

11 A very multicultural part of Paris, in the 18th Arrondissement.

12 Close to the Goodwill stores.

13 Christine Angot and Viriginie Despentes are very successful contemporary women writers.

14 Spitting Images.

15 Le Ventre de Paris is a novel by Zola about the place in Paris where food used to be supplied and sold in the 19th century, hence in extension commercial places.

is friendly with a bunch of young punks, jobless and moneyless (38) high schoolers or students, "depressed" (33) as she is, very individualistic (33), wearing extravagant headdresses and clothes, spending their time hanging out in coffee shops or dancing in nightclubs, dreaming of becoming famous while their parents encourage them to find summer jobs, training internships or worse, to apply for unemployment. "Andy Warhol foresees that in the future there will be no more famous people, but everyone will be famous for a quarter of an hour in his life." (45) Faced with such hopes, getting back to drawing and then painting is a miracle for Villovitch who would like to consider her future as follows: "Having new ideas, this is how I want to spend my time" (65). At the end of that year she shoots her first filmed self-portrait entitled "I'm 20 years old." The camera placed in front of her "serves as a mirror with the difference that it does not send her reflection back but absorbs her face" (87-88). She films a makeup session which leads to the reconfiguration of her facial features into "a network of crosses and red and black triangles." The budding artist is ready to go back and live in Paris.

Je pense à toi tous les jours is a collection of short stories on some personal events of Villovitch's around the year 1993. One of them, however, goes back to the year 1984, when she had her single internship directly related to her professional training at the Ecole Boulle.[16] This three-month internship, paid at minimum wage, was followed by a short period of freelance (33) at the end of which she is coldly dismissed, however great her enthusiasm to realize her "new ideas" (27). There is no longer a question of working full-time in the field of design, arts, and crafts. Becoming "rich and [above all] famous" is now the subject of impossible dreams while she is working in various companies filling temporary administrative tasks, with three-month contracts, and the hope of getting a six-month one, to finally hitting the jackpot by getting a long-term contract, or working at home in front of her computer. When she has time, she runs arts projects she must promote. Running openings, cocktail parties and dinners in eccentric attire is snake oil. How indeed to be recognized without knowing anyone? How to be known by "people who might be interested in her work" (125)? The challenge is important for her when she goes "from job to job without the time to apply for unemployment between two missions" (101).

With humor based on the dysfunctional relationship between cause and effect, Villovitch recalls her fragmented professional course, unmistakably mirroring her emotional instability. Her life companions come and go, never beautiful, intelligent and earning a good living at the same time, often "good for nothing" (55) until she meets her current boyfriend Jan Peters, a German

---

16 An advanced public school of fine arts, crafts and applied arts in Paris.

filmmaker with whom she shot several experimental films, and to whom she dedicates this collection of stories Je pense à toi tous les jours.

Petites soupes froides has thirteen stories about people in their thirties. With humor, Villovitch reminds us that she has not reached the "fame" of a Stephanie of Monaco, but that all things considered, she believes to have "done as well as she has" (7-8). In her exhibition, a certain Michel invites her to present her film A ma place[17] (1993), a series of seventeen self-portraits of herself made by girls and boys she asked to imitate her telling her life (65), each having to begin with the words: "My name is Helena Villovitch."[18] Self-portraying continues to interest her, and over several years, she experiments shooting herself and reusing the same film she carefully rewinds in the dark so that "the replicas follow (...) next to the original "(86). Satisfied with this intellectual and artistic distance, she amusedly states: "I stand beside myself" (86). This kind of biographical work is the opposite of the videographer Valerie Mréjen's who is interested in the emptiness of language. For her work Portraits filmés (14 souvenirs),[19] Villovitch tells us in Moi aussi[20] (113-115) that Mréjen, when asking her to recall a memory (that she will invent), imposed the colors of her clothing, shortened her text and made a "creature" of her (115). Leaving Mréjen, Villovitch told her that later she "would love to be an artist too" (115), but it is clear that Villovitch is joking and does not think for a moment of imitating her. She succeeds and makes her way, not in the field of video, drawing and painting where the "dampers" are commonplace, but as a novelist and essayist.

Dans la vraie vie brings together ten short stories whose common feature is the gloom generated by the professional and emotional instability of a whole generation of people in their thirties and forties. There are few stories told in the first person, few artists, but groups of employees in Parisian companies, some of which have in hand permanent contracts, while others less fortunate are sacked after temporary three-months, three days or even a few hours contracts. Qu'est-ce que tu vas faire[21] (35-50), a masterpiece of the genre, depicts the woes of a woman for whom the brevity of her professional contracts is consistent with that of her love affairs. "Two months after her arrival in a first company, she signs a fixed term contract of three months." Just at the time when this contract is not renewed, her boyfriend Jacques

---

17 In my position.
18 http://www.paris-art.com/exposition-art-contemporain/%C3%A0-ma-place/villovitch-helena/126.html
19 Filmed Portraits (14 Memories): http://valeriemrejen.com/folio/?skill-type=videos
20 Me too.
21 What are you going to do?

leaves her. Thereafter, she houses an unemployed person named Karim while working in an industrial area for a company that gives her her contract on her last day of work. What luck! She can then benefit from a cafeteria card expiring the very evening. Karim moves out, sets up a business and promises to hire only long-term contracts. During the three days of her third contract, she corrects accounting errors, and establishes a relationship with a temporary employee "based on immediate pleasure" (49). To end it all, she is given four hours of work in the suburbs. On the train back, " she has sex in the toilet with a "blue-eyed, stringy-haired, wearing sneakers" passenger. This completes the demonstration of a depressing experience. In another story, even employees' vacations are a letdown as they arrive at the Grand Canyon by night. In Dans la vraie vie,[22] a beautiful young employee is deceived by the sex of the person she falls in love with on the Internet, but if it is "somebody great," it can be but a man (104). Speed-dating gives Villovitch the opportunity to invent a flood of questions impossible to ask for lack of time. The last story describes a woman who, after failing a job interview and a series of misadventures, finds herself in a train station with no money, sipping a beer with a man without shoes … Insecurity thus has an end but what a disenchanted one!

Villovitch's characters' financial vulnerability also shows in their places of residence. A Paris tiny maid room, located on the seventh floor under the roof, houses students and unemployed in most of her stories. In 1984, her mother gave her "1,000 francs to survive in a maid's room" (Je pense à toi tous les jours, 27). As a dwelling, a studio, an apartment where one lives alone but more often in cohabitation, is also a workplace for Villovitch as a freelance artist and writer.

L'Immobilier depicts individual paths based on the characters' residences. Living in 11 square meters is acceptable for Villovitch as a young student at the Ecole Boulle, but forces her to draw on the floor for lack of space (11), as a young man she meets notes: "It is small" (12). She then moves into a "damp" studio (22). Subsequently, "[she] moves in and out in a manner that witnesses an increase of the number of square meters on which she has an influence over the years" (28). Because of the housing crisis, living alone is impossible for the badly matched couple of the story Chacun chez soi (36-51), whose wife is off on Internet dating sites as compensation. In the short story J'ai quitté Tom, being over-crowded plays havoc. Not parting with "Tom" could have been considered if "[their] apartment had been better designed." Since it did not have any entrance-hall, the "office-lounge-dining room" was used as a passage between "[their] private cell and the outside world" (66), preventing Villovitch from working without being disturbed by Tom's long gossip and

22 In Real Life.

proofs of love whenever he would leave the apartment (67). Had they had a child, they would have had to make love "balanced on a table, a chair or the toilet-bowl", and end with "hate for this offspring who would have reduced their precious meters square" (69).

The Idéal pour investisseur story traces the journey of two friends who met at the " Palais de la femme," a residence for young provincial students in Paris. As "paying rent is throwing money out the window" (31), they buy a cubby to "invest" instead of "squandering" (32). Once the loan is repaid, they embark on investing and being the fleeting owners of a "crooked two-room place," then of several rooms they had rented, later former offices they had had transformed into "lofts" (33), or small areas turned into "small flats." Finally their land revenue is tenfold bigger in the Cyclades, where they acquire a hotel and underpay their staff. The moral of this frantic race to profit: their real estate plans imprison them in bitter regret of missed transactions like the possession of a " Mykonos luxurious thalassatherapy"(35).

Villovitch's entire literary production is characterized by unfailing humor, a willingness to give some space to the postmodern frail elements of society, to the individual as subject of the market economy and bearer of societal changes. Her critical stance towards herself but also towards the global profiteers honors her and makes her an important witness of the increasingly severe economic debacle.

Bibliography

Pagès, Yves. Petites natures mortes au travail. Paris: Editions Verticales, 2000.

Villovitch, Hélèna. Je pense à toi tous les jours. Paris: Editions de l'Olivier, 1998.

--, Pat, Dave & moi. Paris: Editions de l'Olivier, 2000.

--, Petites soupes froides. Paris: Editions de l'Olivier, 2003.

--, Dans la vraie vie. Paris: Editions de l'Olivier, 2005.

--, Le bonheur dans le shopping. Paris: Maren Sell Editeurs, 2005.

--, L'immobilier. Paris: Editions Verticales, 2013.

Films by Héléna Villovitch

Villovitch, Hélèna. Le cercle de mes relations (12 min, 16 mm, 1991).

Quatre portraits miroirs (7 min, 16 mm, 1993).

Moi, moi, moi & moi (5 min, super-8, 1993).

Je tricote (8 min, 16 mm, 1995).

Ne regardez pas (3 min., super-8, 1998).

La vérité (3 min, super 8, double écran, 1998).

Vanité (boucle en super-8, 1999).

À ma place (11 min., béta SP, 2002).

Helena Villovitch, Jan Peters. Bye bye tiger, film (2005).

Don Riggs

Serial Poet

One potential limitation to writing sonnets almost exclusively is boxing yourself in a "small poem" aesthetic. I was once in a workshop led by Diane Wakoski in which she exploded over "workshop poems" that fit nicely on the page, were well-worked and critically unassailable, but lacked the kind of expansiveness of reach afforded by longer poems. Later, like about two decades later, I read the entry on the "Modern Long Poem" in the *New Princeton Encyclopedia of Poetry and Poetics*, and found that many recent poets "of length" attained their size through an agglutinative process in which one poem is followed by another poem in such a way as to imply that the two poems are now stanzas, of sorts, in what is now a longer poem. Hence, once Ezra Pound decided on his Canto structure, he kept on adding to *The Cantos* for the rest of his life, until he hit—I think—number 116 ("I cannot make it cohere").

What I find is that I will write a 14-line poem on a subject, then, feeling that more needs to be said, I'll write another 14-line poem right afterwards. Often I will submit these someplace as a double sonnet or, as most people don't recognize double sonnets when they are confronted by them, simply as a "departure from my customary sonnetary practice."

Little do they know that I still got there by writing individual sonnets, then laying them side by side, "like well-dressed stone," as the *Odyssey* has it (in translation, of course). One of my favorite instances of transcending the individual sonnet length by doing a series was when I was feeling particularly antlike, in relation to the *Fable of the Grasshopper and the Ant*.

Let me admit right away that I always identified with the Grasshopper in this one. This is my translation from the *Fables* of Jean de la Fontaine:

Grasshopper and Ant
A grasshopper, singing all summer,
found the cupboard was bare
when the winter winds came.
She knocked on the door
of her neighbor the ant,
asking if she could please borrow
a crumb or a sliver
of grub or of midge?
"I'll pay you back, animal's word,

both the principal and with interest!"
The ant's no soft touch:
that's the least of her faults!
"How did you spend your summer?"
she asked. "I sang and I fiddled,"
her long-leggéd friend said,
"and wove my words in
with the warm southwest wind!"
"You sang?" said the ant.
"Okay; so now you can dance!"

My self-perception, developed over the course of many years in grade school, college, and graduate school, was of the last-minute essay-writer, the three-in-the-morning epiphany intellectual on the morning the paper was due, of the *gaudeamus igitur* school. That is, the grasshopper. As a result, my grade average was often widely erratic, depending upon whether the particular courses required slow and steady drudge work or sudden brilliant intuitive insights. As a result, moving right along in a cause-and-effect chain that, like the mills of the gods, grinds exceedingly slow but exceedingly fine, I find that now I must do the careful, meticulous antwork that I avoided for years, and do it over and over and force undergraduates to do it as well, as a purgatorial penance for my youthful insouciance. So, that's the dynamic I explored in the following series (with my commentaries inserted between sonnets):

1. The Educated Grasshopper
They say that if you put a grasshopper
in a jar, he will learn that he can jump
only as far as the invisible
but impenetrable surface will allow. Even if you let him out in the
wide world after a while, his leaps will always be limited intrinsically
by what he learned in that little environment, where his horizons were brought forcibly against his most delicate man-
dibles and his forehead was battered by
something he couldn't predict would be there,
and even the broad sky was distorted
by the vector of a translucent curve.

Number one comes from what probably is an urban, or rural, myth that someone told me over after-dinner drinks once. I myself have never experimented with raising young grasshoppers, least of all in jars, but it seemed like such a forceful analogy that I grasped it and applied it to my life. Please notice that my self-imposed formal restraints include having exactly ten syllables per line; this means that here, instead of coming up with other wording to match the lines exactly, as I ordinarily do, I allow the line break to chop the word in half. Someone suggested that I break the word at the end of every line, but that struck me as being the foolish consistency of which Emerson speaks.

2. Fall

The grasshopper everybody admires—
that Romantic, sky-leaper, denizen
of summer, surrounded by supple stalks
of froth-topped grasses that dance with the wind.
Is it the grasshopper who fiddles, or
is it his cousin the cicada? No
matter: we're not entomologizing
here, we're ruminating about fables:

the grasses, much more lithe than the rigid
oak, still fall to the scythe, the cicada's
cadences fall with the flamboyant leaves,
and the grasshopper's balletic legs seize
up, grinding at the joints, his carapace
a hollow husk. The ant wins in the end.

In this one I decided to leave behind the behavioral conditioning of the first sonnet and to celebrate the ideal of the grasshopper. It is flavored a little with memories I have of tall grasses from the property around my elementary school; I loved to pluck one of them and fiddle around with it, imagining the busby-like seed head of the stalk to be the uniform hat of one of the guards of the Wicked Witch of the West—all *WE are / we OWE her*—this practice of mine gave me the nickname "the Fiddler" in elementary school. After the turn, in the sestet, I return to the formican reality principle.

3. Sparrow

The ant wins in the end. The sparrow, drunk
on pyracantha berries, smacks against
the living room's plate-glass window, neck snapped,
thuds on the lawn. An hour later, ants
form a two-way assembly line, bucket
brigade lugging the blood and whatever
other furniture they can dismantle
from the body the sparrow's abandoned.

This was no skylark, connecting this earth
with the realm of the Luminosities,
occasional Bridge that made daring raids
on the Infinite. This was a bundle
of feathers and twigs for gleaners to pick
apart as grammarians grade papers.

For a brief time, I have switched into the mode of a "Crown" of sonnets, where the last line of one sonnet becomes the first line of the next; the final sonnet, the seventh or the fourteenth, depending upon your ambition, ends with the first line of the first sonnet. I don't go that far here, though. "The ant wins in the end" seemed like too good a sentence to waste in one sonnet, even though it does give it some good closure.

The scene of the bird having broken its neck on the picture window comes from a house I visited regularly in Norfolk, Virginia: there, birds would eat the berries of the pyrecantha bush which, particularly in the autumn, when they would ferment, would make the birds drunk. Not seeing that the large opening was in fact a slab of glass, a bird would confidently zoom right into it. The bit about the skylark and the realm of the Luminosities came from a book on the esoteric cosmology of the English Romantic poets. Unfortunately, I have no idea whatever happened to that book; I'd love to find it and read it again, but if that is to be, then it will happen.

4. Subway
As grammarians grade papers, so ants
file through the bodies of the world, the black
lines flexing in the sunlight, blood pulsing
without the vessels to contain them. They

contain themselves, the ants crawling over
each other so as not to fractal off
and subdivide the stream with the threat of
chaos. The ants are orderly, like a

muscle fiber, like commuters on the
subway, like a python that engorges
a jungle boar and widens all along

itself, accommodates that bulk as it
is stripped of tough hide, muscle, tendon, fat,
and clean bones are delivered at the end.

From "the ant wins in the end" to "as grammarians grade papers" may seem a bit of an unjustified leap, but I'm writing about my life here, and I'll follow my unconscious mind as it makes connections. After all, I am using the strictly decasyllabic line as a way of diverting my conscious mind's attention from the content, so there must be some use in letting the other mind hold the reins and steer the chariot for a while. When I was at a reading being given by Kevin Varrone, and it came time for audience members to read one poem if they wanted, I read this one even though I had not been planning to, because the python's thorough digestive process resonated with the uncompromising physicality of one of Kevin's images. We're definitely in the Dionysiac realm here!

5. Ant, Alone
From one of those glistening files of ants
that connects a sudden source of food—road
kill, fish flopped out of water, seagull dropped
from the sky—you will occasionally

notice a single ant that has struck out
into a divagation from the flow
of the collective. In a wavering
loop, the ant will stagger beneath its crumb,

bump against pebbles and glebes, its spindles
pick out the pathways the water has gouged,
all the while its antennae frantically

trying to figure out how to get back
into the comforting compaction crowds
exchange for the nakedness of freedom.

As you can tell, I abandoned the "Sonnet Corona" principle here; otherwise I would have started with "Clean bones are delivered at the end." That's not a bad idea, but I wanted to start with the file of ants, and explore the possibility of the exile from a commuter community. Here we touch on the Steppenwolf, the Lonely Crowd, the Organization Man—all sorts of touchstones of my youth in the late 1960s, where nonconformity was *de rigueur*. There is also a hint of T. H. White's *The Book of Merlyn* here, where the wizard turns Wart into a goose flying with a flock and an ant working in a colony with Borg-like mental loudspeakers.

However, I think that I stumbled onto the origin of my antishness below, in a recollection of my habitual behavior on weeknights from seventh through twelfth grades:

Fourth House Thumbnail

That tiny bedroom, maybe ten by twelve,
is not just where I slept, but where my desk
and chair under the built-in bookcase sat.
I had a dictionary and a lamp—
harsh fluorescent white—a can of pencils,
pens, and a compass on my right, the window
also on my right but behind my back.
There I'd perch on weekday nights for six years,
when I would stay at school and walk home late
just in time for dinner, then climb upstairs
while the rest of the family watched TV.
Three closed doors kept most of the laughter out
of my ears. My consciousness was an ant
that slowly would meander across the page.

Being an ant was a self-imposed punishment for having tried to be a
grasshopper, unsuccessfully, earlier in the day, just as being an ant now is just
such a punishment for trying to have lived the grasshopper lifestyle before
"settling down."

Gail D. Rosen

Tiny Furniture more than a Small Film

"I am in a postgraduate delirium," says Aura (Lena Dunham), the main character in *Tiny Furniture*. That may be true, but this small film is more than an indie postgraduate comedy. *Tiny Furniture* contains memorable characters, a good cast, and a fresh new voice. It made me laugh and it also moved me.

After graduating college in Ohio, Aura (Dunham) returns home to New York to live with her artist mother Siri (Laurie Simmons) and overachieving 17-year-old sister Nadine (Grace Dunham). Aura reconnects with old friend Charlotte (Jemima Kirke) as she attempts romance with the wrong men and struggles to find her place in the world as an adult. Does it make things more interesting to know that writer/director/star Dunham graduated from college in Ohio and that her real mother and sister play Aura's mother and sister? Yes, but that is only part of the appeal. Perhaps there is something to that adage about writing what you know.

Dunham creates characters who are likable (Siri, Charlotte, and Aura) and characters who are unlikable (Jed and Keith), but all of the characters are recognizable; at times they seem uncomfortably real. It is obvious that Aura lived a somewhat privileged life, but this has not done much for her self-esteem. Aura wants to be a filmmaker, but her mother's success as an artist feeds her insecurity. Aura may be smart, naïve, and vulnerable, but she is never annoying. I wonder why she is attracted to a pompous loser like Jed (Alex Karpovsky), but on some level I understand it. Jed has achieved some YouTube notoriety as The Nietzschean Cowboy (the shots of him pontificating while on a rocking horse are hilarious) and is described as "a little bit famous in an Internet kind of way." His claims of meetings with people at Comedy Central are obviously false or exaggerated, but Aura is feeling so down on herself that she allows him to use her for room and board. Chef Keith (David Call) seems like a better choice, but he talks in clichés and wants her to get him drugs. Aura is sharp enough to notice these shortcomings, but too insecure to challenge these guys. I enjoyed the scenes of Aura's changing relationships with old friend Charlotte and college friend Frankie (Merritt Wever), but what resonates the most for me is Aura's journey. She wonders what kind of adult she should be and is afraid to leave the safety of her family. In one of the more revelatory scenes, she argues with her mother after her mother objects to her inconsiderate behavior. "Do you like living here?" Siri asks. "I love living here," Aura admits. Throughout the film Dunham's dialogue is sharp and incisive, but never mean.

Dunham the actress is extremely appealing. By Hollywood standards, she may not be model perfect, but she has a vulnerability and sweetness that I found moving. Her deadpan delivery of the film's funnier lines made them even funnier. When asked if she smokes, Aura replies, "I could." Laurie Simmons reminds me of Allison Janney, Grace Dunham is just right as Aura's know-it-all little sister, and the three have great chemistry together. They are a believable family, perhaps because they are a real family. Jemima Kirke is delightful as the affected and flighty Charlotte, who is a good foil for the more down-to-earth Aura. I loved their scenes together. Alex Karpovsky is perfect as the annoying Jed, delivering Jed's cringe-worthy dialogue with the required arrogance.

The title of the film refers to Siri's work photographing miniature objects. They are present in many scenes, and at one point Aura touches them with a certain amount of wistfulness. At times Aura seems to feel that she is living a miniature adult life. But Dunham straddles the line between reality and fiction like a seasoned pro. She is close to her subjects, but maintains the right amount of distance to make a good film, a film that won at the South by Southwest Music and Media Conference and Festival. *Tiny Furniture* reportedly was made for the tiny sum of $25,000, a rare occurrence in an age of ridiculously expensive films. This small low-budget film will stay with me for a long time.

Tiny Furniture. Directed by Lena Dunham. Lena Dunham (Aura), Laurie Simmons (Siri), Grace Dunham (Nadine), Jemima Kirke (Charlotte), Alex Karpovsky (Jed), David Call (Keith), and Merritt Wever (Frankie). IFC Films, 2010.

Don Rutberg

In and Out of the Nielsen Family

My wife and I were selected by the Nielsen TV Ratings to join their family. This was no ordinary super-important responsibility. We were to represent 28,100 homes in our area, with each household averaging 3.5 persons. Our viewing habits, our approval or disapproval of television shows 24 hours a day, 365 days a year, registered in Nielsen's Florida home office as 98,350 votes!

A Nielsen field representative came to our apartment, near Philadelphia. Once he learned that we had no little kids hogging the tube, he rubber-stamped us and explained how we would be assimilated into the family. We told him we didn't mind the responsibility or loss of privacy because we considered ourselves sophisticated and intelligent viewers, eager to endorse worthwhile productions. No wrestling or survival shows; no Hollywood Insider-type productions for us.

If he would've left immediately, everything would've been fine. But as this man kept talking, we became less enthusiastic about joining his family.

"The first thing we do is tear apart your TVs," Mike, the Nielsen rep, said.

"You mean, you open up our TV sets and insert your tracking devices?" I asked.

"Uh-huh."

"Can't you just stick a magnetized chip on the side of the TV?"

"No. We have to get inside; both TVs and both DVRs."

My wife asked, "Suppose you break one of the TVs or DVRs?"

"If your devices stop working because of our messing around in there, we'll pay you 50% of the value of the TV or DVR."

Our TV is probably worth $300 but would cost $800 to replace.

"That means you'll give us $50 for any TV you break?" I asked.

"Sounds fair," he said with a smile.

"That hardly ever happens, I'll bet."

Mike didn't answer.

My wife broke the silence.

"So you'll know everything we watch *and* tape."

"Exactly. The next thing we'll do is tear up your carpeting in the living room, dining room, hallways, and bedroom."

My wife gasped.

Mike explained, "We'll run wires along the walls and floorboards, into the telephone jacks."

"Uh, we only have one phone jack in the front of the apartment and that's in the kitchen," I said.

Mike inspected our walls. The last time someone looked so closely at our walls, the person was about to saw through them in order to rescue a baby squirrel.

"No problem," Mike replied. "We'll run the wires near the door alongside the heating and air-conditioning systems, into the kitchen, then ... hmmm, you'll have to remove the phone from the wall-mount and put it on the kitchen table."

"Won't there be a lot of wires on our kitchen walls?" my wife asked.

"You won't even notice them," Mike promised.

That's what the cable company had promised my wife. She's still mad at them.

"It sounds complicated," I mentioned. "How long will it take to install?"

"Five or six hours."

"It'll take a guy five or six hours just to install a monitoring system?"

"No, it'll take a team of three to four men five or six hours to install the system."

"We could put in a whole new kitchen with that kind of time and manpower," I suggested.

"We'll want to get this in motion as soon as possible," Mike said. "The day after tomorrow works for us. Is seven a.m. too early to get here?"

"Yes!" I replied. "I go to bed late."

"We'll work around it. How about Friday night, from 5-11 pm, give or take?"

"We have the Mexican fiesta party at the clubhouse on Friday night," my wife reminded.

We were going to need a few margaritas to say "Yes" to this deal, especially if they wanted to bring in jackhammers, port-o-potties, and cots.

"Why does it take so long?" I wondered.

"We have to rewire all your equipment. We'll bring in a few computerized boxes, hide them nicely in cabinets, then they'll record all your info ...."

"We don't have cabinets near the TV's," I said.

The fact that we had no children was a plus but having no cabinets, well, that seemed unnatural to the man.

"Don't worry," Mike replied. "We'll hide the boxes somewhere."

"Not in the fireplace," I mumbled.

Mike coughed up an insincere chuckle.

"Here's the neat part," he said. "The boxes will be hooked up to your phone line and they'll auto-dial our home office in Florida every night about two a.m."

"Say that again," I instructed.

"The computer is set to auto-dial."

"I make phone calls to the West Coast at two a.m. Are you telling me that when I try to make a call, the Nielsen box will be on the phone, calling in a report?"

"It won't take long."

"The box isn't going to call its friends in Australia and talk for an hour, is it?" I joked.

Mike didn't answer.

My wife broke the silence.

She asked, "So how much do you pay us for all our help?"

I could see her ears perking up.

"A dollar a month."

"Excuse me?" she blurted out, her head tilted.

"For each TV and DVR," Mike said, adding incentive.

"Four bucks a month?" my wife screamed.

"Before we pay you, you have to sign a contract for two years," Mike told us.

"Two years!" I repeated.

"If you move, you can quit."

"Gee, thanks," I said. "It really *is* a free country."

"And we pay you six months in advance!" Mike advised.

"Wow, 24 dollars in one lump sum," my wife, the accountant, whispered.

At that moment, executives from my wife's favorite network, Lifetime, should have jumped in and offered her ten thousand dollars to sign the contract. Lifetime would have made a hundred times that sum every year from sponsors and could have out-rated all the major networks. The Philadelphia Eagles, Flyers, 76ers, and Phillies should have been there to offer me incentives, since they would have been guaranteed 98,350 registered viewers every time they played, even exhibition games.

(I mentioned earlier that we *considered* ourselves sophisticated and intelligent viewers. That doesn't necessarily mean that we are.)

My wife and I are complementary in nature and have very different tastes. I often joke that, since she mainly uses the left side of her brain and I use the right, together we use one complete brain. In this case, however, we were thinking exactly alike. I could feel her on my wavelength. It was time to let Mike in on our telepathic secret.

We admitted that we weren't going to live in a construction zone and give up our privacy for $4 a month. We said we weren't up to the challenge. (We weren't psyched to climb Mt. Everest for two bucks apiece, either). He told us he understood but then stood up in a huff and packed his papers, using body language to question how we could turn down this great opportunity.

We looked with relief at the clean walls and smooth carpeting and wall-mounted phone. I told Mike that we always watched *NCIS*.

"It's the number one show, anyway," I said with a consoling shrug. "You don't need us. *NCIS* doesn't need us."

Mike flew out the door.

"Keep your hands off our TV!" my wife shouted out the window.

Alone in our apartment, feeling as if we had regained our rights as private citizens without taking part in a bloody coup, my wife and I hugged. Lifetime network executives, somewhere, were sobbing at their lost millions. But the truth was, we would've paid the Nielsen family four bucks a month just to leave us alone.

Sheila Sandapen

Reading... Passing it on.

I am a bookaholic.

I share a spiritual kinship with Eramus who once said—or so I read— "When I get a little money I buy books; and if any is left I buy food and clothes." I, too, have been known to spend money earmarked for something dull such as groceries on books. Big coffee-table-sized books with glorious colorful pictures and pages that are stiff to the touch. Small books with closely written words on tissue thin pages that tear if you don't use care. Illustrated children's books. Remaindered classics and former best sellers. Secondhand books that hold the marginalia of a previous owner's thoughts.

It was through no fault of my own that Borders bookstore went bankrupt a few years ago. On that day I mourned. I had to say farewell to the staff members at my local store who, while not quite family, were well-liked neighbors. I drove 10 miles out of my way to snap up "bargains" at another store because I didn't want the people at "my" store to witness my glee as I reaped the benefits of their misfortune.

Whenever I move into a new neighborhood (and there have been a few), I seek out the local library. Currently, I am a card-carrying member of multiple libraries in three counties. I am not counting my access to the online databases at several universities.

My books are visible to all who visit my home. They line shelves in the dining room, are piled up in the family room, and the bedrooms each have a nice selection. When we moved a year ago, the movers carried in box after box loaded with books. The boxes had been gleaned from the state liquor store and they looked at me quizzically. When I explained they were books and not booze one of the men asked if I had not heard of the Kindle or Nook.

Yes, I have.

But I am a *book* person.

Let me amend that statement: My daughter and I are *book* people.

My daughter is beginning to read now. It has been a long, slow process. One that bore careful repetition and endless patience.

When she was a baby and would wake screaming in the night there was Dr. Seuss—*A Wocket in My Pocket* and *Mr. Brown can Moo, Can you?* were particularly favored ones. Whenever there is a storm I still have a tendency to quote: "Boom. Boom. Boom. Mr. Brown makes Thunder!"

For the last four years—three quarters of her life—my daughter has been horse mad. We sit together and read books on horses. Ponies. Riding. Rodeos. Unicorns. *Black Beauty. The Black Stallion. Ponyella. Goldilicious.*

One of the first things I taught her was how to handle books with care. No tearing of pages or scribbling over the text. Today when we borrow a book from a library and she notices a previous patron has scribbled in the book, she is indignant for the book's sake.

Now she is sounding out words and reading simple sentences. *Horse* is one word she has long known by heart. *See He To Do Not A The What When* are among her other "sight" words. She is beginning to read simple sentences. I see the excitement in her eyes when she completes a sentence and it creates meaning.

We are starting to talk about the process of reading books and how they are formatted to create meaning. We talk about book titles and pictures and summaries on the backs of the books. What they say and don't say. The function they serve. Whether she thinks the summary on *Pal the Pony* is a good one.

Now when bedtime comes we take turns reading the words on the page. It is a bittersweet process. I am so proud of my budding reader but I am sad that I will soon no longer be her reader.

I will need to create a new role for myself: As an active listener when she tells me about her books.

Alan Soble

Sexual Duties, Sexual Supererogation

Never reach out your hand unless you're willing to extend an arm.
[Pope Paul VI / Elizabeth Fuller]

When I was in graduate school, I had a sexual encounter about which I wished I had thought more carefully before it occurred. (I wish that I had thought more carefully about most of my encounters before they occurred, even at the expense of spontaneity.) The encounter was with a woman, a student, in her early twenties, slightly younger than I. Toward the sex that was soon to occur I felt the pull of *moral* obligation: either I veridically sensed a duty or I tricked myself into imagining it. We were only acquaintances. A complication was the nagging thought that I should be faithful to my emerging libertine ideals (a matter of personal integrity), about which she knew, and she also knew that I knew that she knew (a matter of public integrity). The woman in this encounter was "Ø," ordinarily taken in our society to be a revolting physical property. Given my tastes at the time, I experienced no sexual desire for her, so I was not under the spell of physical appetite. She approached me tentatively, shyly, and made her request. I agreed. The issue that concerns me now, in retrospect, is whether taking on and fulfilling this task was merely morally permissible, if even that, or, more stringently, morally required, an obligation, or was even morally exemplary.

In a touching and, as always, absurd episode of the animated *Family Guy* ("New Kidney in Town," 2011), Peter Griffin needs a kidney transplant and the only medically satisfactory donor is Brian, the family's dog. Because dog kidneys are small, Brian would have to donate both kidneys to save Peter. Still, Peter's best friend decides to forfeit his life. "Morally supererogatory" is the term we use for Brian's decision: it benefits another person through self-sacrifice, going "above and beyond" what duty demands, and is, as a result, praiseworthy.

Two features of this scenario reduce the level of Brian's supererogation. First, Brian and Peter are friends and family members. We have duties of benevolence toward friends and family members, so although Brian's gift goes beyond the reach of these duties, his supererogation is not as grand as a stranger's bestowing both kidneys to save Peter's life. Second, the evening before Brian will lose his kidneys, he asks Lois (Peter's wife, for whom Brian pines) if she would allow him to hump her leg to completion. Because he gains something desirable he otherwise would not have obtained, the quality of Brian's supererogation is lessened, but not by much; his purpose in donating his kidneys was not to hump that leg. Lois's gift to Brian is also supererogatory. She offers herself, or her leg, as an object to be used by Brian, which she finds demeaning. And Lois makes a deeper psychological sacrifice, if she is pained by the adulterous, incestuous nature of this perverted (by her own standards) sexual act. The joke is that Brian ejaculates way sooner than the fifteen seconds allotted to him by Lois. (What has become of television since Philip Larkin and 1963?)

In the sexual domain of our lives, as in other domains, we distinguish sexual acts that are morally *permissible*, for example, consensual intercourse between two adults, from those that are *prohibited*, such as rape. (For one long list of prohibitions, see Leviticus 18:6-23.) Depending on the moral perspective or religious allegiance presupposed, actions that fall into the permissible and prohibited categories vary. Nonetheless, the notion that a sexual act is a moral *duty* mostly enters our discourse about sexuality only through the backdoor, or negatively: we have duties *to refrain* from engaging in acts that are prohibited. A duty *to* engage in (joyous) sex has the weird flavor of a duty to, say, eat (delicious) pizza. But if we have, in some circumstances, a positive duty *to perform* sexual acts (circuitously: a duty prohibiting failing to engage in sex), then we have this third moral category (beyond prohibited and permissible), one that is underutilized in our discussions about sexual morality. Further, we then have also a fourth (and underutilized) category, sexual supererogation— sexual acts that go above and beyond what our duties demand of us.

Female nurses in Amsterdam have had to insist that providing sexual services to their patients is not in their job description; it is not one of their professional tasks and patients should not expect to receive sexual care. But when I am almost ready to go, and not even the lure of an easy noncoital buck will convince a prostitute to try her skills on me (not to mention the problem of sneaking her past the guards into my nursing home room), perhaps a Dutch nurse on the staff with the heart of Mother Teresa will be kind to an old man, going the extra mile beyond the chores the commercial home has contractually agreed to pay her to do. Comedians, primarily, pay attention to supererogatory sexual acts, but they deserve serious exploration, which we'll try to do here. We need not go whole gushing hog, however; it is not doing it for free that would make a prostitute's or nurse's acts supererogatory, but doing it *at all* with someone repulsively old as I would be, even if she is paid handsomely to do so. The quality of her supererogation is lessened by the payment, but not erased.

The idea that we might have obligations to engage in sex will seem odd only as long as we deploy the analogy with a duty to eat pizza or embrace the equally odd notion of a "duty to self." If we have obligations to engage in sex, they will be grounded not in our own pleasure (or whatever else it might be that we want for ourselves from engaging in sex), but in the pleasure, value, or significance of the act for the other person. Once we recognize that if we have duties to engage in sex, our goal must be the benefit for other people of our acts, we have a foundation for claiming that our general duty of benevolence (or beneficence), to which almost all religious and secular moral codes ascribe, applies in the sexual domain. Surely, we have duties to help other people, to be of assistance to them, to attend to their pain and suffering. These duties might be weak, not requiring much effort or cost on our part to satisfy, and perhaps ignorable in order to fulfill other duties. Or some of these duties might be strong, requiring substantial inconvenience and effort and not easily overridden by other duties. Why is it rarely proclaimed that some sexual activity might be mandatory by our commonly shared general duty of benevolence? Whether the duty would be weak or strong is not the pressing philosophical problem. The problem is deriving *any* obligation to engage in sex from our general duty of benevolence. Alternatively, we could turn the tables, and lessen the difficulty, by asking how it could be that the duty of benevolence does *not* justify more widespread sexual activity. After all, our duty of benevolence implies that we must feed the starving. The ordinary thinker replies, "Feeding a starving person is required to save his or her (physical) life, but people can remain alive without sexual contact. I reply, "Kind sir or madam, you are not taking the duty of benevolence seriously enough, nor are you showing sensitivity to the psychological death that accompanies severe sexual malnutrition."

The idea of an obligation to engage in sexual activity is actually of ancient origin. One location in scripture is Paul's letter 1 Corinthians 7:1-9, from which theologians have reasonably extracted two doctrines. First, that marriage serves as *ad remedium concupiscentiae*: entering marriage provides spouses with sexual satisfaction so that they thwart the temptation, which they felt while unmarried, to fall into promiscuous fornication and opportunistic same-sex encounters. Paul's second doctrine is the "marriage [or conjugal] debt": a spouse has a *duty to* engage in sex with the other spouse pretty much on demand. Exceptions include when the spouse is ill or is getting closer to God. So, "Not tonight, Dear, I have a headache" is supplemented with, "Not right now, Dear, I'm praying," but not with, "I really want to watch the game." Putting a 20th-Century spin on Paul, Elizabeth Anscombe's version of the marriage debt does not allow a spouse to "insist . . . [on sex] against *serious* reluctance of one's partner." (Is wanting to watch a game sufficiently weighty? Is giving up the game therefore supererogatory? Note that once sex becomes a duty in marriage, logical space is created for supererogatory sexual acts in marriage.) Paul's welding the marriage debt to marriage's purpose as a remedy against sin makes sense: if a spouse feels sexual itches and has them dutifully and reliably scratched by the other, marriage may well succeed as a remedy. As we expected, the rationale of the obligation to engage in sex with the other spouse is that doing so benefits the other person. If each spouse fulfills the duty, they help each other avoid a sexual-spiritual disaster. By the way, the promotion of marriage as a remedy against sin and the accompanying marriage debt existed earlier, in ancient Judaic teachings; in Talmudic fashion, a sailor owes his wife fewer sexual acts than does a scholar.

Nowadays, apart from densely Catholic precincts, Western culture does not advocate the marriage debt, as most of my female students tell me, perhaps influenced by the announcement by feminism of a woman's inalienable right to control what happens to and in her body, a right that prohibits rape and permits abortion. To some extent, the ancient-medieval question of what the spouses owe each other sexually has been replaced, in contemporary secular approaches to the problem of sexual parity and compromise in marriage or partnerships, by discussions of justice, even the notions of distributive justice and microeconomic "welfare functions." (One simple function is "tit for tat.") Sexual duties remain, even if the dialogue sounds different. Other contemporary approaches steer away from moral duties. For example, if a person X loves another person Y or cares about Y's psychological and physical well-being, X might agree to have sex with Y even if X prefers to watch the game. In this alternative approach, X is not fulfilling a duty of morality but a distinct duty of love. Another approach points out that a spouse who asserts the absolute right to say "no" is in jeopardy of alienating the affections of the other, of driving the other spouse to "sub-monogamous" ways of achieving sexual satisfaction—online cybersex with anonymous chatters. The absolute "no" (fueled by a gender-neutral right to control one's body) endangers the viability of the relationship. Maybe a spouse does not want to have sex exactly here and now and in this position, but the spouse might also want to maintain the relationship, and not necessarily for base or dire economic reasons. This assent to engage in sex is motivated pragmatically. It involves doing what the marriage debt requires, but doing it for self-interested reasons (unless it is claimed, disingenuously, that X's maintaining the dyad is primarily for Y's benefit). Consider this common scenario: X does not enjoy a certain sexual act, maybe is even repulsed by it. X does it anyway, purely for the sake of the other person Y or to preserve their relationship. Would Y request or permit X to do it, knowing how X feels about the act? (This thoughtfulness did not dissuade Brian.) The situation is uncomfortably ironic: Y might not permit X to do the act, thereby preventing X from achieving saintly supererogation, or preventing X from acting according to a duty of morality or of love, or preventing X's attempt to solidify the relationship. The intended beneficiary of a sexual act refuses to be a beneficiary. (Out of perverse malice?) Even so, if Y cares for and about X, too, Y would similarly refuse. There was no reason to expect that the sexual domain would be immune from this paradox of altruism: Y out of love or respect for X insists on doing it; X out of love of respect for Y insists that Y not do it.

Nevertheless, if we accept the plausibility of an innocuous version of the marriage debt, the central issue remains: why must the scope of sexual duties be so severely restricted? Paul did not encourage any unmarried people to have sex with other people to help the latter avoid sexual-spiritual disaster. Why not? Because any such sexual benefactor would be engaging in exactly the promiscuous fornication Paul was attempting to curtail. *So what?* One person's being promiscuous to save others from promiscuity seems like the majestic kind of self-sacrifice exhibited by Jesus. This case, however, shows how difficult it may be to distinguish duty from supererogation. To risk or abandon one's soul or salvation by promiscuously satisfying the sexual needs of other people, so that they do not fall into promiscuity, might not be demanded by "Love Thy Neighbor," but it seems morally exemplary in going beyond what that commandment requires. Yet self-sacrificial promiscuous behavior does seem required by the *agape* promoted by Paul in 1 Corinthians 13. A duty to engage in sex with other people for their good seems a duty of "Love Thy Neighbor" as well as of our general (secular) duty of benevolence. Denying that Christian love includes benefiting other people sexually makes *agape* stingy. It no longer bears all things, believes all things, hopes all things, and endures all things.

In trying to decide whether giving sexual pleasure to other people is a duty, at least on some occasions, or is altogether supererogatory, perhaps Luke 10:25-37, on the Good Samaritan, will help. Is the Good Samaritan a role model for sexual supererogation? The problem for me is that I'm not convinced that the Good Samaritan was supererogatory. (That is, I do not think that the Good Samaritan was a Good Samaritan.) True, the Samaritan tended to the wounds of the injured man, a perfect stranger, and paid for a room in an inn where he would rest and heal. A modern secular consciousness judges this behavior to be supererogatory. But before and after the description of the Samaritan's behavior in Luke, we are told that these kinds of acts are those that will earn us "eternal life" *and* that we are commanded to do them by Jesus. On the one hand, we are rewarded by being good Samaritans; self-interest that also benefits others is our motive. On the other hand, taking responsibility for a stranger's life is commanded, is our duty. If so, the Good Samaritan doesn't come close to being supererogatory. Maybe, though, we've learned a lesson: either we bestow, as our duty, sexual pleasure on other people as our neighbors, or we give them sexual pleasure out of a rarefied and sophisticated self-interest that also happily benefits them. (Adam Smith's "invisible hand" enters the stage.) The only logical space for sexual supererogation are cases in which we benefit others sexually and get nothing out of it, not even the pleasure of being pleasurable, or, better, tangibly suffer as a result. The proof that we are really doing our best to benefit others sexually for their sake alone is that in doing so, we suffer (as did Christ).

None of this philosophy saves me when morally evaluating my agreeing to play a part in the "pity sex" (that's how it seemed to me, although maybe she thought she was giving me pity-sex) with the Ø-woman. My fulfilling her request for sexual activity seems not to have been supererogatory. I had nothing to gain, but I also had nothing to lose, except a few hours of my day: we had our encounter in the privacy of her well-kempt, clean bedroom, her personal hygiene was impeccable, we engaged only in safe acts, and she was not married. Any benefit would be hers, and fulfilling my agreement did not harm me (or not immediately). I did not deserve any praise for sleeping with her. Supposing my actions were not supererogatory, did I nonetheless have a duty to have sex with her? I *felt* that I did, but did I *really*? I'd like to think that I did, that my moral sense was not faulty, that providing pleasure for other people is a weak duty of benevolence, or at least we have a duty to provide sexual pleasure for those who might otherwise not have many such experiences, or who especially need it.

In the *Family Guy* episode "Peter-assment" (2010), Angela, Peter's boss, is suicidal and desperately pleads with Peter to have sex with her. Perhaps for Peter to have sex with her would be supererogatory; perhaps he had an obligation. In any event, what should we make of Peter's duties to other people who might be harmed? In particular, do the obligations created by Peter's marriage vow take precedence, or does he have a more important duty to save this woman, and we hope that Lois would agree? Maybe Angela was lying. If she had been successful in getting Peter to have sex with her, she would have been guilty of "fraud in the inducement," a kind of rape. She would have been taking advantage of Peter's generosity or his sense of duty. But my Ø-partner did not lie that she was Ø. Nor did I have a commitment to another person the terms of which would have been violated by my having sex with this Ø person or anyone else. There is apparently nothing getting in the way of concluding that I had a duty to her which I satisfactorily fulfilled.

There is, however, one detail of our encounter that I have so far not mentioned. Before I agreed to have sex with her, I asked her to promise me that she would abide by a certain proviso, that we would engage in sexual activity once and only once, to which proviso she smilingly and eagerly assented. This is why I was bothered, later, by the thought that it was morally wrong for me to have sex with her under the condition I imposed on her. The modern consciousness would reply: "Mr. Philosopher, you laid out the contract clearly, and you did not trick or cajole her into accepting the proviso. Her free and informed consent, and your free and informed consent, both guaranteed that what you did was morally permissible." I am not sure that this well-intentioned defense is convincing. In extracting the promise, I was not being morally decent. To be able to extricate myself from any further obligations toward her, to make sure that our encounter would be perfectly casual with no strings attached, I relied on her present neediness. I made her make a promise that neither she nor I could know, at the time when it mattered, that she could keep. By agreeing to have sex with her I might have created for myself (through "invisible strings") an obligation to do it again, despite the legalistic proviso. Casual sex is often not so casual.

Accepting her invitation to engage in sex was, due to my naïveté about sexual relations, also a pragmatic blunder. She spent the next month or so popping up wherever I was, bearing a sad doggy face, her signal (I suppose) to me that she'd be happy, instead of sad, if she received more of the same. I had, contrary to my intentions, made her worse off by having had sex with her; hence the encounter was not, after all, morally permissible. Now I had a duty to extricate her from the edge of doom, toward which I had pushed her. In her eyes, and perhaps in mine, I had made an implicit promise to her that I ignored at my moral peril. As a result, the encounter turned out to be more than a minor inconvenience for me. A better calculation, in advance of what the encounter might cost me, had to be made, and I suspect that had I realized that she would not be satisfied with one encounter, that she would not abide by the proviso, and that she would plague me for more, I would (and should) have refused her original invitation. My having sex with her was, after all, supererogatory, although not knowingly and intentionally, because the subsequent stalking to which I had made myself vulnerable was a significant harm. We cannot rest, however, with the judgment that I had been supererogatory. My vague but palpable feeling of guilt, if I were to trust it, told me I had done something morally wrong, somewhere.

Mary V. Spiers

Neuroenhancement: Do "Smart Pills" have Limits?

Limitless (2011) USA; Directed by Neil Burger

What if there was a "smart pill" that could help you excel at everything? *Limitless* (2011) examines the power of the mind and how one struggling writer, Eddie Morra, played by Bradley Cooper, deals with his newfound super-mental powers. The film begins by re-asserting the popular myth that we use only a small portion of our brain's potential (Beyerstein, 1999) and proceeds to show both the upside and downside of neuroenhancement.

The inciting incident of the movie occurs when Eddie, a down-and-out writer, first takes the smart pill, NZT, given to him by his shady former brother-in-law. Eddie is now able to effortlessly write his novel. He composes and writes like a speed demon, finishing his manuscript in days. Any trace of writer's block is gone and, according to his editor, he produces a masterpiece. Eddie is hooked. He quickly discovers that his abilities extend beyond just enhancing his previously learned skills. He has access to every incidental memory in his life. He feels he can "tap into" his unconscious. This is more than just the rote retrieval of photographic memory. Like a dream come true, he uses his memory of obscure references to seduce his despised landlord's girlfriend, a law student, who is impressed by the analysis he offers on her paper. Whereas Eddie's previous life had become the paragon of sloth, procrastination, timidity and disorganization, NZT now gives him a boost in executive functioning; he becomes a self-starter, gets himself and his apartment spiffed up and organized and is undaunted in his response to any new situation. Eddie Morra is now competent, self-assured, and on-target. Not only are his intellectual abilities enhanced but he is also more socially and emotionally aware. He can read others' emotions, apparent needs, and intentions. Soon Eddie yearns to reach beyond his life in the publishing world. He is taken in by the allure of big money to be made as a day trader. Even better than having the primed and plastic brain of a child, he learns complex equations and digests trends in minutes. If he needs to learn Mandarin Chinese, he can do that, too. He is soon the hottest trader on Wall Street.

Limitless is timely in that it echoes the current interest in neuroenhancement. It has been estimated that more than 100 drugs may be under consideration as cognitive enhancers (Soyka, 2009). For example cholinesterase inhibitors were originally developed to delay memory decline in dementias such as Alzheimer's disease, and prescription stimulants are routinely used to improve attention and focus in disorders such as attention deficit hyperactivity disorder. They are now being used "off label" and are increasingly sought by healthy people of all ages with no diagnosed medical condition who want to sharpen their memory, attention, and focus (Larriviere, Williams, Rizzo, & Bonnie, 2009; McCabe, Teter, Boyd, Knight, & Wechsler, 2005). In addition, cognitive enhancement can also occur through the use of non-invasive brain stimulation techniques such as transcranial magnetic stimulation (TMS) and transcranial direct current stimulation (tDCS). Currently in clinical use for treating depression (D. R. Kim, Pesiridou, & O'Reardon, 2009), brain stimulation has also been demonstrated to show improvements in healthy people in working memory (Ohn, Park, & Yoo, 2008), language learning (Floel, Rosser, Muchka, Knecht, & Breitenstein, 2008), and complex motor tasks (Y. H. Kim, Park, Ko, Jang, & Lee, 2004).

There is much debate in the medical and psychological community pertaining to the ethical use of medications to enhance neural performance and *Limitless* speaks largely to the personal safety issue. One of the primary dangers of NZT is that its physical addiction creates life-threatening peril. Eddie begins to have memory "blackouts." Without NZT, his mind and body crash, he can't concentrate, and he goes through a physical withdrawal that could kill him. While the film's depiction of addiction may be played up in the name of dramatic tension, prescription drugs and brain stimulation used to enhance cognition for healthy people is not without risk. For example, prescription drugs carry a variety of risks related to safety and addiction, and TMS carries a risk, albeit rare, of seizures (Wassermann, 1998). These risks have led some experts in the field of addiction research to raise serious concerns about the use of neuroenhancement (Soyka, 2009).

There are a number of larger ethical questions that neuroenhancement brings up. For example, do cognitive-enhancing drugs create unfair academic and work-related advantages similar to those discussed in sports-doping debates? Will neuroenhacements be able to alter not only cognition, but social and moral thought? NZT does give Eddie Morra an unfair advantage in every area of his professional life. He secretly employs his power to gain personal wealth and fame. While his power is initially used for his personal gain, after a number of personal crises, in the end, Eddie turns to politics. Whether this choice is pro-social or the ultimate in power seeking is left up to the viewer. The issue of how the "self" may be altered by neuroenhacement is broached more directly by Eddie's girlfriend Lindey. After she takes NZT she admits she may have done things that she wouldn't have done without the pill. Eddie, however, argues that he is the same. This issue, although just hinted at in the film, represents perhaps one of the more contentious issues related to the future of neuroenhancement. Studies using neurostimulation suggest that people can be influenced to alter aspects of their moral reasoning. TMS to the right parietal junction influenced participants to disregard the intention of an act in favor of a morally reasonable outcome (Young, Camprodon, Hauser, Pascual-Leone, & Saxe, 2010) and inhibitory stimulation to the frontal cortex had an effect such that "self-interest" often trumped a more typical "fairness" response in a reward seeking task (Fecteau et al., 2007).

If neuroenhancement can affect not only cognition, but mood and social and moral reasoning, do we then move into the brave new world of altering or creating entirely new selves? Currently there is no one drug that is *Limitless*. Even in this film, the pill's effect is largely on learning and cognition. But *Limitless* opens the door to bigger questions: How far can neuroenhancement take us beyond our current limits, and do we want to go there?

References

Beyerstein, B. L. (1999). Whence Cometh the Myth that We Only Use 10% of our Brains? In S. D. Sala (Ed.), *Mind Myths: Exploring Popular Assumptions About the Mind and Brain*.

Fecteau, S., Knoch, D., Fregni, F., Sultani, N., Boggio, P. S., & Pascual-Leone, A. (2007). Diminishing risk-taing behavior by modulating activity in the prefrontal cortex. *Journal of Neuroscience*(27), 12500-12505.

Floel, A., Rosser, N., Muchka, O., Knecht, S., & Breitenstein, C. (2008). Noninvasive brain stimulation improves language learning. *Journal of Cognitive Neuroscience*(20), 1415-1422.

Kim, D. R., Pesiridou, A., & O'Reardon, J. P. (2009). Transcrannial magnetic stimulation in the treatment of psychiatric disorders. *Current Psychiatry Reports*(11), 447-452.

Kim, Y. H., Park, J. W., Ko, M. H., Jang, S. H., & Lee, P. K. (2004). Facilitative effect of high frequency subthreshold repetitive transcranial magnetic stimulation on complex sequential motor learning in humans. *Neuroscience Letters*(367), 181-185.

Larriviere, D., Williams, M. A., Rizzo, M., & Bonnie, R. J. (2009). Responding to requests from adult patients for neuroenhancements. *Neurology, 73*(17), 1406-1412. doi: 10.1212/WNL.0b013e3181beecfe

McCabe, S. E., Teter, C. J., Boyd, C. J., Knight, J. R., & Wechsler, H. (2005). Nonmedical use of prescription opioids among U. S. college students: prevalence and correlates from a national survey. *Addictive Behaviors*(30), 789-805.

Ohn, S. H., Park, C. I., & Yoo, W. K. (2008). Time-dependent effect of transcranial direct current stimulation on the enhancement of working memory. *Neuroreport*(19), 43-47.

Soyka, M. (2009). Neuro-Enhancement aus suchtmedizinischer Sicht. *Der Nervenarzt,* *80*(7), 837-839-839. doi: 10.1007/s00115-009-2800-7

Wassermann, E. M. (1998). Risk and safety of repetitive transcranial magnetic stimulation: report and suggested guidelines from the International Workshop on the Safety of Repetitive Transcranial Magnetic Stimulation. *Electroencephalography and Clinical Neurophysiology*(108), 1-16.

Young, L., Camprodon, J. A., Hauser, M., Pascual-Leone, A., & Saxe, R. (2010). Disruption of the right temporoparietal junction with transcranial magnetic stimulation reduces the role of beliefs in moral judgements. *Proceedings of the National Academy of Sciences USA*(107), 6753-6758.

Scott Stein

A Knife to Set Things Right

An older brother's job is to protect his younger brother or sister. That's what I'd always been told by my parents, and that's what I'd seen. My older brother protected me.

Jason wasn't a fighter—back then, I think it would be fair to call him a shy boy. But he was athletic and strong, and older, and he defended me whenever I needed defending. I was short and, for a time, when I was still in elementary school, I was sensitive about it. My brother knew this. One time this bigger, older kid bullied me at Peter Pan, the local arcade, and called me a shrimp because I wouldn't give up my spot to let him play the game I was playing, and my brother stepped in. They were about the same age and size. Jason told the kid to leave me alone and not to tease me. The kid didn't like being told what to do, and called me a shrimp again, and that was enough to send the both of them rolling around on the ground. It was a real dust-up. Finally, an adult pulled them apart and the other kid was kicked out of the place for starting it. It wasn't life and death or anything, but I always remembered it, and the other times he never hesitated to stick up for me.

I was just as protective of my younger sister, Amy. When I was 10, it was high drama the time I threatened to break an eight-year-old boy's legs because he wouldn't stop pushing my sister, who was seven. She'd told my parents that this kid, who towered over her, was pushing her every day and teasing her. It wasn't gentle "he-probably-just-has-a-crush-on-you" pushes. He really shoved her around. When a phone call to the boy's mother from my mother did no good, my father told me that I was to make it very clear to this boy that his pushing days were over. At that age, I had a hell of a temper. I might have been the shortest kid in the class, in nearly the whole fourth grade, but I didn't get picked on much. Maybe it was my sparkling personality, my disarming humor and quick wit, but it probably also had something to do with my penchant for punching other kids in the face at the least provocation. I didn't have to hit the second-grade boy. He left Amy alone after our little talk. I'm sure he moved on to shoving a different girl who didn't have older brothers.

Like my brother, I took my duty seriously. But when the stakes were higher, when it wasn't just a kid shoving, but something more dangerous, I failed. It happened at the movies. My friend Danny and I must have been around 12, which means Amy was nine.

We were in the theater, watching Superman III, Danny, me, and Amy, sitting in that order. An old man was sitting next to my sister. Halfway through the movie, my sister said she wanted to leave. She was very upset. So we left. It was a few minutes after we left the theater and were walking home before she would say what was bothering her. The old man, that sick fuck, had taken out his penis and was playing with it, and was trying to get my sister's attention, trying to make eye contact, so she would see what he was doing. All while sitting right next to her and two seats down from me.

We didn't have cell phones back then, and were already almost home. When we got to my house, we told my mother, who rushed with all of us to the movie theater. The manager was sorry, and offered us free tickets to see the movie again, which was starting in a little while. I learned that one of our mistakes was sitting my sister on the end. My mother said she should have been in the middle, where it was safer. And that's where Amy sat that afternoon, between me and Danny, while we again watched Superman III.

The old man was gone by then, of course. I can still see his face today, a white-haired, mostly bald, hunched-over old man with a big nose. Everyone seems so old to a 12-year-old. Maybe he was 70. An old 70. He's probably dead now, dead maybe a couple of decades or more. Who knows what he had done, what he went on to do, whether he ever went beyond exposing himself and molested some little girl somewhere?

That day, I wasn't thinking of protecting society or other potential victims or anything else. I was a 12-year-old, thinking of my sister, and the old man. I sat there in the dark of the theater and wished desperately that he would come back. Before leaving my house to return to the theater, I'd grabbed my pocketknife. It didn't have more than a three-inch blade, but it was sharp, and I hardly paid attention to the movie, just fingered the knife the whole time and wished for the man to come back, so I could stab him in the stomach. I wanted to stab him. If he had come back, I would have stabbed him. But he never came back, so I never did.

Kathleen Volk Miller

You Might Not Have ADHD: You Might Just be Tired

The *NY Times* recently fanned the flames of the controversy over whether many cases of ADD and even ADHD are actually cases of sleep deprivation. Every time this idea hits big media the same reactions happen—other media picks it up, overgeneralizes and twists it, camps are formed, and people go to (verbal) war.

I saw one Huff Po post that called ADHD a mental illness, which seems more of a brutal word choice than semantics should allow, as this same author accused parents of hoping for the diagnosis so that their child might get "homework medicine." I saw a piece that called parents of ADD- and ADHD-labeled children "lazy" and poor parents who simply can't control their kids. I saw many, many pieces blame the phenomenon of high rates of diagnosis on our culture's favorite topic, hobby, tool, and scapegoat: technology, in all its forms.

I don't know that much about ADD and ADHD. I know I have a dear friend whose son and husband have been diagnosed, and whose daughter has a more controllable, less severe case of ADHD. To reach those diagnoses her family members took tests, the children were observed at school by a clinician, the children's teachers filled out questionnaires that went directly to the doctor so that the teachers could answer without any fear of blowback from the parents.

They ruled out other causes of distraction, dreaminess, and difficulty in learning in the traditional "taught to the middle" classroom, including adenoid issues and sleep deprivation.

ADD and ADHD is a real issue; it's estimated that 3-5 % of Americans aged 12-17 have it. But those numbers don't add up with other current data. A report by the Centers for Disease Control tells us 6.4 million American children have been diagnosed with ADHD. One out of every five high-school boys has been diagnosed with the disorder.

The issue couldn't be more complicated: we're applying science to a condition that cannot be clinically proven. The symptoms are inattention, hyperactivity, and impulsivity, distraction, fidgeting, losing things, daydreaming, talking nonstop, touching everything in sight, having trouble sitting still during dinner, being constantly in motion, impatience, interrupting conversations, showing their emotions, acting without regard for consequences, and having difficulty waiting their turn. Sounds like a middle school cafeteria. (Or maybe even the Dunkin' Donuts on 20th and Chestnut.) The point is, where does the line between "disorder" and personality meet and cross over? What's "normal"?

Things are going to get more complicated before they get easier: Criteria for the proper diagnosis of ADHD, to be released next month in the fifth edition of the Diagnostic and Statistical Manual of Mental Disorders, have been changed specifically *to allow more* adolescents and adults to qualify for a diagnosis.

We're at an all-time high of 11% of *all* school-aged children in America being diagnosed as ADD/ADHD, depressed, or suffering from severe anxiety. Are we smarter and more savvy at catching conditions early on? Sales of stimulants to treat ADHD have more than doubled to $9 billion in 2012 from $4 billion in 2007. The fastest growing market for antidepressants is preschoolers.

Um... should we do anything about that?

A friend's son went away to Penn State and when he came home for Christmas break told her that he'd been taking his roommate's Ritalin and it made him better able to focus. He asked her if she could take him to his pediatrician or *just call him up*, and get a prescription. When my friend started to explain to him that that wasn't how it worked, that diagnosis of ADD or ADHD was a process, he was flabbergasted: all three suitemates had 'scripts, as well as other kids on his floor, and everyone shared pills all the time. He wanted to have his own 'script so he wouldn't have to pay his friends for individual pills. This parlays right into numbers that show 7% of college students report using prescription stimulants for cognitive performance; that number grows to 25% at elite universities.

About a month after my husband died, I was having trouble sleeping. I went to my GP and she asked me if I was depressed. When I answered that I damn well better be she suggested Wellbutrin. I also smoked, then, and she said we'd have a "two-fer." I did not like the idea, but I wanted to sleep and I did want to stop smoking as well.

Two weeks in to taking the drug I was standing outside the Kenneth Cole on Walnut Street, screaming into my phone, and I had this strange experience of being able to see myself, marching on the street, talking too loud, never quite sure of what I was doing or what I should do next. Even in my grieving state my hyperkinetic personality went into overdrive on the Wellbutrin. I felt (and often looked) like the Tasmanian devil, whirling about, wild-eyed.

Growing up, my teachers called me "Chatty Kathy." My father still loves to tell people I "came out talking." I can't help but wonder if I had been raised in the '90s instead of the '70s if I'd be labeled ADHD too. And what would be different about me now if I had?

I don't know the answer: kids that aren't diagnosed until later are often found to self-medicate, and often suffer from academic failure and low self esteem.

Dr. Ned Hallowell has been the talking head on ADD, and arguably one of the leading experts. But all the new CDC data, and news reports of young people abusing stimulants, has left him reassessing his role.

He has concern for the undiagnosed right alongside acknowledgment that the diagnosis is "being handed out too freely." For years Hallowell's much-quoted opinion on Adderall and other stimulants was that they were "safer than aspirin." Last month he said, "I regret the analogy... I won't be saying that again."

Kathleen Volk Miller

Remember, Your Kids are Your Free Labor

In two weeks, both of my daughters are leaving for college, and I am very worried about my 14-year-old son, who will still be with me at home: Will he be too lonely without them, or will he revel in his new role as "only child"? He will be a latchkey kid three days a week: Will he be scared to enter the empty house, or will he love the privacy and independence? How will I monitor his gaming habits? But the question that weighs on me the most is: Will I ever again have an empty dishwasher without asking for it?

The girls are not perfect, of course. When each of them was a senior in high school, something kicked in and they constantly cleaned up, and did extra lovely things like making fresh-squeezed lemonade and baking batches of cupcakes. I'd go down to the laundry and see a load of freshly folded towels that I hadn't done myself. Since they have grown, and the oldest has had her own place, their focus is less on the family home and more on their own lives, of course. But they do tend to pick up a dirty glass as they walk through the living room, empty the kitchen recycling can when it overflows, etc. My son Chris, however, does absolutely nothing that he isn't told to do.

My boy is 14 years old and like most 14-year-olds, he's complicated. He's young enough to still list "blue" as one of his favorite flavors, but old enough that blue drinks stain his incoming silky mustache. He answers his phone in a deeper register than I ever thought possible, but can still whine and make his complaint sound: a kind of low, guttural grunt he has made since he was a toddler. He has not yet hit his growth spurt, but we stand literally eye-to-eye, if not always figuratively.

He's starting ninth grade. I'm starting to panic. There's so much to worry about. Will high school be dramatically different than middle school? Will he handle the workload? If he's not in the coolest of crowds, will he at least blend in? Will he stay with his group of friends from middle school, or start to hang out with kids I don't know? Can he handle French 2 and TV Production? Will he keep his straight-edge philosophy, or will he become "under the influence" and start experimenting with alcohol and pot? Will I know if he does? Will company be able to use the second-floor bathroom before the girls come home for Christmas break?

Some of the chores around our house have traditional gender roles attached, I must admit. But though the girls have never mowed the lawn and Chris does that chore, he has been in the dishwashing rotation. Each child has, for the most part, done their own laundry from the time they hit about 12. Now that I think about it, the girls don't do any chore that Chris doesn't also do, but many are his alone, like the aforementioned lawn mowing, and taking out the garbage. I push him into the male role so wholeheartedly, I even tell him he has to kill the aberrant bug that invades our space.

It seems to me, though, that like older male/female house and chore sharers, Chris is happier to do project-oriented tasks. While some of his responsibilities are repetitive, garbage only needs to be taken out once a week. Lawn mowing gives him a sense of satisfaction for two weeks. Emptying the dishwasher is invariably followed by loading the dishwasher; believe me, I get his disdain.

I hate cleaning so much that I have tried to find someone to swap chores with me, i.e., I will cook meals for you if you clean my house. I would rather cook for three hours than clean for 30 minutes. I haven't felt bad about doling out tasks to my kids; I figure over the course of a lifespan, the window of opportunity I have to take advantage of them is very small. In their early years, kids basically suck your life's blood, as well as your breast milk. Once they're 12, you can start to ask them to do stuff, even though you are still giving them much more time than they are giving you. Once they move out, they're gone, so your opportunities for free floor Swiffering are long gone. Once they are living on their own, it would be socially unacceptable to hand them the Windex and point them to the smudged storm door when they come over for dinner, but it's almost expected that they still ask you for cash as well as advice. An inequitable relationship to say the least, right? So. Why not get the air conditioning registers dusted while you can?

The girls are still home with me for a few weeks (Drexel's unusual quarter system), but I dropped Christopher off for his first day this morning. He let out one big exhale, opened the car door, and walked away from me. So much can happen in the next four years. I watched him walk toward the doors of his high school, and the last thing on my mind was dirty dishes.

Scott Warnock

Writing for Dummies: Standardized Tests are Destroying Education, Part 3 (of a Plethora)

The art of writing. The mysterious skill of writing. Writer Jack Dann once said, "For me, writing is exploration; and most of the time, I'm surprised where the journey takes me." Alas, for many of our children, writing will never be about exploration, discovery, art, or the challenge of learning complex technical skill. Instead, writing will be standardized, boxed-in, formulaic. It will be an obstacle they need to figure out strategies to get around. Lucky for me, a pre-teen who may or may not live in my home, bless her heart, always has it all figured out. More about that in a moment.

You know that writing components have been added to many standardized testing systems, including the SAT. It's just a part of the broader movement to narrow the band of education.

Now, using valuable time they might have spent gaming the multiple choice sections of tests like the SAT, students have to figure out how to game the writing sections. They learn to throw in big words. They learn to write long sentences. They learn to make arguments fit five-paragraph essays: Thesis, point one, point two, point three, conclusion. They learn the value of writing a lot, no matter how much they really have to say. They learn the preeminence of neat handwriting.

But what they don't learn is how to write. They don't get better at writing by thinking about these writing tests, by practicing for them, or by being evaluated for them.

Evaluated? They just get a number, and there is increasing interest in having that number generated by a machine. In a *New York Times* article about these "robo-readers," writing researcher Les Perelman discussed his analysis of some of these automated graders, based on his own experiences writing for them. One slight problem, Perelman says, is that truth is unimportant. Robo-graders don't care if you don't know your facts. They can't tell. Also, they like long sentences (sorry Hemingway). They prefer longer essays. They don't notice if you throw in a random line or two about an unrelated topic. If you take your sentences that start with "and" and "or" and switch them to "however" and "moreover," Perelman says, these machines see you as having more "complex thinking."

And so on.

These students learn strategies revolving around using big words and writing long. They learn writing formulas that help them write exactly one kind of writing: The standardized test. Forget the damning generational accusation I often hear: "These kids can't write." For every 18-year-old you show me who has writing issues, I'll show you two forty-somethings with similar issues, even if clear writing is crucial to their field. The students I know are extremely smart, and what they are lacking—when they are lacking—in their writing is not the skill, broadly conceived, but instead the creativity to think outside the five-paragraph format of the standardized test. Gun control: Good. Pollution: Bad.

These students, bred in the era of the five-paragraph standardized testing essay, can produce that five-paragraph argument about almost anything. But I find that when I ask them to, say, toss in that sixth paragraph, they're confused, cagey. "But where would it go?" they wonder. "In an appendix?"

The world, of course, is not broken up into five-paragraph problems. Yet make no mistake about it: The form in which you are trained to write becomes a form that governs the way you think. So they try to see the world in terms of the five-paragraph essay: Contained, neat, easy.

I'm not blaming them. I don't blame their teachers, either. The stakes in this mad game of educational assessment are too high for their individual classes. It's hard to blame administrators. In the absence of thoughtful ways of evaluating the overall success of their schools, these tests carry incredible weight; the results are connected to real dollars.

I want to blame the government, but this is the US, and we are the government. Anyway, in his January 2013 State of the Union Address, President Obama said, "Stop teaching to the test." Then, in a February interview with Jon Stewart, Secretary of Education Arne Duncan said the same thing. Yet teacher-blogger Anthony Cody asked a reasonable question on his blog, *Living in Dialogue*: "How is it that with both our President and Secretary of Education so firmly against teaching to the test that we have states dramatically increasing the stakes for these tests?"

I suppose, like with most things, we only have ourselves to blame for the growth of this testing farce. So our kids are just going to have to continue to figure out ways to please/beat the system.

Which brings me back to that pre-teen who may or may not live with me. She was getting ready for the written component of her recent battery of standardized tests. "Are you ready for your writing test?" I asked. "Oh yes, I'm ready," she said, eyes gleaming with confidence, lips pursed, head nodding wisely. "I'm going to use the word 'plethora'.

Contributors

Marquerita Algorri is a senior, double-majoring in nutrition and English, living in Philadelphia. She hopes to develop a career in literary publishing or microbiology after graduation. Her hobbies include writing, painting, knitting, and studying biology.

Ronald Bishop is a professor in the Department of Culture and Communication at Drexel University in Philadelphia. His third book, *MORE: The Vanishing of Scale in an Over-the-Top Nation*, was published in 2011 by Baylor University Press. His two previous books, *Taking on the Pledge of Allegiance* and *When Play Was Play: Why Pick-Up Games Still Matter*, were published by SUNY Press. His research has been published in a variety of journals across many disciplines, including the *Electronic Journal of Communication*, the *Journal of Popular Culture*, the *Journal of Sports Media*, the *Journal of Communication*, *Addiction Research and Theory*, the *International Journal of Progressive Education*, and the *Journal of Poverty*.

Caitlin Bubel is a mechanical engineering major from Dallas, Texas. She plans on pursuing a career in automotive design. Her favorite hobby is rowing for the Drexel Women's crew team.

Amanda Margaret Busch is a junior in the School of Biomedial Engineering, pursing a neuroengineering concentration, in addition to a psychology minor. Growing up in quiet Ambler, Pennsylvania afforded her plenty of time to fall in love with reading and writing, and to become enthralled by historical crime investigations, the psychology behind crime, and the science behind psychology. After graduating in 2015, she plans to pursue a career in medical or pharmaceutical research.

Samantha Cassel is a freshman biomedical engineering major from Chalfont, Pennsylvania. She plans to pursue a concentration in biomaterials and tissue engineering, as well as a minor in Spanish. Outside of the classroom, Sam enjoys playing trumpet in the concert band and playing softball.

Paula Marantz Cohen is Distinguished Professor of English at Drexel University and the author of four non-fiction books and four novels, as well as numerous stories and essays in publications like *The Yale Review*, *The Chronicle of Higher Education*, *The New York Times*, and *The Times Literary Supplement*.

Len Finegold is a physics professor at Drexel University and finds his true home in the desert, preferably the Colorado Plateau (centered on the Four Corners region, with red rocks—hence the name). Since 50% of his knees do not permit backpacking, he camps near a car. His research is in biophysics and his published articles include, "Biological Sensing of Static Magnetic Fields" in the *American Journal of Physics*.

Valerie Fox recently published *Poems for Writing: Prompts for Poets*, co-authored with Lynn Levin. Her books of poems include *The Glass Book* (2010) and *The Rorschach Factory* (2006). She has published poems in *Ping Pong, Hanging Loose, Per Contra, Apiary,* and many other journals. She earned her PhD from Binghamton University and also studied at Temple University (for MA) and Shippensburg University of Pennsylvania (for BA). She teaches writing at Drexel University.

David Georgeanni is a physics major from Burlington, New Jersey. He plans to continue physics in graduate school. He is passionate about space exploration and aspires to a career as an astronaut.

Hannah Mindl Gittler is an aspiring writer who works as an editorial staff member at *Painted Bride Quarterly*. Her work can be seen at www.hannahgittler.blogspot.com

Grant Grothusen is a first-year biological science major from Haddon Township, New Jersey. He plans to attend medical school after the completion of his studies at Drexel. His hobbies include running and playing drums.

Evan Higgins is a senior business student graduating from Drexel University in the spring of 2013. His majors are finance and management information systems. After graduating, he plans to start doing consulting work for the Big 4 firm KPMG. His favorite books are *48 Laws of Power* by Robert Greene and *Revolutionary Suicide* by Huey P. Newton.

Maria Hnaraki is the Director of Greek Studies at Drexel University. She is author of *Cretan Music: Unraveling Ariadne's Thread* and *Sing In Me, Muse, and Through Me Tell the Story: Greek Culture Performed* (forthcoming). Her wide-ranging circle of activities includes, among others, international publications of articles and book reviews in journals and periodicals, translation as well as instruction, presentations, and performances on several aspects of the Greek culture.

Rebecca Ingalls is an associate professor and Director of the First-Year Writing Program at Drexel University. Her work in composition and cultural rhetoric may be found in *invention; Academe; The Review of Education, Pedagogy, and Cultural Studies; POROI; Harlot;* the *Journal of Teaching Writing;* the *Journal of Popular Culture;* and *Writing & Pedagogy.* She is co-editor of the book *Critical Conversations about Plagiarism* (Parlor Press, 2012).

Henry Israeli's books include *New Messiahs* (Four Way Books: 2002), *Praying to the Black Cat* (Del Sol: 2010), and *god's breath hovering across the waters,* forthcoming from Four Way Books. He is the translator of *Fresco: the Selected*

Poetry of Luljeta Lleshanaku (New Directions: 2002), *Child of Nature* (New Directions: 2010), and *Haywire: New and Selected Poems* (Bloodaxe, 2011). Henry Israeli is also the founder and editor of Saturnalia Books (www.saturnaliabooks.com).

Dawn Kane teaches English to international students in the English Language Program at Drexel University. Prior to taking the Drexel position in 2012, she taught elementary school to English language learners in south Philadelphia. She has instructed for teacher training programs in Mexico, South Korea, India, and for Drexel University. She is currently a volunteer with Project Kenya Sister Schools, which promotes cultural exchange and improvement in rural Kenyan public schools.

Helena Krobock is a freshman biology major from Harrisburg, Pennsylvania. She currently is a research assistant with the Department of Biology, a STAR Scholar, and a member of Active Minds. In the future, she plans to pursue a minor in psychology and continue writing as a hobby throughout her life.

Marcus Kunkle is a sophomore English major from Lehighton, Pennsylvania. His hobbies include whitewater kayaking, rock climbing, and songwriting.

Lynn Levin, poet, writer, and translator, is adjunct associate professor of English at Drexel University. She is the author of four collections of poems: *Miss Plastique* (Ragged Sky Press, 2013); *Fair Creatures of an Hour* (Loonfeather Press, 2009), a Next Generation Indie Book Awards finalist in poetry; *Imaginarium* (Loonfeather Press, 2005), a finalist for *ForeWord Magazine*'s Book of the Year Award; and *A Few Questions about Paradise* (Loonfeather Press, 2000). She is, with Drexel colleague Valerie Fox, the author of a craft-of-poetry book, *Poems for the Writing: Prompts for Poets* (Texture Press, 2013).

Joanna Lyskowicz, originally from Poland, has been a Spanish instructor at the Modern Language Program at Drexel for the past eight years. Although her primary subject taught is Spanish, she speaks several foreign languages and has taught French and Portuguese in the past, which has influenced her major research interest: comparative linguistics and translation. She hopes to make the language learning process easier for potential students.

Christiny (or Chris) Martin is a junior screenwriting and playwriting major, with a minor in film. She is from Philadelphia. Chris aspires to move to LA after graduation to pursue a career in television.

Harriet Levin Millan is the Director of the Certificate Program in Writing and Publishing. Her two poetry books include *The Christmas Show* (Beacon Press), which won the Barnard New Women Poets Prize and the Poetry

Society of America's Alice Fay di Castagnola Award, and *Girl in Cap and Gown* (Mammoth Books), a 2009 National Poetry Series finalist. The first chapter of her novel-in-progress, *Yalla!*, appears in the Winter 2011 issue of *The Kenyon Review*.

Paul Martorano is a freshman chemical engineering major from Coral Springs, Florida. He plans to pursue nuclear research after graduation.

David Nehring is a sophomore majoring in both chemistry and biological sciences with a concentration in organismal physiology. He is from West Chester, Pennsylvania. After graduation, David hopes to attend medical school with aspirations of becoming a surgeon. His hobbies include playing ultimate Frisbee for Drexel's "Spitfire Ultimate" and volunteering at the Lombard Central soup kitchen.

Nahjan Amer Nordin graduated from Drexel University in spring 2013 with a bachelor of science in environmental engineering. She will enroll in the masters of environmental engineering program at Stanford University in fall 2013, where she hopes to concentrate specifically on water resources. During her free time, she enjoys writing, which she actively does through a blog, and reading.

Anne-Marie Obajtek-Kirkwood is an associate professor of French and head of French Studies at Drexel. She teaches French and Francophone 20th- and 21st-century literature, culture and film, and Women Studies and International Area Studies with a focus on the Maghreb, the Middle East, and Iran. Her research and publications include the above topics, as well as minorities in France, autobiography, and war (WWII, 9/11, the Iraq War). She has published *Signs of War: From Patriotism to Dissent* (Palgrave MacMillan 2007) and on many contemporary French writers.

Araks Ohanyan is a pre-junior studying biology, with a concentration in ecology. Originally from southern California, she hopes to pursue field biology and conservation. Her hobbies include hiking, bird watching and photographing wildlife.

Evangelia Papoutsaki is an associate professor in international communication at Unitec, Auckland, the co-author of *Media, Information and Development in Papua New Guinea* and *South Pacific Islands Communication: Regional Perspectives, Local Issues*, and facilitator of the South Pacific Islands Communication Forum (SPICF) research collective.

Don Riggs has been writing a sonnet each morning in or around his bathtub, on the basis of which he pretends to some internal expertise on the genre, at least in its formative stages. Other publications include a translation of

François Cheng's analysis of traditional Chinese poetics, a revelation of the true natal horoscope of Michelangelo and its late-15th century significance, and parallel appearances of the Mother Goddess in works by Marie de France and Marion Zimmer Bradley. His analysis of the relevance of J.R.R. Tolkien's *The Hobbit* for a child's moral development appeared in an international anthology of essays on fantasy published in Wroclaw, Poland.

Gail D. Rosen teaches English at Drexel. She holds a BA from Temple University and a JD from Temple University School of Law. She has written weekly film reviews for *When Falls the Coliseum*.

Don Rutberg has a Master of Fine Arts degree from USC and is a published author of books, children's books, stage plays, comic books, and magazine articles. His cookbook, *We'll All Be Eating In 15 Minutes ... No Matter What* is available at ebooklit.com. His book, *A Writer's First Aid Kit* (Pale Horse Publishing) is a proactive approach to writing and selling books and scripts. Don is an adjunct professor at Drexel University (communication) and Community College of Philadelphia (writing).

Kate Rosenberger is a junior business administration major from Philadelphia. Her hobbies include writing and running.

Marie Ruisard is a freshman at Drexel majoring in architecture. After graduation, she hopes to continue writing while pursuing her architectural career. She enjoys reading, track and field, and horseback riding.

Sheila Sandapen is an associate teaching professor of English at Drexel University and teaches in the First-Year Writing Program. She also works in the Drexel Writing Center.

Mik Schulte is from Raleigh, North Carolina. Going into his third year at Drexel, he enjoys writing for his blog on *The Huffington Post*, working at a Center City law firm, and serving as secretary general for the 2014 Washington Model OAS. He is an international studies and philosophy double major.

Vaughn Shirey is a first-year environmental sciences major from Pottstown, Pennsylvania. He hopes for a career in either geology or botany after graduating from Drexel. He writes for the opinion section of *The Triangle* and also writes short stories in his free time.

Alan Soble has been, since spring 2007, an adjunct professor of philosophy at Drexel University. He regularly teaches Propositional Logic, Critical Reasoning, Introduction to Western Philosophy, and the Philosophy of Sex and Love. He has written or edited a dozen books in the latter field, including *The Philosophy of Sex and Love* (Paragon House, 2nd edition, 2008), *The Structure* *of Love* (Yale University Press, 1990), and *The Philosophy of Sex: Contemporary Readings* (Rowman and Littlefield, 6th edition, 2012).

Mary V. Spiers is an associate professor of psychology in the Department of Psychology at Drexel University and a licensed clinical psychologist specializing in neuropsychology. She received her Ph.D. in clinical psychology from the University of Alabama at Birmingham. She is the co-author of two textbooks in neuropsychology and has published and presented over 30 papers, articles, and chapters.

Scott Stein is a teaching professor of English at Drexel University and co-director of the Drexel Publishing Group, author of the novels *Lost* and *Mean Martin Manning*, and founding editor of *When Falls the Coliseum: a journal of American culture (or lack thereof)* <whenfallsthecoliseum.com>. His short fiction has been published in *National Review, Liberty, The G.W. Review*, and *Art Times* and his essays and reviews have appeared in the *Philadelphia Inquirer, New York* magazine, *Liberty*, and PopMatters.com.

Zachary Stockmal is a first-year animation and visual effects major from Lafayette, New Jersey. He hopes to work in California at a movie studio. His hobbies are reading, singing badly, and taking too many naps.

Nathan Tessema is a freshman biomedical engineering major from Addis Ababa, Ethiopia. He plans on concentrating in devices and imaging. His hobbies include listening to music, working out, and playing sports.

Virginia Theerman is a sophomore design and merchandising major from Paeonian Springs, Virginia. As an old soul who loves new shoes, vintage clothing, and classic literature, she intends to go to graduate school for the history of design and hopes to one day curate a historic costume collection.

Allison Tipton is a pre-junior dual biology and psychology major from Lansdale, Pennsylvania. Although undecided about her ultimate career choice, she is considering medical school or a Ph.D. in clinical psychology. Currently, she works in an eating disorder research laboratory and enjoys spending her free time with friends or with her pets.

Julia Turner is a freshman mathematics major from East Berne, New York. She plans on pursuing a degree in education as well. She likes to plot graphs and analyze data in her spare time.

Kathleen Volk Miller is co-editor of *Painted Bride Quarterly*, co-director of the Drexel Publishing Group, and a teaching professor at Drexel University. She is a weekly blogger (Thursdays) for *Philadelphia Magazine's Philly Post*. Volk Miller writes fiction and essays, with work in publications such as Salon.

com, *Opium*, thesmartset.org, the New York Times *Motherlode* and with upcoming work in *Drunken Boat*. She is currently working on *My Gratitude*, a collection of essays. Recently, Kathleen Volk Miller was named a Creative Connector by Leadership Philadelphia. Follow her on Twitter @kvm1303.

Scott Warnock is an associate professor of English and Director of the Writing Center and Writing Across the Curriculum at Drexel University. He writes "Virtual Children," a bi-weekly column/blog, for the site *When Falls the Coliseum*.

James Warren is a sophomore environmental science major from Schwenksville, Pennsylvania. He plans to go on to get his Ph.D. in ornithology after graduation. His hobbies include distance running, birding, and photography.

Joshua Weiss is a freshman communications major with a concentration in public relations. He is from Cherry Hill, New Jersey, and plans to continue a career in writing after college. Other than writing, his hobbies include fishing, cooking, reading, and film appreciation.

Tristan Winick is a freshman physics major from Allentown, Pennsylvania, whose interests include martial arts, scuba diving, reading (primarily in the genres of fantasy, science fiction, and satire), and electronic music composition and production. Alongside his pursuit of higher education and a yet-undecided career, he hopes to eventually produce his own album.